File Systems

Structures and Algorithms

Thomas R. Harbron

Anderson University

PRENTICE HALL, Englewood Cliffs, New Jersey 07632

Library of Congress Cataloging-in-Publication Data
Harbron, Thomas R.,
    File Systems : structures and algorithms / by Thomas R. Harbron.
        p.   cm.
    Includes index.
    ISBN 0-13-314709-6
    1. File organization (Computer science) 2. Data structures
(Computer science) I. Title.
QA76.9.F5H37 1987
005.74—dc19   87-32675
                                                        CIP

Editorial / production supervision
and interior design: Carolyn Fellows
Cover design: Wanda Lubelska Design
Manufacturing buyer: Barbara Kittle and Cindy Grant

Cover Art:
The cover illustration is a tree that shows how the file
structures described in this book are related. A traversal of
this tree will produce an outline of the contents.

 © 1988 by Prentice-Hall, Inc.
A Division of Simon & Schuster
Englewood Cliffs, New Jersey 07632

Printed in the United States of America
10 9 8 7 6 5 4 3 2 1

ISBN 0-13-314709-6   025

Prentice-Hall International (UK) Limited, *London*
Prentice-Hall of Australia Pty. Limited, *Sydney*
Prentice-Hall Canada Inc., *Toronto*
Prentice-Hall Hispanoamericana, S.A., *Mexico*
Prentice-Hall of India Private Limited, *New Delhi*
Prentice-Hall of Japan, Inc., *Tokyo*
Simon and Schuster Asia Pte. Ltd., *Singapore*
Editora Prentice-Hall do Brasil, Ltda., *Rio de Janeiro*

*This book is dedicated to my mother
at whose knee I first learned to value good books.*

Contents

Preface

This book is intended as a textbook for a one-semester course in file systems. The course is similar in content to the ACM curriculum '78 course CS 5, but differs in that a course in data structures is assumed as a prerequisite. There are two reasons for this difference. First, many of the standard topics of a data structures course are either directly applicable to file system problems, or are very similar to the structures and algorithms used in file systems. This makes a good foundation for the study of files.

Second, the pattern used in both courses is one where a data structure is defined, then algorithms and applications are discovered that are appropriate to the structure. Comparisons of structures and algorithms are encouraged in both courses. Thus, file systems is a very natural extension of data structures both in subject matter and methods.

To define a data type it is necessary to define four aspects of the data type: (1) a set or range of values, (2) an external representation of those values, (3) an internal representation of those values, and (4) a set of operations that can be performed on the values. This book focuses on the latter two aspects of data types, the internal structures and the operations, for various classes of external file data types. It is emphasized that, to the use of files, operations or algorithms are just as important as the structures.

The student who has completed this course will be prepared to study database systems without becoming distracted by the workings of the underlying file systems and techniques upon which all database systems are built.

Throughout the book, algorithms are described in a nonspecific, block-structured language. This may be regarded as a "pseudocode" or process design language and is suitable for guiding the student in developing procedures and programs on a real computer system. A pseudocode has several advantages over use of an actual language. It is possible to describe complex algorithms without inserting the syntactically required details of a particular language that do not aid in the conceptual understanding. Thus the algorithms can be stated concisely enough to be readily comprehended. Moreover, students cannot simply copy the code from the book, but must think it through for themselves as it is translated to a real language.

Similarly, the file system used throughout the text is "generic" and may be readily adopted to most file systems and operating systems that students are likely to encounter.

There is a deliberate attempt throughout the book to use three pedagogical devices to motivate and assist students in mastery of the subject. First, an attempt is made to raise questions in a student's mind as to how the necessary file functions can be performed efficiently. A cardinal sin that we, as educators, frequently commit is to answer questions that students are not asking. This produces poor motivation, and motivation is the key to effective learning. Thus problems will be posed early in the text for which there are no obvious or efficient solutions. Throughout the remainder of the book, progressively better solutions will be developed by introduction of more sophisticated structures and algorithms. This has proven to be very effective in motivating students to eagerly seek out and learn the more sophisticated methods.

Motivation is also greatly aided by having the student implement solutions on a computer system. It is entirely too easy to gloss over fundamental aspects of file systems if one is not forced to completely solve all parts of the problem. Moreover, this gives an opportunity for the student to experience the delays caused by inefficient algorithms. The exact form of the programming assignments will necessarily vary, depending on facilities available and the abilities of the students. However, it is vital that some of the problems be more than "paper exercises." Several nontrivial file system problems are described in detail in Appendix B and referenced by problems at the end of the chapters.

Second, a standard problem will be used throughout to illustrate the strengths and weaknesses of each method. The problem is complex enough to give a realistic picture of the effectiveness of each method. At the same time, it is simple enough to be easily understood. By using a constant and diverse application, the student can compare all methods with the single application, thus eliminating differences due to different illustrations, and emphasizing the differences due to the methods.

Third, a consistent approach is used for all file structures. A structure is first described, and the primitive operations that can be performed on it are introduced. Then the algorithms appropriate to these structures and operations are developed. Next, a set of standard functions is evaluated in terms of the number of logical and physical accesses required. Finally the standard problem is solved using the best methods introduced to that point.

Chapters 1 and 2 present the foundational concepts for the study of files. Most students will already be familiar with simple files and understand these concepts at an intuitive level. Consequently, much of the material will be a review and consolidation of concepts. Chapters 3 through 10 constitute the technical core of the subject. New structure concepts are introduced, developed, and applied in each chapter. As each chapter builds on the previous ones, they should be studied in sequence, with the possible exception of Chapters 7 and 8.

Chapter 1 introduces the basic ideas of files, including records and entities, fields and attributes, and keys. Chapter 2 examines the constraints imposed by the physical memory devices commonly used in computer systems.

Chapters 3 through 5 introduce elementary concepts with the simplest of file structures. There may be a reaction, when reading these chapters, that the file structures introduced there should not be used to solve some of the example problems. This would be true for real problems; however, the student has not yet studied the more sophisticated structures and does need to know why the elementary structures are not suitable for many applications.

Chapter 6 introduces the idea of key transformations (hashing) which is expanded in Chapter 7 to include a rudimentary form of indexing with the extendible hash file. Chapter 8 introduces indexing with a different vehicle, the indexed sequential file. Either or both of Chapters 7 and 8 may be omitted without doing great harm to the sequence of concepts in the book.

Chapters 9 and 10 expand on the use of indexes, focusing first on the structure of the indexes themselves, and then on their applications in file systems.

The final chapter on database systems is not to be considered more than a culmination of the study of file systems. Many real problems, including the standard problem used throughout this book, cannot be solved well without using database methods. This is especially true where multiple entities are involved. This does not mean that an actual database management system is necessary to solve these problems, but rather that some fundamental database concepts must be applied to file systems to solve most real problems satisfactorily.

Much of the material in the appendices is integral to a study of the subject. It has been placed in the back of the book so as not to create digressions from the topics of the chapters. Appendix A contains descriptions of file systems as supported by typical operating systems. The generic file system that is used in the algorithms is described in detail as well as partial descriptions for two real machines: the Digital Equipment Corporation's VAX series and Hewlett-Packard's 3000 series.

Appendix B contains detailed descriptions of three file application problems. These may be used as programming exercises or study problems for any of the file structures from Chapter 3 onward. The first problem, the student records problem, is used as an example throughout the text, but the parameters may be altered so as to make a different problem of it.

Appendix C simply shows how to calculate logarithms to bases not usually found on calculators or in library functions. Although this is nothing more than simple algebra, many students seem unaware of the technique. Appendix D gives a syntactical description of the pseudocode that is used to describe the algorithms throughout the book.

It is neither possible nor helpful for a textbook to attempt to cover, or even enumerate, all of the file structures that have been invented over the years. Few areas of computer science have known such a variety and quantity of solutions for a problem. The attempt here is to cover a sufficient number of the most useful file types so that the student will be able to make informed choices and be able to study and understand other types as the need for them arises. Those whose favorite structure has been omitted, please accept my apologies.

One of the problems with a young discipline such as computer science is that the vocabulary has not been standardized. Consequently, one finds the literature filled with a variety of names for the same concepts. Again, the area of file systems seems to have more than its share of confusion with nomenclature. Throughout this book, an attempt has been made to use terms that are accurate and descriptive. In a few places these qualities have been valued above the standard of most popular usage. For example, the literature uses the terms ''collisions'' and ''synonyms'' to refer to keys that hash to the same address. However, a collision is an event that can occur for several different reasons, while ''synonym'' is a mathematical property of the keys and hashing algorithm. Thus the latter has been used in preference to the former when discussing the problems of managing direct access files.

External sorting is sometimes a topic in file system courses. Most of the common algorithms for internal sorting are usually covered in a data structures course and so are not repeated here. The problem of extending an internal sort to an external sort is more properly the subject for a book than for a chapter. Consequently, there is no attempt made here to cover the subject in any depth. However, the student should become familiar with the sort utility that is available, including the algorithm and statistics that characterize it and how it can be used.

ACKNOWLEDGMENTS

The many pioneers who have developed and analyzed file and database methods over the past thirty years are too numerous to mention. However, without them we would still be using the crude forms of card decks and magnetic tape. I wish to thank them for their contributions, both to this book and to the state of the art. May their inventive and scholarly spirit continue in all who read this.

Many people have been helpful and supportive of the effort to write this book. I would especially like to thank R. Waldo Roth of Taylor University, for his encouragement and considered comments; Jack Anderson of Anderson University, whose considered analytic judgements have been most helpful;

Maxine Loeber, for her careful proofreading and suggestions; and Chris Funk of C. M. Funk & Company, without whose help and support the writing of this book would not be possible.

Finally, I would like to thank all the students who, over the years, have motivated me to refine and hone the materials upon which this book is based. It has been their insightful questions and responses that have developed this material into a pedagogically sound presentation.

Thomas R. Harbron
Anderson, Indiana

1

Basic File Concepts

1.1 ENTITIES AND ATTRIBUTES

Computers exist to process data. Usually the data represents information useful to people for some purpose. Frequently, the data is of a simple, scalar nature: for example, the number of gallons of gasoline in the tank, or the total sales volume for the month. More often, however, the data concerns a large number of similar objects, or *entities*: for example, the employees of a company, or the transactions made in the accounting system.

It is often the case that the entities of a system are not immediately obvious. It is probably wiser, in the system analysis phase, to collect information on the data needed and defer the decision of naming the entities involved. The question of formally recognizing entities is called "normalization" and is properly part of the study of databases.

Entities are described in the computer system by one or more *attributes*. These are characteristics that describe an entity and allow us to distinguish one entity from another. For example, the entity "employee" might have attributes of name, address, employee number, department, pay rate, job class, and so on. Attributes relate to entities in the manner that adjectives relate to nouns (i.e., they describe the object).

It may seem strange at first that the data representing an entity consist only of attributes of the entity. However, to include the entity name as an attribute would be highly redundant and totally unnecessary. For example, no information would be added if we included the value "employee" with the data on each employee. We already know that these entities are all employees. To repeat this with each occurrence of an employee would not help in any way.

1

On the other hand, it is usually necessary or desirable to be able to distinguish uniquely between similar entities. Thus we often find a somewhat artificial attribute, such as employee number, that serves to uniquely identify one entity from all other similar entities.

Another troubling aspect of classifying everything as either an entity or an attribute is that those things that are properly attributes in one context may be entities in another context. Consider an automobile dealer who wishes to keep data on automobiles that he has in stock. "Automobile" is properly the entity to be used and will have attributes such as make, model, vehicle identification number, engine, color, and so on. The attribute "engine" may have values such as "4.5 liter V-8", "2.2 liter 4", and "3.4 liter V-6." However, the service department of the same dealership may wish to keep data on items requiring service. In this context, "engine" might be an entity with attributes such as displacement, horsepower, interval between oil changes, type of sparkplugs used, and so on.

Usually, it will become clear, in the process of developing a system, which items are entities and which are attributes. However, it is a matter upon which reasonable people can disagree. When this happens after careful study, it is usually true that there will be little difference in the functioning of the system, regardless of which choice is made.

1.2 RECORDS

The attributes that describe an entity will usually be represented by a variety of data types. For our employee entity, name and address might be character strings of some definite lengths, while employee number and pay rate might be fixed length integers. Department might be a three-character mnemonic code where only certain values are legitimate.

Since each attribute, in general, may be of a different data type and length than the other attributes, we cannot employ the familiar device of an array to store our entities. The array requires all elements to be of the same form. We need a structure that will accommodate an aggregation of dissimilar data types that represent one occurrence of an entity. This object is commonly called a *record*.

Each record contains all the attributes to describe one entity. Thus we may have an employee record that contains a *field* of 30 characters for the name, a field of 40 characters for the address, a field consisting of a 32-bit integer for the employee number, and so on. as shown in Figure 1.1. The exact bit pattern of each field depends upon the specific codes used to represent data in a particular machine. The figure shows the location of each field within the record, its length, and name.

Records for one entity type are usually all of the same form. That is, they each have the same fields in the same quantity, order, and length. Records of this type are called *fixed-length records*. However, there are exceptions to this

Name	Address	Emp Nbr	Dept	Pay Rate	Job Class

|← 30 bytes →|← 40 bytes →|← 4 bytes →|← 3 →|← 4 bytes →|← 2 bytes →|

Figure 1.1 Employee record with fixed length.

rule. Records that are not necessarily all of the same length are called *variable-length records*. There are three kinds of variety that may cause records to have a variable length: variable-length fields, variable format records, and repeating groups.

Variable length fields usually result from efforts to conserve space where a field may contain widely varying amounts of data from record to record. For example, an employee's full name might vary from "Jo Fox" (6 bytes) to "Elizabeth Josephene Throgmorton" (30 bytes), or longer. If a fixed-length field is used, its size must be determined by the longest name to be stored, and since the average length is considerably less, much space will be wasted. A variable-length field would allow exactly the amount of space required for each name.

Variable format records result when data on different types of entities are stored in the same file. For example we may wish to have two types of employees, hourly and salary. Differences will occur in that we will need to record the hours worked for hourly employees, but not for salary employees. Similarly, the rate shown for hourly employees is probably an hourly rate, whereas that for salary employees is probably a monthly rate. Should these be confused, we might see a salary employee receive a very large paycheck that was calculated by multiplying a monthly rate by hours worked. This would doubtless make the employee very happy, unless he was also the analyst or programmer who made the mistake and joined the ranks of the unemployed as a result. Figure 1.2 illustrates a variable-length record caused by having a variable format.

Type = "H"	Name	Address	Emp Nbr	Dept	Hourly Rate	Hours Worked	Job Class
Type = "S"	Name	Address	Emp Nbr	Dept	Monthly Rate	Job Class	

Figure 1.2 Variable-length employee records

When variable-format records are used, it is essential that the program processing them know how long the records are and which format to use with them. In many cases it may be possible to imply the format from the length. However, there may be situations in which several different formats have the same length. For example, in our employee record the only difference may be that the pay rate for some employees is hourly whereas for others it is monthly. We might be able to distinguish by selecting some value (say, $250) as a boundary. We would assume that rates below this value are hourly and those above are monthly. Such ad hoc rules usually fail sooner or later due to the vagaries of inflation or other unanticipated circumstance, and are not recommended.

A better solution is to qualify the record in some explicit manner to absolutely identify the record type. For example, in Figure 1.2 we have an attribute called "type." Type is allowed to have one of two values: "H" for an hourly record and "S" for a salary record. By first examining type, we can determine the format of the remainder of the record. The Pascal "variant record" feature was designed to allow for this type of variable-format record.

Variable-length records may also result from having a *repeating group* within the record. Repeating groups occur when there is an attribute or group of attributes that may be repeated an indefinite number of times. For example, we may wish to keep insurance information about each employee and information about the dependents of the employee for insurance purposes. Since each employee may have zero or more dependents, we might have a repeating group of the attributes called "dependent name" and "birthdate." An employee with no dependents would have no occurrences of this group in his record. An employee with six children would have six such groups and hence a longer record. See Figure 1.3, for example.

Name	Emp Nbr	Insurance Type	Dependent Name	Dependent Birthdate	Dependent Name	Dependent Birthdate	. . .

Figure 1.3 Employee insurance record with repeating groups.

As will be seen later, repeating groups are troublesome both in the physical storage arrangements, and especially in the algorithms we use to find data. Consequently, when sufficiently powerful tools, such as database systems, are available, we will usually not allow them to exist. Where they are used, it is necessary to know how many repeating groups are contained in the record. This may be done by having a field that contains a count of the repeating groups. For example, the record of Figure 1.3 might have an integer field called "number of dependents" that would serve as a count on the repeating group.

Variable-length records are less common than fixed-length records largely because they are more difficult to handle, they tend to complicate our storage schemes, and are unworkable for some structures. When they are used, we need to have several items of information about each record.

First, we need to know how long the record is. This information may be returned by the file system as a separate parameter from the actual data, or it may be returned with the data, say as an integer which is the first attribute.

Where fields are variable in length, it is necessary to find the field length. Again, it may be given explicitly by an integer field, or it may be necessary to search for an end-of-field sentinel such as a period or other special character. Where the format can vary, some attribute must be used to determine which format is to be used. The "tag field" is used for this purpose in Pascal variant records.

1.3 FILES

When all the records representing entities of one type are collected together, we call the aggregation a *file*. Files can be viewed as both logical and physical entities. For the moment we consider only the logical aspects of files.

A file may be thought of as a two-dimensional organization of data. The horizontal dimension contains the fields of the record. It may range from a few bytes to thousands of bytes, but typically most files range between a dozen and a few hundred bytes in width.

The vertical dimension of a file represents the number of records. This may range from zero to millions of records. Typically, most files contain between 100 and 100,000 records. In these respects a file looks like a table where rows represent entities and columns represent attributes. Figure 1.4 shows a tabular representation of a text file used by a text editor. Each row represents one line of text. There are two attributes, line number and line text.

Line Numbers	Text
1.0	Mary had a little lamb
2.0	its fleece was white as snow
2.1	(the reference to snow is poetic
2.2	license, as lambs fleece is more
2.3	an off-white or cream color)
3.0	And everywhere that Mary went
4.0	the lamb was sure to go.

Figure 1.4 Editor text files.

The total space required for a file depends both on its logical size (the sum of the size of all records) and the particular physical storage arrangements made for it. For example, where records are allowed to have repeating groups, we may wish to set an upper limit on the number of repeating groups allowed and then allocate sufficient space for each record to have the maximum number of repeating groups. Thus our file has logical records that are variable length, but physical records that are fixed at the maximum length. Other considerations, such as blocking which is discussed in Chapter 2, also affect the total physical storage required.

The concept of a file as a single object is very useful both in thinking about the logical file, with its data, and in implementing the physical file. Files may, for example, be passed as parameters between programs and procedures as with scalar objects.

1.4 KEYS

There are times when the data in a file can be processed without regard to the number or order of records being processed. For example we might wish to write a program to calculate the monthly payroll liability from our employee file. This would require the record for each and every employee to be read, an estimate to be made of the monthly pay, and this added to a cumulative total. The order in which the records are read is not important.

This type of processing is not the normal mode for using a file. Usually when a file is used, one or both of the following conditions are imposed on our access to the records: Either we wish to access only certain records, or we wish to access the records in a specific order. For example, we may wish to have the names and pay rates of all employees who work in a certain department. Moreover, we would like to have the list in alphabetical order by name.

We call attributes that are used to select or order records *keys*. A key may be a single attribute, or a combination of attributes. A file may have no keys, or it may have many keys. Any and all attributes may be keys, or parts of keys, or both at the same time.

Often, one key will be designated as the ***primary key*** for a file. This means that this key can always be used to uniquely select one record from the file and distinguish this record from all other records. For example, employee number would be a good primary key since it is unique to each employee. Name would not be a good choice since names are not always unique or consistent. An employee might spell his name "John Carl Smith" one time and "Jack C. Smith" another.

A primary key is often the basis for locating the physical position of the record within the file. When this is done, and there are also other keys that may be used to find records in the file, the nonprimary keys are called ***secondary keys***.

In some files, the primary key may be of a type called an ***external key***. An external key is one that is not composed of one or more attributes of the logical record, but rather is derived from some characteristic of the physical record. For example, in many types of files it is standard practice to assign a unique number to each record. The first record may be assigned "0", the second record "1", the third record "2", and the last of N records may be assigned "$N - 1$." This external key is commonly called the ***record number***. Since record numbers are assigned systematically rather than being derived, they are unique and frequently are used as primary keys. Many of the algorithms we will study depend on record numbers used as keys. Figure 1.5 shows the text file from Figure 1.4 with the addition of record numbers. Notice that record numbers and line numbers are different things and have different values.

Record Number	Line Number	Text
0	1.0	Mary had a little lamb
1	2.0	its fleece was white as snow
2	2.1	(the reference to snow is poetic
3	2.2	license, as lambs fleece is more
4	2.3	an off-white or cream color)
5	3.0	And everywhere that Mary went
6	4.0	the lamb was sure to go.

Figure 1.5 Editor text file with record numbers.

Keys do not have to be able to uniquely define a record to be useful. In the example cited earlier, we wished to select employee records based on the value of the "department" field. We would expect there to be many employees in each department, so this is definitely not a unique key. Similarly, we may select records based on a range of values of a key instead of a single value. For example, we may wish to select the records of all hourly employees whose pay rate is equal to or greater than $10.00 and less than $12.00 per hour.

1.5 SUMMARY

In this chapter we have seen that a large number of similar objects called *entities* are each described by the values of a set of *attributes*. The collection of all attribute values for one entity is stored in a physical *record*. Each attribute value occupies one *field* in the record. Both fields and records may vary in length. Records may also vary in format. A group of one or more attributes may be repeated zero or more times in a *repeating group*.

Records representing similar entities are stored together in a *file*. *Keys* are attributes, or combinations of attribute values that are used to order and/or find records within a file. *Primary keys* are able to uniquely identify a record and may be the basis for assigning a location to the record within the file. Sometimes a primary key may be artificially assigned. Such an artificial key is called an *external key*. A *record number* is an example of an external key assigned by the file system.

1.6 PROBLEMS

1.1. Name three entities and list at least five attributes for each.

1.2. Explain the difference between an entity and a record.

1.3. Explain the difference between a field and an attribute.

1.4. Describe two record formats that might benefit from variable-length fields.

1.5. Describe an entity that would employ variable-format records.

1.6. Give an example of a record with a repeating group.

1.7. When would it be appropriate for an attribute to be neither a key, nor part of a key?

1.8. How many bytes are required by a logical file of 15,000 records with the following fields?

Attribute	Field Length (bytes)
Name	30
Identification number	6
Street address	26
City	16
State	2
Zip code	5

1.9. How many additional bytes would be required for the file of Problem 1.8 if the zip code were expanded to 9 bytes?

1.10. Which attribute(s) or combinations of attributes might be a good choice for a primary key for the file of Problem 1.8?

1.11. Companies that maintain mailing lists frequently collect names and addresses from a variety of sources. This practice leads to many duplicates, which can be annoying to the recipient and expensive for the company. Describe an algorithm that will flag suspected duplicates. You may assume the following:

1. The duplicates have the same name, but with variations: W. F. Smith, William F. Smith, Bill Smith, W. Frank Smith, and so on.

2. The identification numbers can be different for the duplicates.

3. The street address will be the same but may be in different forms: 123 West Elm Street, 123 W. Elm St., and so on.

4. The city, state, and zip code will all be identical for duplicates.

2

The Constraints of Physical Devices

2.1 STORAGE CHARACTERISTICS

If computers had perfect memories, the study of files as a separate topic would never exist. However, computer memories are not perfect. They are less than perfect in two important respects. First, they are limited in size. There are several reasons for size limitations, the most important being cost and address space. There seems to be some kind of natural law at work which says that no matter how much memory a computer system has, there are always applications that would work better if there were more memory available.

Second, computer memories are usually volatile. That is, they lose data that has been stored in them simply because their supply of power has been interrupted for one reason or another. This is an inconvenient but tolerable situation for the small amounts of data involved in executing a program, but it is not feasible where large amounts of "permanent" data need to be saved for repeated use and updating.

Thus we find a need for another form of data storage that is nonvolatile and, if not unlimited, is much larger than the memory found in computers. This has led to the distinction between primary memory and secondary memory in computer systems. *Primary memory* is the main, working store of a computer. It is characterized by high speed, random access, (usually) volatility, and high cost. *Secondary memory* is a lower level of storage characterized by lower speed, less random access, (usually) nonvolatility, and lower costs.

The principal force in shaping memory systems is economics. Storage devices can be made with access times that are a fraction of a nanosecond. However, they are prohibitively expensive for use, even as primary memory.

Conversely, devices such as magnetic tape are very inexpensive, but are so slow that they can be used in only a limited number of applications. Thus we see that there is a relationship between access time and cost for storage devices.

A plot of cost per bit as a function of access time for commercially competitive devices yields an interesting relationship as shown in Figure 2.1. When plotted on logarithmic coordinates, all devices cluster along a straight line. Those that fall well above this line need some special characteristic, such as low power consumption, to remain commercially feasible. As the technology develops, new devices appear below the line because they are cheaper and/or faster than the devices they replace. Thus, over a period of years, the line tends to move downward on the graph.

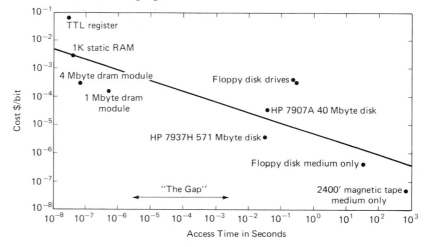

Figure 2.1 Cost of storage versus access time.

An important characteristic of the data in Figure 2.1 is the *gap* that appears between the fastest disks and drums, and the slowest devices used as primary memory. This gap typically represents a ratio of 1000 in access time. Although there have been many devices designed to fill this gap, all have proven to have costs that place them well above the line, and hence are not competitive.

Consequently, we find that for most computer systems there is a considerable gulf in both cost and access time between the primary and secondary storage devices. This gap is created by the need for a low storage cost for permanent data and causes the slow access time of secondary devices. Our study of file systems is largely a search for methods to minimize the effects of this slow access time.

2.2 MAGNETIC TAPE

One of the first secondary storage devices invented and still one of the most popular in use is magnetic tape. While magnetic tape is made in many sizes and used in a variety of devices, we shall focus our attention on the half-inch tape that is commonly used in most standard tape drives associated with computer systems. This form of tape is stored on reels up to $10\frac{1}{2}$ inches in diameter which contain lengths up to 3600 feet. Tape is easily the least expensive medium of data storage commonly used. It is also a strictly *sequential access device*, that is, a device that allows records to be read or written only in the physical order in which they are stored.

The physical medium used to record the data consists of a thin, plastic tape, coated on one side by a thin layer of magnetic material. The magnetic material, when exposed to a strong magnetic field, becomes magnetized in the direction of the external field. It retains this magnetism until another external field is used to change it. Data is recorded on the tape by passing the tape over a *head* which contains electrical and magnetic circuits capable of selectively magnetizing very small areas of the tape. The same head is also capable of detecting the magnetism on subsequent passes of the tape and converting the magnetic patterns into electrical impulses.

A small length of tape is represented in Figure 2.2. The head records data on nine parallel *tracks*. Each track represents a series of binary digits or *bits*. Standard tape densities are 800, 1600, and 6250 bits per inch (bpi). The density used by a particular tape drive is determined by the electronic circuits used, the method of coding bits into magnetic patterns, and especially the design of the head. Some drives are capable of operating at more than one density, although the same density is always used throughout the length of any one tape.

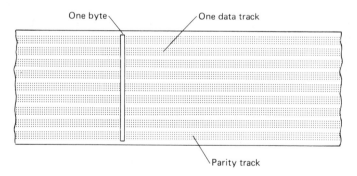

Figure 2.2 Length of magnetic tape with nine tracks.

Data is usually communicated between the computer and the tape drive in units of 8-bit *bytes*. A byte may represent one alphanumeric character, or may be part of a larger unit of data, such as a 64-bit floating-point number. Tape drives record a byte on tape by writing the 8 bits, one on each of eight different tracks, all in one vertical column, as seen in Figure 2.2. Thus the abbreviation bpi can mean both bits per inch (per track) or bytes per inch (for the whole tape).

The ninth track is used to record **parity bits**. The parity bit for one byte is set to a one or zero so as to make the total number of 1-bits in that column odd. This bit is used to check for errors when reading back the data. Parity bytes are commonly added as well to provide longitudinal parity checks.

The tape must move over the head at a precisely controlled speed whenever the tape is being read or written. If the tape were to move constantly, as for example an audio tape moves, the computer would have to be able to transmit or receive data continuously. Since this is seldom feasible, or even desirable, a method is needed to start and stop the tape. However, since the tape cannot be read or written unless it is running at a fixed speed, there will be gaps without data where the tape stopped and restarted during recording. These gaps can also be used to stop and start the tape during reading. These gaps are called **interrecord gaps** and are illustrated in Figure 2.3. The minimum gap size for standard half inch tapes is 0.5 inch. Most drives write a slightly longer gap with a nominal size of about 0.6 inch. However, any drive that is capable of reading standard tapes must be able to start and stop in a half inch or less. This requires a very high acceleration. One of the more significant cost factors in the manufacture of a tape drive is the mechanism for accelerating the tape to full speed in 0.25 inch.

Some tape drives are designed to write interrecord gaps without stopping. These are called **streaming** tape drives and are used in special applications such as in backing up disks. It is still necessary to insert the gaps since, when the tape is read, it may not be possible to process the data as quickly as it can be read. Streaming tape drives typically have slower start/stop times and are not able to stop or start in the space of the interrecord gap. Such drives will overshoot the gap and must then back up to a point before the gap to make a "flying start" on the next block. This process requires considerably more time than the start/stop times of a nonstreaming tape drive.

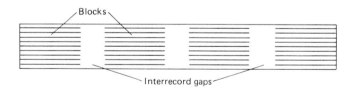

Figure 2.3 Blocks and interrecord gaps.

The unit of data between interrecord gaps is called a **block**. Typically, one block will contain a number of data records. The number of records per block is called the **blocking factor**. Blocks are limited in size since the computer system must allocate primary storage space to store at least one block. This space is called a **buffer**. The block size can also be limited by the tape drive and the scheme used to encode the data on the tape.

While the block size is limited, it is very important that it not be too small. If the block is too small, most of the length of the tape may be wasted with interrecord gaps, and most of the time required to read or write the tape will be spent in starting and stopping the tape drive. For example, consider a text file with 10,000 records of 80 bytes each. At a tape density of 1600 bpi, the actual data would require $10,000 \times 80 \div 1600 = 500$ inches. With a blocking factor of 1 and interrecord gaps of a $1/2$ inch, the gaps would require $10,000 \times 0.5 = 5000$ inches. Thus our file would be 5500 inches long and the tape storage efficiency would be $500 \div 5500 = 9.09\%$. To make matters worse, the tape would have to start and stop 10,000 times while processing the file which would take a considerable time. Figure 2.4 illustrates such a file.

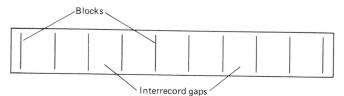

Figure 2.4 Small blocks with interrecord gaps.

The same file with a blocking factor of 60 would require $10,000 \div 60 = 167$ blocks. The total file length is $500 + 167 \times 0.5 = 583.5$ inches. The storage efficiency is much better at 86% and the required start/stop time is only 1.67% of the previous case. Higher storage efficiency requires larger block sizes. A block size of 8000 bytes at 1600 bpi will yield an efficiency of 91%.

The modes of access for magnetic tape are fairly simple. All blocks must be processed in sequence. Thus the usual logical operations are: read next block, write next block, and rewind. Some systems have the capability to read or write in reverse; however, these operations are useful in only a few circumstances and we will not consider them further. Blocks are usually written only at the end of the file, or ***appended***. The reason for not writing or updating elsewhere is that it is very difficult to overlay one block exactly with another.

Magnetic tape is useful because the cost per bit is extremely low. Since blocks can vary in length, it will accommodate variable-length records easily. However, because the access is sequential, the number of algorithms that can be used with tape is limited. Characteristics of some common magnetic tape drives are listed in Figure 2.5. Figure 2.6 shows a $1/2$-inch magnetic tape drive.

2.3 HARD MAGNETIC DISKS

Magnetic disk is the most important form of secondary storage today. Disks can take on many different forms, including floppy disks, cartridge disks, and fixed-head disks. The most common type used in mainframe computers is the hard, moving-head disk, and it is this type that we will concentrate on.

Manufacturer and Model	Tape Width (inches)	Mode[a]	Maximum Tape Length (feet)	Number of Tracks	Bits per Inch per Track	Read/Write Speed (in./sec)	Rewind Speed (in./sec)	Average Transfer Rate (Kilobytes/sec)
HP 9142A	0.25	S	600	16	600	62.5	90	33
HP 7970E	0.5	C	2400	9	1600	45	160	58
HP 7974A	0.5	S	2400	9	800/1600	100	200	133
HP 7978B	0.5	S	2400	9	1600/6250	75	250	367
HP 7980A	0.5	S	2400	9	1600/6250	125	320	611
DEC TK50	0.5	S	600	22	303	75	—	45
DEC TA78	0.5	C	2400	9	1600/6250	125	440	611
DEC TA81	0.5	C	2400	9	1600/6250	25	192	122
DEC TU80	0.5	S	2400	9	1600	100	192	125
DEC TU80	0.5	C	2400	9	1600	25	192	31
DEC TU81+	0.5	S	2400	9	1600/6250	75	192	367
DEC TU81+	0.5	C	2400	9	1600/6250	25	192	125
IBM 3480	0.5	S	600	18	16,900	40	150	1160

[a] Mode: C, conventional start/stop; S, streaming.

Figure 2.5 Magnetic tape drive characteristics.

Figure 2.6 Half-inch magnetic tape drive. (Courtesy of Hewlett-Packard Co.)

Hard disks are made of sheets of metal cut into disks, usually between 3.5 and 18 inches in diameter. The disks are coated with a thin layer of magnetic material similar to that used on tape. Several disks are mounted on a common axis or hub to form a *disk pack*. Typically, a half-dozen to a dozen disks are mounted in one pack, as shown in Figure 2.7. All the surfaces of the pack except the top surface of the top disk and the bottom surface of the bottom disk are used for recording. Sometimes one surface is used for permanent tracks that aid in positioning the heads on the other tracks. These are called servo tracks and cannot be used for data.

The recording is done on each disk surface on a series of concentric tracks. The tracks are separate and do not form a spiral as do the grooves of a phonograph record. Each track is usually divided into a series of fixed-length physical blocks called *sectors*. The sectors are separated by interrecord gaps. Each sector begins with a sector address, which is unique on the disk pack, followed by the sector data. Typically, each sector will contain a few hundred bytes of data. The data is recorded serially on the sector, meaning that the bits of each byte follow one another along the same track. Figure 2.8 shows how one track might look on a disk surface.

Figure 2.7 Disk pack.

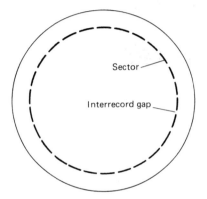

Figure 2.8 One track with sectors.

The reading and writing of the tracks is performed by heads. Usually, there is one head for each disk surface. The heads do not touch the disk, but fly aerodynamically a few dozen microinches above the surface. Because of the high speed with which the disk moves past the head, contact between head and disk is destructive to both. Thus it is imperative that such contact be avoided at all costs.

The heads fly on a boundary layer of air that moves with the disk in much the way a water skier "flies" on the surface of the water. Dust and other contaminates on the disk surface are a major cause of "head crashes." Figure 2.9 illustrates the size of several common disk contaminates relative to the head-to-disk clearance. Because foreign particles on the disk present such a serious hazard, disks are assembled in "clean rooms" with a dust-free atmosphere and sealed, or are supplied by the drive with a constant flow of filtered air to prevent the entry of contaminated air.

Since there are usually a few hundred tracks on each surface, but only one head, it is necessary to move the head from track to track to reach all the tracks. This is done by a mechanical arm to which all the heads are connected as shown in Figure 2.10. The arm is powered by a mechanism that is designed to

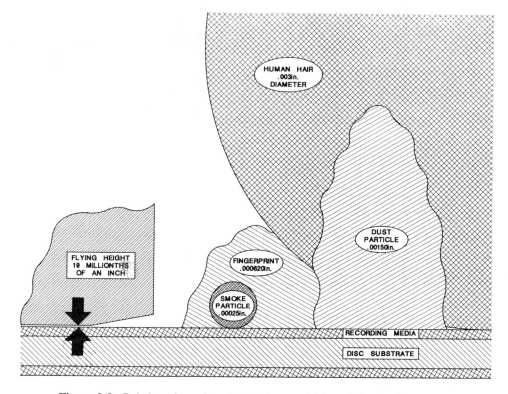

Figure 2.9 Relative size of contaminating particles and head clearance. (Courtesy of Hewlett-Packard Co.)

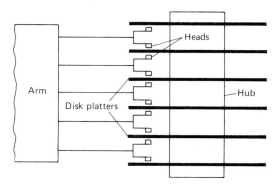

Figure 2.10 Heads and arm mechanism.

Figure 2.11 A 3.5-inch hard disk with 10 megabyte capacity. Note the arm supporting the head. (Courtesy of Hewlett-Packard Co.)

move the heads very precisely in a minimum of time. A hard disk with the head supported by the arm is shown in Figure 2.10.

The heads are mounted on the arm so that they are aligned vertically with one another. Thus if the head on the first surface is positioned over, say, track 479, all of the other heads will be positioned over track 479 on their respective surfaces. All of the tracks that are under the heads at the same time are called a *cylinder*. The sectors of a disk pack are ordered so that all in one cylinder have consecutive addresses. Thus, when processing data sequentially, all sectors or tracks in a cylinder can be accessed before the arm must be moved. This is important, because moving the arm takes far longer than any other aspect of accessing disk data. Only one head is selected at a time for reading or writing. Switching between heads is done electronically and is therefore very fast. Figure 2.12 shows a removable disk pack.

Disks are frequently referred to as random access devices because, unlike tape, any part of a disk pack may be reached in a small fraction of a second. However, a true *random access device* is one in which all addresses are equally accessible. This is clearly not true of a disk. The most accessible sectors are those which will pass next under the heads. The next most accessible are those on the same cylinder. Those on distant cylinders will require the most time to reach because of the time needed to move the arm. Thus it is more appropriate to refer to disks as *pseudorandom access devices*.

The total time required to transfer data to or from a disk has three components. First is the time required to reposition the arm, called *seek time*. This usually varies from a few milliseconds for a one-track move to scores of milliseconds or more for a move from one end of the disk to the other. Most drives

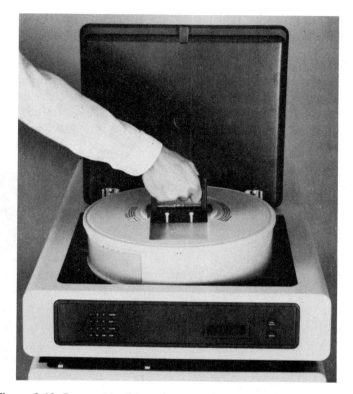

Figure 2.12 Removable disk pack (inside cover) with capacity of 404 megabytes. (Courtesy of Hewlett-Packard Co.)

give a specification for an average, or random, move, which should be used in calculations.

The second component is the time from when the arm is positioned to when the first sector of the transfer moves under a head. This time is called *latency* and depends on the speed of rotation of the disk. In the best case there would be no wait at all, while in the worst case where the beginning of the sector had just been missed, the wait would be the time required for a full revolution. On the average, the latency will be equal to the time required for the disk to turn half a revolution. For example, at 3600 rpm the disk turns 60 revolutions every second. Thus a full revolution requires 16.7 milliseconds. The average latency is the time required for half a revolution, or 8.3 milliseconds.

The third component is the time actually required to transfer the data. If we assume that the transfer is done within the bounds of one cylinder, which will usually be the case, the time will be that required for the sectors involved to pass, one at a time, beneath the head or heads. For example, a disk spinning at 3600 rpm, with 40 sectors of 256 bytes each per track, will require $(1 \div 60) \cdot (5 \div 40) = 0.00209$ second or 2.09 milliseconds to transfer a block of five sectors which contains 1280 bytes. Average transfer rates should always be calculated on the basis of the time required for the data to pass the head. The specification given for transfer rate on disk drives is frequently the peak or burst rate. This is always higher than the average rate due to the gaps between sectors.

Seek time dominates the total time required for a disk access, typically followed by the latency time, and finally the data transfer time. When it is possible to do a transfer without moving the arm, there is a great savings in the total time, and there are some schemes that attempt to minimize the arm travel for this reason. Figure 2.13 shows a cabinet containing two disk drives.

Figure 2.13 Two 571 megabyte disk drives in one cabinet. (Courtesy of Hewlett-Packard Co.)

Disk operations are simple, because the disk driver and controller usually take care of automatically moving the arm to the required cylinder, selecting the appropriate head, checking the sector addresses, and handling any errors. The basic operations are thus reduced to reading or writing a specified number of sectors, beginning at a given sector address. Data transfers must always be for an integral number of sectors. It is not usually possible to transfer a fraction of a sector. Thus the block sizes used with disks are always multiples of the sector size. Characteristics of some common disk drives are listed in Figure 2.14.

2.4 OTHER DEVICES

There are numerous devices on which files may be stored. These include floppy disks, punched cards, and others. In many ways these devices are similar to hard disks or magnetic tape, and the same methods that are applied to disks or tapes may be applied to these devices as well.

Floppy disks are organized similarly to hard disks. They differ in several important respects. First, they are made of plastic and are flexible (or "floppy"). They are not stacked in packs but are used as single platters, either with only one side, or with both sides having data recorded. They are enclosed permanently in small plastic envelopes and may easily be carried about or mailed.

Second, floppies have both less area available for recording and a lower recording density. Hence they hold much less data than one platter of a hard disk pack. For example, one platter of a hard disk may hold as many as 100 million bytes of data, while one floppy may hold fewer than 1 million bytes. Consequently, the size of files that may be placed on a floppy disk is limited.

Third, floppy disks are considerably slower than hard disks in all three parameters of disk speed: seek time, latency, and data transfer time. Consequently, similar operations may take more than 10 times longer when done on a floppy as compared to a hard disk. Since floppies are usually dedicated to one task, and the files are relatively small, the difference in speed may not be as noticeable to the user.

Fourth, while the heads on hard disks must never make contact with the disk surface, heads for floppy disks are in direct contact. This greatly simplifies the structure of the heads and their supports but also restricts the speed of the disk relative to the head. This makes floppy disks both less expensive and slower than hard disks. The heads are pressed against the disk only when reads and writes are actually being done. During idle time the head is removed from contact or the disk is stopped from rotating to minimize wear. Figure 2.15 shows both floppy and hard disks.

Many clever schemes have been invented to prevent unauthorized copying of programs or data from floppy disks. All of these involve a departure from the standard recording techniques on at least a small portion of the disk. These methods include placing tracks at irregular intervals; using sectors of odd lengths; writing (and subsequently reading) a track while the access arm is in motion so that the track forms a short spiral instead of a circle; and recording a sector with a noise pattern which, when read back, gives unpredictable and inconsistent results. This last method is verified by reading the "noise" sector several times and comparing the results. If they are not different, the disk is a copy. All of these methods require direct control of the disk read/write hardware by the program, thus bypassing the file system and operating system.

Cards are archaic and little used for files anymore. They are characterized by a fixed record length, usually of 80 bytes. They are unusual in that a card

Manufacturer and Model	Disk Type	Diameter (inches)	Capacity per spindle (megabytes)	Number of Date Surfaces	Bytes per Sector	Sectors per Track	Tracks per Surface	Average Seek Time (milliseconds)	Average Latency (milliseconds)	Transfer Rate (kbytes/sec)	Tracks per inch
IBM 3330	Hard		200	19	13,030[a]		808	30	8.3	806	
IBM 3340	Hard		70	12	8,368[a]		696	25	10.1	442	
IBM 3350	Hard		317	30	19,069[a]		555	25	8.3	1198	
IBM 3375	Hard		410	12	35,616[a]		959	19	10.1	1859	
IBM 3380 AD4	Hard		630	15	47,476[a]		885	15	8.3	3000	
IBM 3380 AE4	Hard		1260	15	47,476[a]		1770	17	8.3	3000	
HP 7907A	Hard	8.0	40.1	4	256	64	627	30	8.5	1000	
HP 7935A	Hard	15.3	404	13	256	92	1321	24	11.1	1000	
HP 7937H	Hard	5.25	571	13	256	123	1396	20.5	8.3	2350	1121
HP 7958A	Hard	5.25	130	8	256	64	1019	29	8.3	1250	
HP 9154A	Hard	3.5	10	2	256	28	703	75	10	500	1100
HP 9554B	Hard	3.5	20	2	256	28	1408	75	10	500	1850
HP 99133L	Hard	3.5	44.8	2	256	32	977	40	8.3	625	960
HP 9153A	Floppy	3.5	0.788	2	1,024	5	80	175	50	62.5	135
HP 9127A	Floppy	5.25	0.360	2	512	9	40	93	100	31	48
HP 9121S	Floppy	3.5	0.270	1	256	16	70	370	50	41	135
DEC RA60	Hard		205	6	512	42	1588	42	8.3	1980	779
DEC RA81	Hard		456	7[b]	512	51	2496[b]	28	8.3	2200	960
DEC SA82	Hard		664	7.5[b]	512	57	2846[b]	24	8.3	2400	1063

Figure 2.14 Disk drive characteristics.

[a] Bytes per track (IBM disks are not sectored.)
[b] These drives have two heads per track, which logically doubles the number of tracks per cylinder and halves the number of cylinders.

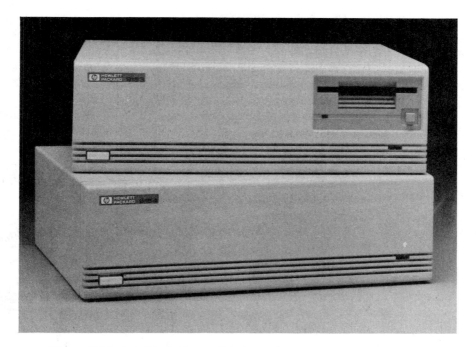

Figure 2.15 A 3.5-inch floppy disk drive (top) with a capacity of 788 kilo-bytes and a 3.5-inch hard disk drive (bottom) with a capacity of 10 mega-bytes. (Courtesy of Hewlett-Packard Co.)

file may be written on exactly once. Thereafter, it may be read any number of times, but can be updated only by manual methods. It also is very limited in access modes, which are strictly sequential or manual. Some of the methods that have been developed for card files, and are now nearly forgotten will doubtless be rediscovered when "write once" devices such as optical laser disks become common.

Optical disks are of two types: read-only (ROM) and write once, read mostly (WORM). The disks are similar, the fundamental difference being whether or not the disk drive has the ability to write on the disk. ROM disks are used for large, published sets of data such as an encyclopedia or large, static databases. The files can be structured for the most convenient retrieval since they will not be updated or added to.

WORM disks, however, need to be used with very carefully designed file structures since records cannot be updated, even to flag them as deleted. Moreover, since records are frequently added to a file over an extended period, it is likely that records from a single file will be scattered over a wide area of the disk and be intermingled with records from many other files. A sophisticated directory is necessary for WORM disks to keep track of which records are active or inactive, and where the physical records are located on disk. Since the directory must be frequently updated, it is likely that part or all of it will reside on a more conventional medium such as magnetic disk.

Technologies such as charge-coupled devices (CCD) and bubble memories have some promise and a few applications for storage of files. Each presents unique problems for the file designer. This is due largely to the constraints of access, which is pseudorandom. Doubtless a somewhat different set of algorithms will emerge for these devices if and when they become popular for file storage.

Another technology that is becoming increasingly common and which mimics older technologies in access modes is telecommunications. Frequently, one computer system will access files on another, remote computer system. The remote system may be using fast hard disks, but the intervening communications link is frequently a slow, serial channel which may make the remote file behave more as though it were on a slow, sequential device.

Figure 2.16 A 0.25-inch cartridge tape drive (left) with a capacity of 60 megabytes per cartridge. The units on the right are hard disk drives with capacities of 10 and 20 megabytes. All are designed for use with microcomputer systems. (Courtesy of Hewlett-Packard Co.)

2.5 BLOCKING AND EXTENTS

Blocks of records were discussed earlier as a requirement if magnetic tape is to be used efficiently. We have also seen that blocks of data can be transferred to or from disks only when their lengths are multiples of the sector length. In both of these situations, it is important that the file designer select the blocking factor with considerable care. A poorly chosen blocking factor can result in the file occupying many times the necessary space and having greatly degraded performance owing to more physical transfers being used than are necessary. Thus the problem of calculating and selecting appropriate blocking factors deserves some study.

Block design is relatively simple for magnetic tape. Basically, the larger the block, the more efficient will be the space utilization, and the fewer will be the number of physical transfers with their attendant starts and stops. The limiting factors on block size are the size of the buffer required in primary memory and the limit of block size that the tape I/O system can handle. Those using tape files on a given computer system are usually aware of these constraints and can factor them into the tape file design.

There are several problems that occasionally arise when tape files are used to transfer data from one computer system to another system of a different type. First, the tape density must be the same. If one system writes a tape at 6250 bpi and the other can only read at 1600 bpi, it will not work. Second, the internal structure of the files must be compatible. Frequently, only the simplest file structures are internally compatible. Consequently, a common form such as plain text files is frequently used to exchange data. Third, the coding scheme must be compatible. For example, most IBM systems use a code called EBCDIC for encoding alphanumeric characters into bytes, while much of the rest of the world uses ASCII. One system or the other will have to have a program to convert the codes if the machines use different codes. Fourth, some systems have difficulty handling files with records or blocks having an odd number of bytes. It may be wise to use an even number of bytes for record length when transmitting files by tape to another type of computer. Finally, do not choose a block size that might be too large for another system to handle.

2.5.1 Disk Blocking

Disk file blocking is a more complicated problem. All of the factors that were considered for magnetic tape also apply to disk. However, there is also the problem of fitting some integral number of records into an integral number of sectors. Unless this is done with care, a significant waste of disk space can occur. Consider a file with a record length of 160 bytes that is stored on a disk having a sector length of 256 bytes. The table in Figure 2.17 shows the result of choosing blocking factors from 1 to 8. Notice that the storage efficiency varies from a low of 63% to a high of 100%. Very low storage efficiencies can result from using low blocking factors with short records. For example, a record of 30 bytes stored with a blocking factor of 1 in sectors of 256 bytes will give an efficiency of $30 \div 256 = 12\%$.

The problem of matching sector length and record length is illustrated in Figure 2.18. Ideally, we would like to find a blocking factor for which we come out even, that is, where the length of B records exactly equals the length of N sectors. In actual practice, this happens only occasionally. Most of the time we

Blocking Factor	Logical Block Size	Sectors per Block	Physical Block Size	Storage Efficiency (%)
1	160	1	256	63
2	320	2	512	63
3	480	2	512	94
4	640	3	768	83
5	800	4	1024	78
6	960	4	1024	94
7	1120	5	1280	88
8	1280	5	1280	100

Figure 2.17 Table of block sizes for 160-byte record with 256-byte sector.

must be satisfied using most of the physical block and wasting a little space in the last sector.

Figure 2.18 Matching sectors and records.

There is no easy formula to calculate an appropriate blocking factor to use for a given file, although it is possible to write a program to do such a calculation. The storage efficiency can be calculated as follows:

$$E = (R \cdot B) \div (S \cdot N) \tag{2.1}$$

where:

$$N = (R \cdot B) \div S \cdot \quad \text{(rounded up)}$$

and R = record length
S = sector length
B = blocking factor (records per block)
N = number of sectors per block
E = storage efficiency

A typical disk file blocking problem will include upper and lower limits on block size as well as record and sector information. A lower limit on block size may be imposed to prevent an excessive number of data transfers while processing the file. This is very important if the file is processed sequentially or when records that may be processed together can be grouped together. An upper limit on block size may result from concerns over the buffer size or the time required to transfer data.

For example, consider the HP 7935A disk drive shown in Figure 2.14. If 1000 consecutive sectors on one cylinder were read in sequence, the total disk time required would be 1000 times the sum of the average latency of 11.1 milliseconds and the transfer time for one sector of 0.24 millisecond for a result of 11.34 seconds. The same data in blocks of 20 sectors would require 50 times the sum of 11.1 milliseconds latency and 4.83 milliseconds transfer time or 0.796 second. The difference would be even greater if the arm were repositioned between reads.

Where the records are processed in random order, a large block size will not significantly reduce the number of physical transfers but will increase the transfer time and buffer size, and is thus counterproductive.

A simple algorithm for calculating an optimum disk block size is to produce a table of blocking factors and storage efficiencies for all block sizes between the upper and lower limits for block size, and then select the factor giving the highest efficiency. For example, given a sector length of 200 bytes, a record length of 86 bytes, a lower limit of 2000 bytes, and an upper limit of 3000 bytes for block size, what is the best choice for blocking factor? The lower limit on blocking factor is 2000 ÷ 86 = 23.3, which is rounded down to 23. The upper limit is 3000 ÷ 86 = 34.9, which is rounded down to 34. Hence we must consider all blocking factors from 23 to 34. The table in figure 2.19 shows the data calculated for this problem.

Blocking Factor	Logical Block Size	Physical Block Size	Storage Efficiency (%)
23	1978	2000	98.9
24	2064	2200	93.8
25	2150	2200	97.7
26	2236	2400	93.2
27	2322	2400	96.8
28	2408	2600	92.6
29	2494	2600	95.9
30	2580	2600	99.2
31	2666	2800	95.2
32	2752	2800	98.3
33	2830	3000	94.6
34	2924	3000	97.5

Figure 2.19 Table of block sizes for 86-byte record and 200-byte sector with block size limits.

Obviously, a blocking factor of 30 is the best choice with a storage efficiency of 99.2%. We might also notice that the best choice will always be one that most nearly fills a physical block. Thus, in the table of Figure 2.17, only the blocking factors of 23, 25, 27, 30, 32, and 34 need be considered. These factors can be determined by dividing the record size into multiples of the sector size and rounding down. Thus we find $2000 \div 86 = 23.3$, $2200 \div 86 = 25.6$, and so on. This will reduce the number of cases that need to be considered and thus the amount of calculations required.

Blocking design is not difficult, but a poor design can cause considerable problems when the file is implemented. Therefore, it is a task that should always be approached with care.

Some file systems calculate the blocking factors automatically and the designer has little or no control of it. Others are capable of spanning records across block boundaries and are thus able to use 100% of the file space. Spanning, however, requires that the file system use more sophisticated buffer management methods when a record spans two blocks.

2.5.2 Extents

Besides dividing a file into records and blocks, many file systems divide a file into sections called extents. An *extent* is a portion of a file that contains many blocks and is physically in one contiguous portion of the disk. Usually, extents are all of the same size for one file and vary in number from one to dozens.

Although management of extents makes the file system more complicated, there are several advantages to dividing the file physically. First, as files are added and deleted, the free space on a disk becomes scattered into many small, isolated pieces. This is called *fragmentation*. Although there may be ample free space on a disk, there may not be any one contiguous area large enough to accommodate a new file. By breaking the file into several smaller extents, it is usually possible to find free space for all of them.

Second, it is sometimes advantageous to distribute a large file over several physical disks. Obviously, this must be done if a file exceeds the size of one disk. For smaller files there may sometimes be a performance advantage in spreading the file over multiple disks. Such a distribution of a file is called *spanning* the file over multiple disks. Extents are used to effect this spanning.

Third, it is sometimes possible to dynamically alter the physical size of a file by adding or deleting extents. For example, as records are added to the end of a file, the last extent will become filled. If the file is so structured, a new extent will then automatically be allocated when the next record is added. This operation may be handled entirely by the file system and be transparent to the programmer or program. Similarly, if a file has one or more empty extents at the end, these may be deleted automatically when the file closes.

2.6 PHYSICAL DATA TRANSFER CONSIDERATIONS

The actual transfer of data between a secondary storage device and the record buffer of a running process is normally handled by the operating system of a computer. It is not the purpose of this book to explain the functioning of I/O systems, as this is properly the domain of a course in operating systems. Nor is it necessary for the student of file systems to understand the inner workings of operating systems to design and use files intelligently.

However, there are some features of the physical I/O that can bias the statistics of doing file I/O to a degree that they need to be considered when designing files. It is these issues that are addressed in this section.

2.6.1 Buffered Input/Output

All physical transfers are done to or from a buffer in the primary memory of the computer. The operating system usually handles the task of assembling a block from individual records when writing, or separating the records from the block when reading. The programmer or user is not explicitly aware of when the physical I/O is performed. The file system commands at the program level are either built into the language or called explicitly as external procedures. Appendix A shows representative file system commands. The commands that transfer data are record level operations, not block level operations. Thus the file system transmits records to and from the process, but transmits blocks to and from the secondary storage device.

When files are processed sequentially, a technique called *double buffering* is sometimes employed. Two buffers are assigned to the file. Initially, the buffers are loaded with the first two blocks of the file. As soon as the first block of records has been processed, a read operation is initiated to refill it with the third block of the file. This read parallels the processing of the records in the second block so that the third block of records is immediately available to the program when the second block has been completed. Because the reads can be anticipated in sequential processing, it is possible for the two buffers to continue alternating, with one being refilled while the other is being processed, thus reducing the total time for the task. A similar benefit can be realized when writing sequential files.

The file system must manage the buffers carefully. Data can be lost, for example, if buffers are not written back to disk after one or more records have been modified or added. However, buffers should not be written back after every change since there may be many changes made in one block before a write must be performed. If multiple users are accessing the file, the buffer management is made even more complicated since several users may be sharing a buffer.

The cost of moving records between the user process and the file system is negligible compared to the cost of moving blocks between the buffer and secondary storage device. Therefore, we will be concerned with estimating the number of these physical transfers. In many situations it is possible to accurately estimate the number of physical transfers, and we will do this through the remaining chapters. However, the file designer must be aware of the features that may distort these statistics.

The most important such feature is called *disk caching*. A disk cache is a very large buffer that can hold many blocks of file data. When reading a file, for example, the block containing the requested record, and many additional surrounding blocks are all read into the cache with one physical transfer. The one block with the desired record is then transferred to the file system buffer, and finally the requested record is transferred to the requesting process, as shown in Figure 2.20. If subsequent reads are for consecutive records, or for records that are near the first record, there is a good chance that they will be in the cache and another physical transfer will not be needed. Thus an effective disk caching system can significantly reduce the number of physical transfers and consequently increase the speed with which a process runs.

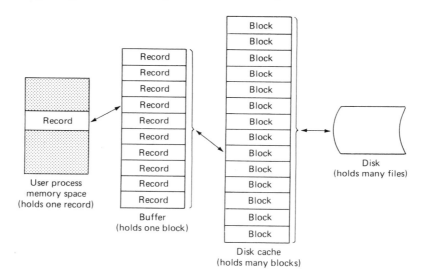

Figure 2.20 Disk caching.

There are many ways to implement disk caching, both physically and algorithmically. For example, the caches may be in primary memory, either in a reserved area, or in competition with process segments in shared memory. Caches may also be located in a dedicated, high-speed memory module in a secondary storage unit or its controller. There are many parameters, including the cache size, the manner in which caches are assigned to files, and when a cache is written to disk that can have a major impact on how well caching will work with a given application. For example, caching is usually very effective when files are processed sequentially, but can actually degrade performance if the file processing is highly random. Thus it is important to have a good understanding of the caching system when designing files for a computer that employs this device.

2.6.2 Memory-Mapped Files

Some computer systems that feature "virtual memory" for management of primary memory also use the same mechanism for moving file data between primary and secondary storage. In these systems, primary memory is divided into a large number of equal-sized segments called *pages*. Typically, page sizes range from 256 bytes to several thousand bytes. In any given system, however, all pages are of the same size.

In such a system, the address space of a process, including code and data, is also divided into pages. A memory-mapping mechanism maps the process address space into the physical address space of primary memory. For a process to be able to run, some, but usually not all pages of the process must be in primary memory, as shown in Figure 2.21. There is no correspondence between the location of a page in the process address space and its location in primary memory. The pages not in primary memory are stored on a fast secondary device, usually disk.

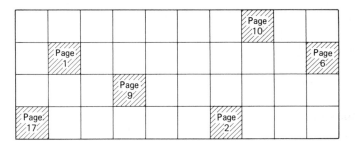

Figure 2.21 Several pages of one process in paged primary memory.

When a portion of process space is addressed which is in a page that is not in primary memory, a *page fault* occurs. The process is suspended while the missing page is read into primary memory. The process may then resume. Thus pages are read in as needed.

Eventually, all of primary memory becomes filled with process pages. A rule is then invoked to determine which page to remove from primary memory each time a page must be brought in. One rule commonly used is to remove the page that has been in primary memory the longest time without being referenced. Pages are also removed when their associated process terminates.

This swapping of pages between primary and secondary memory represents a significant portion of the I/O performed by the system. Memory-mapped files take advantage of this mechanism to perform the file I/O as well.

A *memory-mapped* file is viewed as though the entire file resided in primary memory. The first byte of the first record is at address zero. The first byte of the second record immediately follows the last byte of the first record, and so on. The file is regarded by the memory-mapping mechanism as one contiguous address space.

When a record is addressed, a page fault occurs if the corresponding page is not in primary memory, and the page is swapped in. The record is addressed through the memory-mapping mechanism.

In a sense, the page being addressed acts as the buffer for the records in that page. However, there are significant differences from buffered files. Where a file using conventional I/O will have one or a few buffers, any page of real memory may become the "buffer" for a memory-mapped file. Moreover, if there is ample free primary memory, many pages of the file may reside in primary memory at the same time. Finally, there is no attempt to block memory-mapped files. Records typically span sectors and pages. Thus memory-mapped files make more efficient use of secondary storage than conventional files.

The number of physical I/O operations required is difficult to predict with memory-mapped files. The contention for real memory in particular can cause wide variations in the amount of physical I/O for a given function. Where the active parts of the file can reside in primary memory throughout the time the file is open, there can be a significant reduction in I/O. However, if there is considerable memory contention, the amount of file I/O may actually increase over that of conventional files.

There are other aspects of the physical file systems that may be important to the file designer as well. For example, when several files need to be accessed concurrently, a process may run much faster if the files are placed on separate disk drives. This will reduce the probability that the arm would need to be moved for each access. It also would reduce contention for one disk and allow operations to overlap in time. In a similar way, contention for channels or buses can sometimes be reduced by careful choice of configuration and devices.

2.7 FILE SYSTEMS

In a modern computer system there are many layers of hardware and software that are required to support an end user as shown in Figure 2.22. Each layer depends solely on the layers below it to provide the services and functions it needs for support. In turn, it provides services for the layers above it that are more complex than those provided by the layers below it.

For example, a set of library procedures may provide data to an application program that originates from a disk file. The library calls may completely hide any knowledge of these files from the application program, simply supplying data with no reference to its source.

User commands
Application program
Library procedures
File system
Operating system
Machine instruction set
Hardware

Figure 2.22 Layers of hardware and software.

The library procedures, in turn, call procedures in the file system layer to request that operations be done on the files. These would include opening and closing files, reading and writing, and other services.

The file system translates these requests into calls to the operating system functions to do the physical input/output operations. The operating system will, in turn, execute a "channel program" to cause the transfer actually to take place.

As errors or exceptional conditions occur, each layer attempts to resolve them. Only errors or conditions that cannot be resolved at one level are passed up to the next layer. Several examples will illustrate this principle.

The application program requests data contained in a certain record. The block containing the record spans a cylinder boundary; that is, part of the block is at the end of one cylinder and part at the beginning of the next cylinder. The file system requests the physical transfer whose length equals the block size beginning with the first sector of the block. The operating system transfers the sectors remaining on the first cylinder and reports back to the file system that the transfer terminated, after a certain number of sectors, due to a "cylinder overflow." The file system calculates the appropriate starting addresses in disk and primary memory, and the required length to complete the operation. It then requests another transfer to read the remaining data. The file system reports to the caller that the transfer was completed normally, thus hiding the details of the cylinder overflow from the higher levels.

A hardware condition, such as a disk or tape unit being off-line, may cause the operating system to generate a request to the operator to place the unit on-line. Again, higher layers would not be aware of the condition.

Other kinds of errors and conditions may be detected at higher levels. A request to read a record beyond the end-of-file would be detected by the file system without any calls being made to the operating system. When an attempt to find a record with a key that matches a given key fails, because no such record exists, that failure will be detected at the level of library procedures or, perhaps, even higher up.

Good program design dictates that each level must check for all possible errors and exceptional conditions. Upon detecting such, it must first attempt to resolve them at that level. Failing that, the condition is reported up to the next level for resolution.

A summary of three file systems is presented in Appendix A. The first file system is a simple "generic" system which will be used in algorithms in the remainder of this book. The others are extracts from real file systems. In the case of both real systems, there are additional procedures available for ancillary functions such as returning the parameters of a file or rewinding a tape reel. The ones shown in Appendix A are those necessary for most file access functions.

The algorithms found in this book are appropriate for the library procedures layer and the application program layer. The simpler functions may not warrant separate procedures but can be implemented by direct calls to the file system. Other algorithms are more complex and should be implemented as library functions.

2.8 SUMMARY

Computer storage is usually classified as *primary memory* or *secondary memory*, where primary memory is three to four orders of magnitude faster than secondary memory, but also significantly more expensive. The large span of access time between the slower primary storage devices and the faster secondary devices is sometimes called the *memory gap*. Most secondary storage devices are *nonvolatile*, unlike most primary storage devices.

Magnetic tape is a strictly sequential medium, usually used to store large amounts of data economically. Most tape drives record data in nine parallel tracks on $1/2$-inch-wide tape. Standard *recording densities* are 800, 1600, and 6250 bytes per inch. *Blocks* of data are separated by *interrecord gaps* of slightly more than $1/2$ inch in length. These gaps provide area where the drive can start and stop the tape without losing data. The tape moves over a *read/write* head at a fixed speed when data is being transferred. The peak transfer rate is determined by the tape density and the speed of the tape.

Hard magnetic disks are *pseudorandom access* devices which record data serially on concentric *tracks*. Tracks are frequently divided into *sectors* of fixed length. There is usually one *read/write head* for each disk surface. These heads fly aerodynamically a few dozen microinches above the disk surface, but do not actually touch the surface. Disk platters are commonly stacked to form a *disk pack*. All the heads are supported by a common *access arm* that moves them in unison from track to track. All the tracks that are under the heads at one position of the arm are collectively called a *cylinder*.

There are three components to the time required to transfer data between a specific part of the disk and primary memory. The longest time is required to position the arm at the correct cylinder and is called *seek time*. *Latency* is the time required for the proper sector to rotate under a head. Transfer time is the time required for the sector involved to pass beneath the head(s) while the data is transferred.

Floppy disks use a flexible plastic medium for recording data. They are slower in all respects than hard disks, but also less expensive. The head makes contact with the disk whenever reading or writing is performed.

Blocking on disks maps a discrete number of records into several sectors. The object is to maximize the use of the storage space and minimize the number of physical transfers.

Disk files are sometimes divided into *extents*. Each extent contains many blocks stored in one contiguous area of disk. Multiple extents allow flexibility in distributing a file about one or more disks. They also provide a mechanism for dynamically expanding or contracting a file.

Blocks of data are usually transferred between secondary storage and a *buffer* area in primary memory. Individual records are then transferred by the file system between the buffer and the user's record buffer. *Disk caching* is sometimes used to reduce the number of physical accesses by moving many blocks at one time between the cache and the disk.

Memory-mapped files are viewed as one large address space in primary memory. Segments of fixed size called *pages* are *swapped* between primary and secondary storage as demand dictates.

File use by an end user is usually supported by several layers of hardware and software. These include the hardware, the machine instruction set, the operating system, the file system, library procedures, and the application program. Each layer is supported by those below it and provides higher-level services to those layers above it. Errors detected at any level are resolved at that level if possible. Otherwise, they are reported up to the next level.

2.9 PROBLEMS

2.1. Name three characteristics that usually are different for primary and secondary memory.

2.2. Calculate the storage efficiency for each of the following tape files:
   (a) Block length = 2400 bytes, density = 800 bpi, IRG = 0.75 inch
   (b) Block length = 240 bytes, density = 1600 bpi, IRG = 0 .5 inch
   (c) Block length = 1600 bytes, density = 6250 bpi, IRG = 0.6 inch
   (d) Block length = 8096 bytes, density = 6250 bpi, IRG = 0.6 inch
   (e) Block length = 80 bytes, density = 6250 bpi, IRG = 0 .6 inch

2.3. Calculate the number of bytes that can be stored on a 2400-foot reel of magnetic tape for each of the tape files of Problem 2.2.

2.4. Calculate the optimum blocking factor for a tape file with 72-byte records if the block size cannot exceed 5000 bytes.

2.5. The start / stop times for a nonstreaming tape drive can be estimated closely by assuming linear acceleration and the minimum possible gap size. This translates to a start or stop time of $(0.5 \div v)$ seconds where v is the read / write tape speed in inches per second. Using this method:

(a) Estimate the start/stop time for the HP 7070E tape drive using the characteristics given in Figure 2.5.

(b) Calculate the time required to read a file of 10,000 records of 80 bytes each with a blocking factor of 1. Assume that the tape must stop and start between each block.

(c) Calculate the time required for the same file with a blocking factor of 60.

2.6. Repeat Problem 2.5 for a similar tape drive with a read/write speed of 125 inches per second. Why is the time significantly less than in Problem 2.5 even though the drives in both cases spend most of their time stopping and starting?

2.7. A Hewlett-Packard 7925 disk drive has the following characteristics:

256 bytes per sector
64 sectors per track
9 data surfaces per disk pack
815 tracks per surface

For this drive, how many bytes of data can be stored on

(a) one track?
(b) one cylinder?
(c) one surface?
(d) one disk pack?

2.8. For the HP 7925 disk drive of Problem 2.7, the following times are specified:

Average seek time: 25 milliseconds

Average latency time: 11.1 milliseconds

Data transfer rate: 937,500 bytes per second

What is the average time that could be expected to transfer a block of 5120 bytes?

2.9. Find the most efficient blocking factor for each of the following files if the block size must be between 2560 and 3840 bytes and the sector size is 256 bytes:

(a) Record = 400 bytes
(b) Record = 72 bytes
(c) Record = 64 bytes
(d) Record = 240 bytes
(e) Record = 91 bytes

2.10. Calculate the linear speed in inches per second for each of the following disk drives. Use the speed at the outer rim of the disk. The speed of rotation can be calculated from the latency time. Do your results suggest why the heads do not make contact on hard disks as they do on floppy disks and tape?

(a) HP 7935A
(b) HP 7937H
(c) HP 9127A

2.11. Calculate the acceleration required to start a tape to a speed of 125 inches per second in half of a standard interrecord gap or 0.25 inch. How does this acceleration compare with the acceleration of the earth's gravity at 384 inches per second per second?

2.12. Write a program to calculate an optimum disk blocking factor. The program will accept as input: (1) the record length, (2) the sector length, (3) the minimum allowed block size, and (4) the maximum allowed block size.

3

Sequential-Chronological Files

3.1 DESCRIPTION AND ORGANIZATION

The sequential-chronological file is the simplest type of file we will study. All the methods applicable to this file type are also applicable to nearly every other type of file. While the methods are very unsophisticated, they frequently are the most effective available to solve a particular problem.

The *sequential-chronological file* is organized by appending records to the file in the order that they arrive. Thus the first record found in the file is the "oldest" record, and the last record in the file is the one most recently added. Because of the limited operations that are available for this file type, there is no other way to order the records.

Records may be either fixed or variable in length for this file type. This is a significant advantage, as variable-length records usually make the design of other file types more complicated. Thus, if there is a requirement for variable-length records, this is the type of file structure that frequently will be employed.

The sequential-chronological file is also very compatible with magnetic tape. Magnetic tape is not a feasible medium for most of the more sophisticated file types. Therefore, when a file needs to be stored on magnetic tape, this is one of a very limited number of candidate file types.

3.2 PRIMITIVE OPERATIONS

Primitive operations are those provided by the basic file system of a computer. The operations described in Appendix A are typical file system primitives. These are the elementary file I/O operations upon which all of the file I/O algorithms will be built. Often, languages such as Pascal, COBOL, and FORTRAN will provide high-level constructs to perform these basic operations. Here we will assume that the primitives are invoked by explicit calls rather than implicit high-level instructions.

The set of primitive operations for the sequential-chronological file is small. Central to all of them is the concept of a currency pointer. The *currency pointer* is a logical pointer to the "current record" in the file. Some file systems will have explicit commands to move the currency pointer; however we will assume that the currency pointer is moved implicitly by the primitive operations as noted below. The pointer may exist as an actual pointer within the file system, or it may be implied by a physical state, such as the position of the tape relative to the read / write head.

There are two kinds of logical operations that do nothing more than set the currency pointer. The first positions the pointer to immediately before the first record in the file. This is usually associated with the file open or similar commands. The second positions the pointer to immediately following the last record in the file. This may be done implicitly by the append operation discussed later. Both of these operations may result in a physical positioning of the tape when magnetic tape is used. For example, both rewind and open operations on magnetic tape will leave the currency pointer at the beginning of the file, while the append or find-file-mark commands will leave the pointer at the end of the file.

Primitive operations are those provided by the basic file system of a computer. The operations described in Appendix A are typical file system primitives. While some primitive operations are common to many types of files and devices, others are specific to certain devices, or useful only with particular file structures. Since the sequential-chronological file is appropriate to both magnetic tape and disk devices, the appropriate primitives will be given for both. The primitive operations that are common to both devices are:

> *OPEN* Sets the currency pointer to immediately before the first record and allows access to the file.
>
> *READ-NEXT* Sets the currency pointer to the next record in the file and returns that record to the user. An end-of-file condition is set if there is no next record.
>
> *CLOSE* Terminates access to the file.
>
> *EOF* Returns a value of true if the currency pointer is beyond the last record of the file; otherwise, it is false.
>
> *VALID* Returns a value of true if the previous operation on the file was successful. False is returned if the operation failed for any reason or if a record was read which had been flagged as deleted.

The primitive operation unique to magnetic tape is

> *WRITE-NEXT* Sets the currency pointer to the next record in the file and writes a new record there.

Most file systems with tape drives will also allow other tape primitives, including rewind, backspace, read backward, write backward, and find next file mark (a special symbol used to indicate the end of a magnetic tape file). While these operations are convenient to use, they do not add any capabilities to the magnetic tape primitives given above for building algorithms.

The primitive operations unique to disk drives that are applicable to the sequential-chronological file are:

> *UPDATE* Writes Back the current record in the same location from which it was read. The updated record must be the same length as the record most recently read. The currency pointer is unchanged.

> *APPEND* Sets the currency pointer to immediately after the last record in the file, and writes a new record there.

These primitive operations will be used as the basic building blocks for the algorithms that are employed to manipulate the files. Other file types will allow different sets of primitive operations, which in turn will lead to different algorithms. A complete description of all primitive operations appears in Section A.1.

Throughout the remainder of this book, we will see a recurring sequence of file structure, primitive operations, and algorithms. The primitive operations are determined by the choice of file structure. Similarly, the algorithms are limited by the set of primitive operations. Thus, in choosing a file structure, the designer is also choosing a limited set of algorithms to solve the problem at hand. Consequently, the choice must be made with great care and with foreknowledge of the implications.

3.3 SIX STANDARD FILE FUNCTIONS

There are many kinds of functions we may need to perform on a file, but most file processing consists of six standard functions. Some of these functions are better suited to one type of file, and others to other types of files. However, it is necessary to have methods for doing all six on all types of files. These six functions are defined in this section. Algorithms are developed from the primitive operations to perform each of these functions for each type of file studied. The six standard functions are:

> *Add*. Add a new record to the file.

> *Delete*. Remove a record from the file.

> *Read all records in any order*. It is required that all records be read, but the order is not important. This function is useful when aggregate data such as totals are being developed from the file data.

> *Read all records in key order*. The requirement is to read all records in the order determined by the key values of the record attributes. For ex-

ample, we may wish to read employee records in the order for which the names will be in ascending alphabetic sequence, so as to produce a report ordered by employee name.

Read a record with a specific key value. The requirement is to locate and read a record whose attribute values match a given key. There may be zero, one, or many records satisfying the key.

Update the current record. This is perhaps the simplest standard function since it is usually also a primitive operation. When it is a primitive operation, there is no need to develop an algorithm for it.

In each case, the algorithms for performing these functions must be built using the available file primitives. Thus these six functions represent a higher level of function abstraction than the primitives. The difference in level is usually spanned by a set of procedures that perform the functions and use the primitives.

In this and following chapters we explore algorithms for performing these standard functions. There will be instances where an algorithm is very inefficient or has a contrived appearance. In these situations it is not likely that the algorithm will be used much. This simply illustrates that some file types are not well suited to some functions.

3.4 ALGORITHMS

In this section we discover and analyze algorithms for performing the six basic functions on the sequential-chronological file. Since this file type has a limited set of primitive operations, all reading is done in a sequential mode. For this reason the choice of the blocking factor B will strongly influence all the algorithms examined.

Add (Algorithm 3.1).   Adding records to the sequential-chronological file is a one-operation algorithm. The new records are simply appended to the end of the file. When one record is added, one physical write is required. However, when many records are added, without other intervening operations on the same file, the file system will collect the records in the buffer and write them out a block at a time. Thus, to add M records to a file will require M/B (rounded up) physical writes to the file.

Although it is possible to add records to a disk file at any time, when magnetic tape is used, it is necessary first to find the physical end of file. This may be done by reading through the file until the end-of-file condition becomes true. Some file systems will do this at the primitive level by searching for the file mark.

Delete (Algorithm 3.2). There is no reasonable way to physically delete record from the sequential-chronological file. When disk files are used, records may be logically deleted by flagging them as having been deleted. This may be done by assigning a specific value to some attribute of the record: for example, an employee number of –1. More often, a special field is created for this purpose and allowed to have one of two values to indicate an active record or a deleted record.

Whichever method is used to flag deleted records, the delete function becomes a special case of the update function and uses the update operation to set the flag. This requires that a record must first be read, then deleted by updating. Hence two logical transfers are required to delete a record. If multiple records are being deleted, the blocking factor may reduce the number of physical transfers, depending on the order in which the records are deleted.

Another method that is sometimes used to identify active records in a disk file is a bit map. A *bit map* is a one-dimensional array in which each bit represents a record in the file. The first bit in the array corresponds to the first record in the file, and so on. A bit has a value of zero if the record is not active and a value of 1 if it is active. To delete a record the corresponding bit in the map is set to zero.

The bit map array may be stored in place of one or more records at the beginning of the file. Alternatively, it may be stored separately, in a file header area or even as a separate file. If the file is not too large, it may be possible to have the bit map resident in primary memory while the file is open.

Deleting records by flagging, whether in the record or in a bit map, has an obvious limitation in the sequential-chronological file; eventually the file will become so cluttered with records that have been logically but not physically deleted that processing will become inefficient, and significant storage space will be wasted. To overcome this problem, it is necessary to *reorganize* the file from time to time. Although reorganization is not one of the six standard functions, it is a necessary housekeeping function that must be performed occasionally on the sequential-chronological file, and some others that will be studied later. The frequency of reorganizations will depend on the rate at which records are deleted and the constraints of storage space and processing efficiency.

Reorganization is also the only way to delete or update records on magnetic tape. For this reason, tape is not recommended for use with sequential-chronological files where updating or deleting of records is anticipated. Tape works best with applications that are archival in nature or where the files are copied temporarily to another medium for updating.

Reorganization (Algorithm 3.3). Reorganization is done by copying all unflagged records to a new file and purging the old file. The algorithm is as follows:

```
OPEN(oldfile);   (* set currency pointers to start of files *)
OPEN(newfile);
WHILE not EOF(oldfile) DO BEGIN
        READ—NEXT(oldfile,buffer);
        IF VALID(oldfile) THEN APPEND(newfile,buffer);
                (* copy undeleted records to new file *)
END;
```

Note that the WRITE-NEXT primitive would be used instead of APPEND for a reorganization using magnetic tape.

If the old file contains N records, including those that have been logically deleted, and M unflagged records, the total physical accesses for the reorganization will be $N/B + M/B$. Thus a large blocking factor gives a significant advantage with this algorithm.

Read all records in any order (Algorithm 3.4).   This function is perhaps the one where the sequential-chronological file performs the best. The file is simply read from beginning to end. It is equally applicable to disk and magnetic tape. The algorithm is as follows:

```
OPEN(file);   (* set currency pointer to front of file *)
WHILE not EOF(file) DO BEGIN
        READ—NEXT(file,buffer);
        IF VALID(file) THEN process buffer contents;
END;
```

For a file with N records, including those that have been logically deleted, the total number of physical reads will be N/B. The larger the blocking factor, the fewer physical reads are required. Again, a large blocking factor gives a significant advantage with this algorithm. A large proportion of flagged records will cause the processing to be longer as well as wasting space.

Read a record with a specific key value.   There are three possibilities for this problem: (1) there will be exactly one record with a matching key value; (2) there are several records with matching key values; and (3) there are no records with a matching key value. All cases are treated the same for disk and magnetic tape.

The search is shortest for the first case. The file is read sequentially until the one record is found. The required record could be the first one in the file or the last one. On the average half of the records will be read if there is no significance to the order of the records in the file. Thus the average search requires $(N + 1)/2B$ physical reads. Since N is usually much larger than 1, this is frequently simplified to $N/2B$.

In the following algorithm, the function KEY(buffer) is used to access the value of the key from the record that has been read into the buffer. The algorithm for this search *(Algorithm 3.5)* is as follows:

```
logical function ALGOR3.5(givenkey,file,buffer);
(* returns true iff record in buffer matches the given key *)
OPEN(file);  (* resets currency pointer to front of file *)
ALGOR3.5 := false;  (* in case record is never found *)
WHILE not EOF(file) and not ALGOR3.5 DO BEGIN
        READ-NEXT(file,buffer);
        IF VALID(file) AND KEY(buffer)=givenkey
                THEN ALGOR3.5 := true;
END;
```

Both of the other cases require that the entire file be read. In the case where multiple matches are possible, we usually cannot know when the last match has been found, hence all records must be examined. The algorithm for this case *(Algorithm 3.6)* is only a slight variation from the first case:

```
logical function ALGOR3.6(givenkey,file);
(* returns true iff one or more matching records found *)
OPEN(file);  (* set currency pointer to front of the file *)
ALGOR3.6 := false;  (* in case no matching record found *)
WHILE not EOF(file) DO BEGIN
        READ-NEXT(file,buffer);
        IF VALID(file) and KEY(buffer)=givenkey
                THEN BEGIN
                        ALGOR3.6 := true;
                        process the buffer contents;
                END;
END;
```

the difference being that we cannot escape from the loop after a match is found. Either algorithm gives the same result for the case where no match is found. There is no separate algorithm for this case, since we would not do the search at all if we knew there would be no match. For both cases where the entire file is read, there will be N/B physical transfers of data.

It may seem strange that an unsuccessful search requires more work than a successful one. This is the situation, however, and it will arise again in the context of other file types.

Read all records in key order (Algorithm 3.7).   This is not an appropriate function for the sequential-chronological file. The only reason for including an algorithm for it here is to show how truly bad it is. Where this function is required of a sequential-chronological file, it is much more reasonable to sort it by the key into another file which can then be read sequentially.

In addition to being inefficient, this algorithm requires that the key be unique. It is possible to write a similar algorithm that does not require a unique key, but it would require twice as many accesses for situations where the key is unique. This algorithm is equally inappropriate for disk and tape and is as follows:

```
KEY(buffer0) := min;   (* min is the lowest value the key
    can have *)
done := false;
DO BEGIN     (* one record processed per iteration *)
      KEY(buffer2) := max;   (* max is the highest value the key
          can have *)
      OPEN(file);   (* position currency pointer at beginning of
          file *)
      WHILE not EOF(file) DO BEGIN   (* one record examined per
      iteration *)
            READ—NEXT(file,buffer1);
            IF VALID(file) AND key(buffer2) ≥ key(buffer1) ≥
            key(buffer0)
                  THEN buffer2 := buffer1;
      END UNTIL EOF(file); (* buffer2 now has the record with
      smallest key value larger than that found in buffer0 *)
      IF KEY(buffer2) > KEY(buffer0) THEN BEGIN
            (* call procedure to process buffer2 *);
            buffer0 := buffer2; (* save new minimum key value *)
      END ELSE done := true;
      CLOSE(file);
END UNTIL done;
```

This algorithm requires $N + 1$ passes through a file containing N active records. The extra, last pass is required to tell us that there are no more unprocessed records in the file. The total number of physical reads is $(N + 1)N/B$, which is of order N^2. An alternative would be to count the number of valid records on the first pass, and stop when the number of passes equals that number. This will improve our statistics slightly to N^2/B.

3.5 SUMMARY

The *sequential-chronological file* is formed by adding or *appending* records only at the end of the file and in the order in which they arrive. It is useful only in limited circumstances. Because of its simplicity, it can be used with a variety of media, including magnetic tape and even cards. It is compatible with variable-length records, while most other file types are not. Although records may not be physically deleted from the file, they may be *logically deleted* by *flagging* the records or by using a *bit map* to indicate the active records. Because the logically deleted records continue to be part of the physical file, it is necessary occasionally to *reorganize* the file to remove them physically.

This file type is important because nearly all other file types can also be used as though they were sequential-chronological files. Therefore, the algorithms developed in this chapter are applicable to most other file types.

The algorithms developed for the sequential-chronological file are based on a set of *primitive operations* which are constrained by the type of file device used and the logical structure of the file. Algorithms are developed for the *six standard file functions* using this file type. An algorithm is also developed for *reorganization* of the file as a necessary housekeeping function.

It is not difficult to find ways to improve the structure of this file type and to find more effective algorithms for the improved structures. These improvements, however, result in new file types and so are the topics of other chapters. One variation, which will not be studied further, is to arrange the records so that those with the highest probability of being sought are nearest the beginning of the file. This can produce a much better average search than the $N/2B$ for a single record.

A summary of algorithms available for the standard functions is shown in Figure 3.1. This table will be repeated in the following chapters with the added algorithms and file types.

Function	Algorithm	Sequential Chronological File	
		Magnetic Tape	Disk
Add a record	3.1 Append to file	×	×
Delete a record	3.2 Flag as deleted		×
Read all, any order	3.4 Sequential exhaustive read	×	×
Read all, key order	3.7 Iterative exhaustive search	×	×
Read record by key	3.5 Limited sequential search	×	×
	3.6 Exhaustive sequential search	×	×
Update current record	Update		×
Reorganize	3.3 Copy the valid records	×	×

Figure 3.1 Algorithms for the standard functions.

3.6 THE STUDENT RECORDS PROBLEM

In this section, we examine the process by which a system designer makes the choices that determine the design. The purpose is to arrive at an optimum, or at least acceptable, design. By repeating this process with other file types, we will also have a reasonably complex example that can be a basis for comparing the effectiveness of the different file types.

The reader should, at this point, refer to the description of the ''student records problem'' in Appendix B. This problem will serve as a vehicle for designing and comparing various file systems. It is assumed from here on that the reader is acquainted with this problem.

In this chapter we constrain our solutions of the student records problem to those using a single sequential-chronological file. This constraint will not permit us to find a very good solution, but we can learn some important lessons from the exercise.

Even with such a simple file type as the sequential-chronological file, the designer of all but the simplest systems is faced with large number of design choices. These can be thought of as being represented by a *decision tree*, where each decision is a node, and each choice, another branch. For example, the choices of the entity that will be represented by the records of our file, and whether the records will be fixed or variable in length, result in the tree of Figure 3.2.

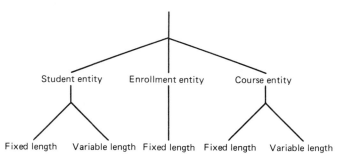

Figure 3.2 First two levels of decision tree.

Other choices will include the blocking factor used, the algorithm used for each of the five functions of the problem, including whether or not the rosters and grade reports will be produced in alphabetic order. Each choice is constrained by those that precede it in the tree. If we were to consider the entire decision tree for this problem, there would be about 40 fundamentally different solutions possible. Ideally, we would calculate the storage and physical access requirements for all 40 solutions and then choose the best one. As a practical matter, this is not feasible. More time would be required than can be justified.

A common method of simplifying our task is sometimes called *tree pruning*. This means that instead of pursuing all design possibilities to the final solution, we may "cut off" a branch of the decision tree that seems unlikely to lead to a good solution. For example, consider the decision tree begun in Figure 3.2. The branch for fixed-length course records might be pruned because the space required is about four times that required by other solutions. It is not always obvious when a tree can be pruned. For example, the algorithms for the remaining file structures might be so much less efficient than those for the fixed-length course records that it would be worthwhile to trade the extra space required for better algorithms. Some experience and insight is required before large branches may be safely pruned. Trade-offs between storage space and speed are especially difficult to make since there is no rule by which they may be compared.

For the purpose of this example, the following pruning decisions will be made. The student will be invited to check the validity of some of these decisions by testing the alternatives in the exercises.

1. Both the rosters and grade reports will be produced unordered.
2. The variable-length course records branch will not be considered since a record would have to be deleted and a new one created each time an enrollment is added to the file.

It is tempting also to prune the fixed-length student record branch since it requires more space than the variable-length student record without any significant difference in the algorithms. However, when the change of schedule function is considered, it becomes apparent that the space occupied by flagged records would more than make up the difference, and the variable-length records would probably require more total space.

The four remaining file designs, with their record sizes and logical space requirements, are shown in Figure 3.3. The record lengths are calculated from the data given in Appendix B as follows. Data for each student requires 85 bytes and includes name, SSN, address, and birthdate. This group appears singly in the student record and the enrollment record, and as a repeating group in the course record. Enrollment data consists of grade, credit, and absences, and requires 5 bytes. This group appears singly in the enrollment record and as a repeating group in all other records. Course data consists of course number, title, instructor, time, and room, and requires 60 bytes. The data appears singly in the course and enrollment records and as a repeating group in the student record.

File	Record Length	Number of Records	Total Space of Active Records
Student, fixed length	$85 + 10(60 + 5) = 735$	N	$735N$
Student, variable length	$85 + 6(60 + 5) = 475$	N	$475N$
Enrollment fixed length	$5 + 60 + 85 = 150$	$6N$	$900N$
Course, fixed length	$60 + 100(85 + 5) = 9060$	$N/5$	$1812N$

Figure 3.3 Four record types with space requirements.

The student record has one repeating group for each course in which the student is enrolled. The average number of courses per student is six and this figure is used for the variable-length version of the student record. If the student record is fixed in length, space must be allowed for the maximum of 10 courses. Data for each course must be repeated an average of 30 times with this record design.

The enrollment record has no repeating groups and contains data for one enrollment, one course, and one student. This is the simplest record design but requires course and student data to be repeated for each enrollment.

The course record contains a repeating group consisting of student and enrollment data. Thus the data for each student is repeated an average of six times in the file; once for each course in which the student is enrolled. The average number of repeating groups per record is only 30, whereas the maximum is 100. The fixed-length record must allow for the maximum number, which seems to give a considerable advantage to the variable-length record. However, a variable-length record cannot be updated if its length changes. It must be deleted and then added back instead. Given the way registration and changes are processed, each course record will be updated an average of $30 + 25 = 55$ times. Thus there would be 55 flagged copies of each course record for each active one by the time changes of schedule are completed. The space required would be prohibitive.

3.6.1 The Fixed-Length Student Record File

The functions for the fixed-length student record file are shown in Figure 3.4. Registration is done by appending student records to the file interactively. This is a sequential operation and the number of physical accesses required is $1/B$ times the number of logical accesses required.

Function	Algorithm	Physical Accesses per Record	Number of Records	Mult.	Total
Registration	3.1	$1/B$	1	N	N/B
Change	3.5	$N/2B$	1	N	$N^2/2B$
	Update	1	1	N	N
Rosters	3.4	$1/B$	N	$2N/5$	$2N^2/5B$
Grades in	3.4	$1/B$	N	$N/5$	$N^2/5B$
	Update	1	30	$N/5$	$6N$
Grades out	3.4	$1/B$	N	1	N/B
Total accesses					$1.1N^2/B + 2N/B + 7N$

Note: For $N = 2000$, $B = 4$, accesses $= 1,115,000$; for $N = 10,000$, $B = 4$, accesses $= 27,575,000$ (N, number of students; B, blocking factor).

Figure 3.4 Function analysis for fixed-length student record file.

Changes are made by locating the record of the student making the change and writing it back with the "update" operation. Most of the accesses are those required to locate and read the correct record. All changes are done with one update.

Rosters are generated by reading the entire file, exhaustively. Each student's record is examined for an enrollment in the course for which the roster is being produced. Since the number of enrollments for the course is unknown, it is necessary to examine all student records. The names on the roster will be in the order they appear in the file and are therefore not in alphabetic order. Exactly the same algorithm is used to access the file for entering grades. The only difference is that when an enrollment is found, the instructor is prompted for the grade that is used to update the record.

The grade output report is produced by reading the file exhaustively, printing out the report for each student as the student's record is encountered. Again, as with the rosters, the students are not ordered by name. As an exercise, calculate the difference that would result from substituting Algorithm 3.7 for Algorithm 3.4 in this function (see Problem 3.1). This would allow the grade reports to be generated in alphabetical order.

3.6.2 The Variable-Length Student Record File

Figure 3.5 shows the function summary for the variable-length student record. It is very similar to the fixed-length student record, differing only in the change function. Since variable-length records cannot be updated if the update changes the length of the record, the old record is deleted by flagging, and an updated version is appended to the file. It is assumed that all changes will result in a change of the number of enrollments, and hence the length.

Function	Algorithm	Physical Accesses per Record	Number of Records	Mult.	Total
Registration	3.1	$1/B$	1	N	N/B
	3.5	$N/2B$	1	N	$N^2/2B$
Change	3.2	1	1	N	N
	3.1	1	1	N	N
Rosters	3.4	$1/B$	$2N$	$2N/5$	$4N^2/5B$
Grades in	3.4	$1/B$	$2N$	$N/5$	$2N^2/5B$
	Update	1	30	$N/5$	$6N$
Grades out	3.4	$1/B$	$2N$	1	$2N/B$
Total accesses					$1.7N^2/B + 3N/B + 8N$

Note: For $N = 2000$, $B = 6$, accesses = 1,150,333; for $N = 10,000$, $B = 6$, accesses = 28,418,333 (N, number of students; B, blocking factor).

Figure 3.5 Function analysis for variable-length student record file.

3.6.3 The Enrollment File

The functions for the enrollment records are shown in Figure 3.6. Registration is again performed by appending records to the file. Now, however, there will be an average of six records per student. Changes are done by first locating each course to be dropped, one at a time. As each course is located, it is updated, either by substituting another course for the one being dropped, or if there are no courses to be added, flagging it as being logically deleted.

Function	Algorithm	Physical Accesses per Record	Number of Rec Records	Mult.	Total
Registration	3.1	$1/B$	6	N	$6N/B$
Change	3.5	$N/2B$	3	N	$3N^2/2B$
	Update	1	3	N	$3N$
Rosters	3.4	$1/B$	$6N$	$2N/5$	$12N^2/5B$
Grades in	3.4	$1/B$	$6N$	$N/5$	$6N^2/5B$
	Update	1	30	$N/5$	$6N$
Grades out	3.7	$1/B$	$6N$	N	$6N^2/B$
	3.6	$1/B$	$6N$	N	$6N^2/B$
Total accesses					$17.1N^2/B + 6N/B + 9N$

Note: For $N = 2000$, $B = 20$, accesses = 3,438,600; for $N = 10,000$, $B = 20$, accesses = 85,593,000 (N, number of students; B, blocking factor).

Figure 3.6 Function analysis for enrollment record file.

Rosters are produced, much as with the student record, by an exhaustive search of the file for all occurrences of the desired course. The difference is that there are six times as many records to search now.

Grades are entered by the same method as that of the student record, searching the file exhaustively, prompting for a grade when an enrollment for the desired course is found, and then updating the record with the grade.

"Grades out" presents a new problem. After the changes are made, there is no assurance that all the enrollments for one student will be in consecutive records, or **contiguous**. For most students the records will not be contiguous. Since we need to have all the grades for each student together, there is a very real clash between the file structure and the requirements of the grade report. A reasonable solution might be to sort the enrollments by name and identification number. However, this would require structures and algorithms beyond those of the sequential-chronological file and we need to solve the problem with the structure at hand if our future comparisons are to be meaningful.

A variation of Algorithm 3.7 will solve the problem. The variant is that we will make two passes through the file for each student. On the first pass, we will determine the identification of the next student in alphabetic order (Algorithm 3.7). On the second pass, we will read all the enrollments for the selected student (Algorithm 3.6). This has the happy property of allowing the students to appear in alphabetic order. Since Algorithm 3.7 requires some key for ordering the records, we may as well take advantage of it.

3.6.4 The Course Record File

The summary for the course record is shown in Figure 3.7. To register each student, it is necessary to search for each of the courses in which the student is enrolled, and update the course record with the student's enrollment when a match is found. It is both possible and efficient to search for all of the student's courses on one pass through the file. Although this does not require an exhaustive search, of the file, the average will be very close to an exhaustive search, and thus the statistics shown are for the exhaustive search. On the average, six records will contain courses for which the student is registering, and these six are updated.

Function	Algorithm	Physical Accesses per Record	Number of Records	Mult.	Total
Registration	3.6	$N/6B$	6	N	N^2/B
Change	3.6	$N/5B$	5	N	N^2/B
	Update	1	5	N	$5N$
Rosters	3.5	$N/2B$	1	$2N/5$	$N^2/5B$
Grades in	3.5	$N/2B$	1	$N/5$	$N^2/10B$
	Update	1	1	$N/5$	$N/5$
Grades out	3.7	N/B	$N/5$	1	$N^2/5B$
	3.6	N/B	$N/5$	1	$N^2/5B$
Total accesses					$2.7N^2/B + 5.2N$

Note: For $N = 2000$, $B = 1$, accesses = 10,810,400; for $N = 10,000$, $B = 1$, accesses = 270,052,000 (N, number of students; B, blocking factor).

Figure 3.7 Function analysis for course record file.

Changes are done by a similar algorithm to registration. One pass is made through the file for each student, locating all courses for which either a drop or add is to be performed. Those course records are then updated, there being an average of five enrollment changes per student.

Roster production and "grades in" are the easiest functions for the course file. In both cases, a sequential search is made for the course. For rosters, the course record is only read, while for "grades in," it is updated as well.

The grade report function presents the same problem as it did with the enrollment records; that is, each student's grades are scattered throughout the file. The solution is also the same; that is, Algorithms 3.7 and 3.6. Two passes through the file are made for each student. On the first pass, the next student is identified, while on the second the courses and grades for that student are produced.

3.6.5 Critique

One final step is required before a fair comparison of the four file types can be made: estimation of the space required. An exact solution will require consideration of blocking factors, which will be left as an exercise. However, the logical space requirements can be accurately calculated now that the algorithms are known.

The fixed-length student file does not require that any records be deleted during the cycle of functions. Therefore, the total logical space required is that shown in Figure 3.3 for the space of active records: $735N$.

Variable-length student records are deleted when a student changes registration. Thus, after changes are done, there will be as much space occupied by deleted records as by active records. The space then is twice that required by the active records, or $950N$.

The enrollment records are also deleted when changes are made, but only by the number of drops in excess of adds which is one per student on the average. Therefore, we may assume that there will be N enrollment records deleted and a like number added during the change function. Thus the total space required is that for $7N$ records, or $1050N$. Since courses are neither added nor deleted during the cycle, the total space for the course file is that shown in Figure 3.3, or $1812N$.

A fair way to compare these four solutions is to place each solution on a two-dimensional plot with log-log coordinates showing the file space and number of physical accesses it requires, as seen in Figure 3.8. A solution lying below and to the left of another solution is the better of the two. Where one solution lies below and to the right of another, a judgment is required as to which is the better solution. This is because the solution on the lower right is faster but requires more storage space.

The requirements for each file design were calculated for N of 2000 and 10,000. A blocking factor was chosen that would give a block size of about 3000 bytes except for the course record, where the blocking factor is 1. As the scatter plot of Figure 3.8 shows, the relative position of each file is about the same for both values of N. The course record file is the worst in terms of both storage space and disk accesses. The enrollment record is the next worst. The two versions of the student record are very close in total accesses, but the fixed-length version uses less space, since records can be updated instead of being flagged as deleted and rewritten. Thus the obvious choice is the fixed-length student record file design.

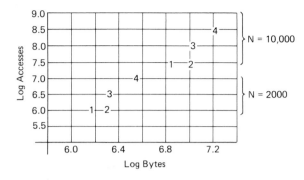

1 = student rec, fixed len; 2 = student rec, var len; 3 = enrollment rec; 4 = course rec.

Figure 3.8 Scatter plot of physical accesses versus storage space.

The functions for all four file designs are of order N^2, and so as N increases by a factor of 5 from 2000 to 10,000, it is not surprising to see that the number of accesses increases by approximately a factor of 5^2 or 25. With this in mind, it is also easy to see why the relative positions of the files in Figure 3.8 remain the same for different values of N. The accesses increased by a factor of 25, while the space increased by a factor of 5. On log coordinates, these changes amount to moving all points by the same amount.

Any solution should be tested for reasonableness and feasibility. This requires that each individual function be examined to determine if the response time is fast enough for on-line functions and if the total time is short enough for batch functions. For example, if we allow 40 milliseconds per physical access, the grades out function for the enrollment record file requires about 333 hours for N = 10,000. This is probably not a feasible solution no matter how attractive other aspects of the file are. Similarly, 6.67 minutes are required to change the schedule of one student for the course record file, which would not be acceptable response time.

Where it is necessary to use the sequential-chronological file for the student records problem, it would be much more effective to sort the file into different orders to perform the various functions. However, this would then become an ordered file, which is studied in Chapter 5.

As other file types are examined, the order of the functions will be very important. Specifically, those with statistics of order $N \cdot \log(N)$ or order N will be much preferred to those of order N^2 which are typical of the sequential-chronological file.

3.7 PROBLEMS

3.1. Calculate the size in bytes of a bit map for a file of 10,000 records. Is this a reasonably sized object to hold in primary memory while the file is open?

3.2. Modify the "grade out" function for the fixed-length student records file so that the reports are produced in alphabetic order by name using Algorithms 3.7 in place of 3.4. Determine the increase in physical accesses as a function of N and B. Calculate the increase in accesses when $N = 2000$ and when $N = 10,000$.

3.3. Calculate the most efficient blocking factor for each of the following files for a sector size of 256 bytes and lower and upper block size limits of 2500 and 5000 bytes.
  (a) Fixed-length student record file
  (b) Variable-length student record file (use average length)
  (c) Enrollment record file

3.4. Calculate the time required for each function of the fixed-length student record file design for $N = 5000$. Assume an average access time of 50 milliseconds.

3.5. Find the best solution for the computer equipment problem described in Section B.2. Use a single sequential-chronological file.

3.6. Find the best solution for the parts supply problem described in Section B.3. Use a single sequential-chronological file.

3.7. Create a file with 1000 records, each record having one field, a 32-bit integer. Fill these records with random numbers. Sort this file into a second file using a sort utility. Print the random numbers from the second file so that you will have all of their values in order.

3.8. Write a small program using Algorithm 3.7 to retrieve all of the records in order from the unordered file of Problem 3.7. Count the number of logical accesses to the file. Verify that the program has functioned correctly by comparing the result to the sorted list generated in Problem 3.7. Compare the number of reads with $N^2/2$. Compare the resources required by Algorithm 3.7 with those required by the sort (if available).

3.9. Write a small program using Algorithm 3.5 to retrieve randomly selected records from the unordered file of Problem 3.7, given their keys (values of the random integer). Count the number of logical accesses to the file required for each retrieval. Repeat until 20 records have been retrieved and calculate the average number of reads required. Compare this number with $N/2$.

4

Relative Files

4.1 DESCRIPTION AND ORGANIZATION

The *relative file* is one in which records can be accessed directly by using their record numbers as an external key. We are no longer restricted to accessing records in the sequence in which they appear in the file. As we saw in Chapter 2, file systems frequently assign a number to each record, the records being numbered from zero to $N - 1$, or sometimes from 1 to N. This type of access is sometimes referred to as *random access*, but it is usually pseudorandom in nature, since it may require more time to locate some records than others.

The file system assumes the burden of calculating the sector address of the block containing a particular record, as well as reading or writing the block. As far as the programmer is concerned, the record number is the address of the record. In this respect, the relative file looks very much like a one-dimensional array where each element of the array is a record and the subscript is the record number.

Record numbers may serve as keys for the data in a file. For example, a company may assign numbers to their employees, which, in fact, are record numbers for the employee file. There are also many functions for converting an internal key, such as name, to a record number. These are discussed in Chapter 6. For the purposes of this chapter, we assume that the record number is known for each record that needs to be accessed.

Since the advantage of the relative file lies in the ability to access a given record directly without having to pass through all the preceding records, it would not make sense to use a sequential storage medium such as magnetic tape for this file type. Thus magnetic disk or other pseudorandom devices are used for this file type.

The task of calculating the exact location of a record from the record number is straightforward when the records are all of the same length. If the records can vary in length, the calculations can only give an approximation of the record location. Consequently, relative files are usually restricted to fixed-length records. Where a file exists in one contiguous extent, the sector address of a block containing a given record can be calculated as follows, using integer arithmetic:

$$SA = FA + (RN / B)SPB \qquad\qquad (4.1)$$

where SA = sector address of the block containing the desired record
        FA = sector address of the first block in the file
       RN = record number of the desired record
         B = records per block
     SPB = number of sectors per block

4.2 PRIMITIVE OPERATIONS

The set of primitive operations for the relative file is similar to that for the sequential-chronological file in several respects. The concept of the currency pointer carries over to the relative file, as do several of the operations. The principal difference is that the currency pointer may now be explicitly directed to a particular record as part of a read or write operation.

With new freedoms usually come new responsibilities. There are two restrictions that must be observed with the relative file. First, a record cannot be read before it is written. This seems logical enough. However, it results in an *exceptional condition*, which is similar to an error condition, if a read is attempted from an empty record. When the file is created, the file system flags all record positions or *slots* as being empty. When a record is written into a slot, the slot is occupied and the record can be successfully read. Similarly, a record can be deleted by flagging it, again, as empty.

The second restriction is that the record number must be within the range of the record numbers (i.e., between 0 and $N - 1$, inclusive). There are no records outside this range and to attempt to address such a record will result in an error. This is analogous to attempting to use a subscript for an array that exceeds the array's bounds.

While many file systems allow the number of available slots, N, to be increased when necessary, there is always a definite value for the number of slots at any given moment.

The primitive operations for the relative file are:

OPEN Sets the currency pointer to immediately before the first record and allows access to the file.

READ-NEXT Sets the currency pointer to the next valid record in the file and returns that record to the user. An end-of-file condition is set if there is no next record.

READ-DIRECT Sets the currency pointer to the slot specified, and returns the record to the user if the slot is occupied. An invalid-record-number condition is set if the slot is not occupied or if the record number is outside the limits of the file.

WRITE-DIRECT Sets the currency pointer to the slot specified and writes a record to that slot, whether or not the slot is already occupied. An invalid-record-number condition is set if the record number is outside the limits of the file.

UPDATE Writes back the current record in the same location from which it was read. The currency pointer is unchanged. May be used to flag a record as deleted.

CLOSE Terminates access to the file.

EOF Returns a value of true if the currency pointer is beyond the last record of the file; otherwise, it is false.

VALID Returns a value of true if the previous operation on the file was successful. False is returned if the operation failed for any reason or if a record was read that had been flagged as deleted.

This set includes all of the primitive operations for the sequential-chronological disk file except append. In the place of append, we have gained the ability to write anywhere in the file as well as to read anywhere in the file. These two operations will add considerable flexibility which will be exploited in the algorithms.

4.3 ALGORITHMS

Many of the algorithms applicable to the relative file are based on operations common to the relative file and the sequential-chronological file. Hence these algorithms are the same. To avoid confusion, new numbers will not be assigned to these old algorithms, nor will they be restated in detail. Instead, the reader will be directed to the older algorithms where appropriate.

Add (Algorithm 4.1). Records may be added at any time and in any slot. The WRITE-DIRECT operation is used. It is the programmer's responsibility to see that no valid records are destroyed by writing a different record over them.

Delete (Algorithm 3.2). Records are flagged as deleted. Some file systems may have a specific operation for deleting records and reinitializing them to the empty state. Otherwise, either the UPDATE or WRITE-DIRECT operations may be used for this purpose. Since slots may be reused, there is no requirement for a periodical reorganization as there was with the sequential-chronological file.

Read all records in any order (Algorithm 3.4).   This function does not differ significantly from the way it is done for the sequential-chronological file. Although it might appear possible to do it by using the READ-DIRECT operation and incrementing the record number with each read, there will usually be many hits on empty slots, where the read-next operation will skip over the empty slots in most file systems.

Read a record with a specific key value.   As with the sequential-chronological file, there are again three possibilities if the key is not a record number: (1) there is exactly one matching record; (2) there are several matching records; and (3) there are no matching records. In these cases, Algorithms 3.5 and 3.6 are the appropriate ones to use. Since these algorithms require sequential searches they are time consuming.

When the key is a record number, or can readily be converted to a record number, a much faster retrieval can be done by using **Algorithm 4.2**. This consists of a single READ-DIRECT operation. One physical access to disk is all that is required. If the read is within the same block as the previous operation, that block will still be in the buffer and no physical access is required.

Read all records in key order.   Here again there is a considerable difference, depending on whether the key by which the records are to be ordered is the record number or some other key. If the record number is the key, and its order is to be significant, there is usually a requirement to attach some other meaning to this number than just that which identifies a record. For example, if turnover is low in a company, we might assign employees' numbers by listing all employees in alphabetic order and then assigning each employee a consecutive even number starting with 2. These "employee numbers" would actually be record numbers in our file. The odd numbers are reserved for new employees, who could be assigned numbers that would still maintain the correspondence between record number order and alphabetic order.

This system has two disadvantages: first, it will eventually break down as old employees leave and new ones are hired. In some intervals there will not be enough numbers to keep everyone in alphabetic order. Then it will be necessary either to be satisfied with an order that is approximately alphabetic, or to assign new numbers to all employees. The second disadvantage is that half of the file space will be wasted with empty slots.

If, however, the record number is the key by which the access to the records is to be ordered, there is a very simple and obvious solution. **Algorithm 4.3** requires only that the file be read sequentially, as with Algorithm 3.4. The difference is that the ordering of the records in the file now has some significance beyond that of chronology. This is possible because the records can be written in any order, not just appended at the end of the file.

For example, the manager of a fleet of automobiles replaces the entire fleet with new vehicles once each year. At that time each vehicle is assigned an identification number consisting of the model year followed by consecutive three-digit numbers. A record is created for each automobile so that the last three digits of the identification number equal the record number.

Thus a sequential read of the file will produce all records ordered by the identification number. While the code for Algorithm 4.3 is identical to that for Algorithm 3.4, it is operating on a different data structure and produces a different result.

Where the file must be read in the order of a key other than the record number, it will be necessary to fall back on Algorithm 3.7, with all of its inefficiency.

4.4 SUMMARY

Relative files allow direct access to each record by using the record number as an address. Since this operation is not feasible with tape, the file type is restricted to random and pseudorandom devices such as disk.

The relative file is a more effective structure than the sequential-chronological file for many applications. There are many situations where a record number may be used as a key. For example, part numbers, inventory numbers, order numbers, and so on, may all be assigned arbitrarily. It is then feasible to assign them values which are actually record numbers. Thereafter, retrieval and updating can be done by accessing the corresponding record directly instead of searching through the file for it. Where this can be done, the efficiency will equal or exceed that of the most sophisticated file types.

There are many variations on the relative file, particularly the ordered relative file and the direct access file. These will be studied in Chapters 5 and 6. The algorithms for the standard functions are shown in Figure 4.1.

4.5 THE STUDENT RECORDS PROBLEM

In this section the student records problem will be reexamined to determine if there is any way to take advantage of the features of the relative file to improve on the solution found in Section 3.6. As noted above, most advantages of the relative file accrue from using the record number as a key. There are no obvious keys that could arbitrarily be assigned to record numbers in the student records problem. However, it is possible to artificially force the record number key on some entities. For example, each student could be assigned a "student number," which, in fact, is a record number. If we can arrange to assign them in alphabetic order, as with the employees mentioned above, the grade reports and rosters can even be produced in alphabetic order with no additional effort. Similarly, it is possible to assign a record number to each course. For this reason, both of these practices are followed at some colleges and universities.

As the decision tree is considered for solving the student records problem with the relative file type, there is some obvious pruning that can be done. The

| Function | Algorithm | Sequential Chronological File | | Rel. File |
		Mag. Tape	Disk	Disk
Add a record	3.1 Append to file	×	×	
	4.1 Write direct			×
Delete a record	3.2 Flag as deleted		×	×
Read all, any order	3.4 Sequential exhaustive read	×	×	×
Read all, key order	3.7 Iterative exhaustive search	×	×	×
	4.3 Sequential ordered read			×
Read record by key	3.5 Limited sequential search	×	×	×
	3.6 Exhaustive sequential search	×	×	×
	4.2 Read direct			×
Update current record	Update		×	×
Reorganize	3.3 Copy the valid records	×	×	

Figure 4.1 Algorithms for the standard functions.

variable-length student record file can be eliminated since relative files use only fixed-length records. The enrollment and course records files will still be considered, but with some suspicion that they will not be strong candidates since they required much more space than the student record file in Chapter 3. There is no reason to expect that the file space requirement will change much with the relative file.

The question of ordering of rosters and grade reports will turn on the feasibility of forcing a correspondence between name order and number order, as noted above. Thus this decision will be left to the final selection of designs.

Space requirements for the records will be the same as shown in Figure 3.3. The number of records will remain unchanged for the duration of one cycle for both the student record file and the course record file, since we assume that neither students nor courses will be dropped or added. However, enrollments will be freely dropped and added during the cycle. This presents two fundamental problems for the enrollment record file.

First, there is no obvious key that could be associated with a record number. Such numbers could be assigned to students and/or courses. It would be very difficult to find any such assignment for enrollments that would not consume inordinately large amounts of file space. The second problem is related to this difficulty; there seems to be no easy way to determine where to store an enrollment. Since neither the student identification nor the course identification is unique to one enrollment, neither can be used as the key to the enrollment. A combination of the two is unique but would waste far too much space. If there are N students and $N/5$ courses, there would be $N^2/5$ unique combinations, which would require a file of 800,000 slots to hold just 12,000 enrollments when $N = 2000$. Thus the enrollment record file will be pruned from further consideration.

4.5.1 The Student Record File

For the student record file each student is assigned a unique record number as an identifier. For N students, all identifiers range from 0 to $N - 1$. Thus there are no unused slots in the file. If the record numbers are assigned to students in alphabetic order, there will be a further benefit in that the rosters and grade reports will be produced in alphabetic order.

As shown in Figure 4.2, the registration is done by directly accessing the student's record with the WRITE-DIRECT operation. Changes are made by again directly accessing the student's record and updating it.

Function	Algorithm	Physical Accesses per Record	Number of Records	Mult.	Total
Registration	4.2	1	1	N	N
Change	4.2	1	1	N	N
	Update	1	1	N	N
Rosters	3.4	$1/B$	N	$2N/5$	$2N^2/5B$
Grades in	3.4	$1/B$	N	$N/5$	$N^2/5B$
	Update	1	30	$N/5$	$6N$
Grades out	3.4	$1/B$	N	1	N/B
Total accesses					$0.6N^2/B + N/B + 9N$

Note: For $N = 2000$, $B = 4$, accesses = 618,500; for $N = 10,000$, $B = 4$, accesses = 15,100,500 (N, number of students; B, blocking factor).

Figure 4.2 Function analysis for student record file.

Rosters require that an exhaustive search of the file be made for all students registered in the required course. Since the search is done in the order of the records in the file and the records are ordered by record number, the records will also be in alphabetic order by name if the record numbers were so assigned. This means that the rosters will also be ordered by name.

Grades are entered by a very similar process. After a student is found who is enrolled in the required course, the instructor is prompted for the grade, and the student's record is updated.

"Grades out" is also accomplished by reading the file sequentially. As with the rosters, the report will be ordered by name if the record numbers were so assigned.

Although most of the functions are now of order N, there are still two of order N^2, which, unfortunately, will dominate the total statistics. Even so, the total accesses have been cut nearly in half as compared to the corresponding solution with the sequential-chronological file structure.

4.5.2 The Course Record File

For the course record file, each course is assigned a unique record number identifier in the range 0 to $(N/5) - 1$. As with the student record file, all slots are occupied. There is no functional advantage in assigning the courses to record numbers in any particular order.

The function summary is shown in Figure 4.3. Registration is done by directly accessing each of the courses for which a student wishes to register, and adding his enrollment to that record. Similarly, changes are made by accessing the record for each course that is being dropped or added by each student and updating it by adding or deleting an enrollment.

Function	Algorithm	Physical Accesses per Record	Number of Records	Mult.	Total
Registration	4.2	1	6	N	$6N$
	Update	1	6	N	$6N$
Change	4.2	1	5	N	$5N$
	Update	1	5	N	$5N$
Rosters	4.2	1	1	$2N/5$	$2N/5$
Grades in	4.2	1	1	$N/5$	$N/5$
	Update	1	1	$N/5$	$N/5$
Grades out	3.7	$N/5B$	$N/5$	1	$N^2/25B$
	3.6	$N/5B$	$N/5$	1	$N^2/25B$
Total accesses					$0.08N^2/B + 22.8N$

Note: For $N = 2000$, $B = 1$, accesses = 365,600; for $N = 10,000$, $B = 1$, accesses = 8,228,000 (N, number of students; B, blocking factor).

Figure 4.3 Function analysis for course record file.

Rosters are produced very easily by accessing the one record for the course directly and reading the enrollments. Grades are entered by the same method, except the record is updated after all grades for the course have been entered.

The only function that does not work well with this design is the grade reports. Here again, the enrollments for each student are scattered throughout the file and must be searched out carefully. There seems to be no option but to again use Algorithms 3.7 and 3.6. This will prove to be disastrous for this design, as the function is of order N^2. Nevertheless, the course records file is about six times more efficient with the relative file design than it was with the sequential-chronological file design.

4.5.3 Critique

It is instructive to note that while both file designs have functions that are of order N^2, different functions are responsible in the two files. The student record file has difficulty with accessing by course in the rosters and ''grades in'' function, while the course records file has difficulty with accessing by student in the ''grades out'' function. Where the access may be done either way, as with registration and changes, both designs work well. This is very typical of real-world file problems. Often, just one function will prove troublesome for a particular file design. When another design is developed to solve the first problem, a different function becomes troublesome. This is a source of great frustration to system designers.

When the functions are evaluated, there is not a clear choice. The course record file requires about half as many accesses, but it uses more than twice the space. This is an example of the classical trade-off between speed and space.

Both files using the relative file design performed much better than did the corresponding files using the sequential-chronological file design. However, a price was paid in the form of an artificial external key—the record number. Some method needs to be found to relate natural keys, such as name or course number to these artificial keys. This will usually take the form of a printed listing which must be at hand whenever the file is to be used. Although workable, this is a considerable inconvenience to users. Designs that do not require such artificial keys will be more welcome.

4.6 PROBLEMS

4.1. Devise an algorithm for the READ-DIRECT operation for a file with variable-length records. Assume that there is available an operation to read block j, named READBLOCK(j). How many physical accesses are required, on the average, for a file with N records and an average blocking factor B?

4.2. Write an algorithm for a file with fixed-length records that implements the READ-DIRECT operation. Include the reading of the block into the buffer using the READBLOCK(j) operation, described in Problem 4.1, and the moving of the selected record from the buffer to the user's work space. Assume a file of N records, each of length L, with a blocking factor of B.

4.3. Why is magnetic tape an inappropriate medium for relative files? Is it possible to implement a relative file on magnetic tape?

4.4. Is it possible to implement an algorithm that will uniquely map enrollments onto a set of record numbers in the range 0 to $(12N) - 1$? (This allows for twice as many slots as actual enrollments.)

4.5. A proposal is made for a design for the student records problem that requires external keys (record numbers) be assigned to both students and courses. The design follows that for the course record file until after the grades have been entered. Then, before the grade reports are produced, the data are moved into a file that follows the student record file design. The SSN field is used to store the student's key (record number). Allowing for the additional function of restructuring the file, calculate the total physical accesses that this design will require as a function of N. Calculate the actual number of accesses for $N = 2000$ and $N = 10,000$. Compare this design with the two in Section 4.3.

4.6. Solve the computer equipment problem described in Section B.2. Use the relative file.

4.7. Solve the parts supply problem described in Section B.3. Use the relative file.

5

Ordered Files

5.1 DESCRIPTION AND ORGANIZATION

Ordered files are files constrained so that the records are ordered by the value of a key. Specifically, for each record i, where i is any record except the first or last, it is always true that $KEY(i - 1) \leq KEY(i) \leq KEY(i + 1)$. This constraint has a great effect on the way the file is built and maintained, but also allows more effective algorithms to be applied.

Ordered files are of two types, ordered sequential files and ordered relative files. Although they share some properties and algorithms, the former is more appropriate for magnetic tape and the latter for disks.

Ordered sequential files are identical to the sequential chronological files of Chapter 3 except that they are also ordered. When used with magnetic tape, this means that records may not be updated or deleted directly, nor may records be appended to the end of the file unless their key values are greater than those found before them in the file. These functions are done instead as part of a reorganization algorithm called a merge. Similarly, magnetic tape does not allow access by record number, which further restricts the algorithms that are usable.

Ordered relative files are identical to the relative file type of Chapter 4 except for three constraints. First, they are ordered as described above. Second, all slots must contain a value of the key on which the file is ordered. This must be true whether or not the record has been flagged for deletion. Third, the record number cannot be used as a key. The record number will be used in the algorithms but cannot be associated with a particular entity as was done with the relative file. The reason is that when the file is reorganized, it is likely that a given record will be assigned to a different record number. There is no way to avoid this if order is to be preserved.

It may seem strange that any benefit could come from restrictions that create such obvious problems as these. However, as will be shown, there are advantages to this organization that more than compensate for the problems it creates. A minor advantage is that magnetic tape again becomes a feasible medium for this file type. The reorganization (Algorithm 5.1) described in Section 5.3 is frequently used with this file type and magnetic tape.

A major advantage is the introduction of the binary search (Algorithm 5.2), which is a very effective method for locating a record with a given internal key. Unfortunately, both of these advantages cannot exist in the same file, as the binary search is not feasible with magnetic tape due to the lack of the READ-DIRECT operation with that medium.

5.2 PRIMITIVE OPERATIONS

The set of primitive operations for the ordered file, like that for the sequential-chronological file, depends on the device being used and whether the file is an ordered sequential file or an ordered relative file. The primitive operations for the ordered relative file are:

OPEN Sets the currency pointer to immediately before the first record and allows access to the file.

READ-NEXT Sets the currency pointer to the next valid record in the file and returns that record to the user. An end-of-file condition is set if there is no next record.

READ-DIRECT Sets the currency pointer to the slot specified and returns the record to the user. VALID becomes false if the slot does not contain a record with a valid key value or if the record number is outside the limits of the file.

UPDATE Writes back the current record in the same location from which it was read. The currency pointer is unchanged.

APPEND Sets the currency pointer to immediately after the last record in the file, and writes a new record there.

CLOSE Terminates access to the file.

EOF Returns a value of true if the currency pointer is beyond the last record of the file; otherwise, it is false.

VALID Returns a value of true if the previous operation on the file was successful. False is returned if the operation failed for any reason.

The APPEND operation is used to write new records since there are no empty slots to which the WRITE-DIRECT operation could be appropriately directed. The APPEND operation is used only when building the file.

The primitive operations for the ordered sequential file are constrained to those feasible for magnetic tape. This is the same set as that used for the sequential-chronological file:

OPEN Sets the currency pointer to immediately before the first record and allows access to the file.

READ-NEXT Sets the currency pointer to the next valid record in the file and returns that record to the user. An end-of-file condition is set if there is no next record.

WRITE-NEXT Sets the currency pointer to the next record in the file and writes a new record there.

CLOSE Terminates access to the file.

EOF Returns a value of true if the currency pointer is beyond the last record of the file; otherwise, it is false.

VALID Returns a value of true if the previous operation on the file was successful. False is returned if the operation failed for any reason or if a record was read which had been flagged as deleted.

5.3 ALGORITHMS

The *add* and *delete* functions share the common fate of being prohibited by the constraints discussed in Section 5.1. Where the ordered relative file is used, it is possible to flag records as deleted, but the key value must remain intact in the flagged records. Similarly, records cannot be added because the file is already full and because there would have to be a vacant slot in the right place in the file to add a new record in key sequence. Therefore, it is generally necessary to reorganize the file to add or delete records, or to change a key value of a record.

Reorganization (Algorithm 5.1).   The file is reorganized by *merging* the original file with a *change file* to create a new file. The original file and the change file may be purged after the new file is built. The change file contains records that are identical in form with those of the original file, except that one additional field is added to indicate the nature of the change. This field indicates whether a record is to be added or deleted during the reorganization. It is referenced by the "flag" function in this algorithm.

The change file is ordered by the same key as the original file. Both are read sequentially, and the new file is written sequentially. The algorithm is as follows:

```
OPEN(oldfile); (* initialize by opening all files and reading
    first records *)
OPEN(newfile);
OPEN(changefile);
READ-NEXT(oldfile,oldbuf);
READ-NEXT(changefile,chgbuf);
WHILE not EOF(oldfile) or not EOF(change) DO BEGIN
        (* loop until there are no more records to process *)
```

```
        IF not EOF(oldfile) and not EOF(changefile) THEN
                (* both files have more records to process *)
                IF KEY(oldbuf)=KEY(chgbuf) THEN BEGIN
                        IF FLAG(chgbuf)="add" THEN BEGIN
                                APPEND(newfile,chgbuf);
                                APPEND(newfile,oldbuf);
                                (* Puts both into new file.  No
                                    action required for
                                    the delete case. *)
                        END;
                            READ–NEXT(oldfile,oldbuffer);
                                (* refill buffers *)
                            READ–NEXT(changefile,chgbuffer);
                END ELSE IF key(oldbuf) < key(chgbuf) THEN BEGIN
                        APPEND(newfile,oldbuf);  (* copy
                            old record *)
                        READ–NEXT(oldfile,oldbuf);
                            (* refill buffer *)
                END ELSE IF key(oldbuf) > key(chgbuf) THEN BEGIN
                        (* add new record *)
                        IF FLAG(chgbuf)="add" THEN
                            APPEND(newfile,chgbuf)
                        ELSE (* error, trying to delete
                            nonexistent record*);
                        READ–NEXT(changefile,chgbuf);
                            (* refill buffer *)
                END;
        ELSE IF EOF(changefile) THEN BEGIN
                (* copy from oldfile to newfile *)
                APPEND(newfile,oldbuf);
                READ–NEXT(oldfile,oldbuf);
        END ELSE IF EOF(oldfile) THEN
                (* copy from changefile to newfile *)
                IF FLAG(chgbuf)="add" THEN APPEND(newfile,chgbuf)
                ELSE (* error, trying to delete nonexistent
                    record *);
                READ–NEXT(changefile,chgbuf);
END;
CLOSE(oldfile);
CLOSE(newfile);
CLOSE(changefile);
```

While this algorithm is appropriate for both ordered relative files and ordered sequential files, the WRITE-NEXT primitive should replace the APPEND operation when it is used with magnetic tape files.

This algorithm builds the reorganized file by comparing the next records from both the old file and the change file. The one with the lowest key value is added to the new file. Where both have the same key value and the change file function is "add," both records are appended to the new file. If the change file function is "delete," neither record is appended, thus deleting the original record. To replace an old record with a new record having the same key value, the change file should first have a "delete" record, then an "add" record with the same key values.

This algorithm will allow multiple records with the same key value. Where the key must be a primary key (unique value), the algorithm may be modified to prevent records with duplicate keys from being written to the new file.

The file may be built originally by using this same algorithm. The old file will be empty initially, and all records will come from the change file. In all cases the change file must be ordered by key value. This will frequently be done by an external sort. Since the change file will usually be much smaller than the old or new files, it is much more efficient to sort only the change file.

Algorithm 5.1 assumes that both the old file and change file are ordered by the key value. Failure of either file to conform to this requirement will result in the new file also failing. Moreover, records may be lost or not properly deleted as a result. Checks could be added to the algorithm to assure that all files are properly ordered if this cannot otherwise be guaranteed.

An error condition will exist if an attempt is made to remove a record that does not exist. Algorithm 5.1 will simply ignore such an attempt, but most real applications will require some sort of error-handling procedure for this case.

Read all records in any order (Algorithm 3.4).   As with most other file designs, there is no better way to perform this function than the straight, sequential read.

Read a record with a specific key value (Algorithm 5.2).   This algorithm is an important reason for choosing the ordered relative file structure. It permits a record to be read based on an internal key value without a long, sequential search.

This *binary search* algorithm is one of a class of searches called *tree searches*. Tree searches are distinguished by having statistics of order $\log(N)$. These are much more efficient than the exhaustive searches which have statistics of order N.

The binary search algorithm, as applied to the ordered relative file, is as follows:

```
logical function BINSRCH(file,buffer,givenkey,n);
(* returns true iff record found. n is number of records in file *)
lo:=0;  (* pointer to the lowest-numbered record
    of interest *)
hi:=n-1; (* pointer to the highest numbered record
    of interest *)
found:=false; (* a logical variable *)
WHILE not found and lo ≤ hi DO BEGIN
```

```
              (* search until match found, or no records of interest
                 exist *)
              rec:=(lo + hi)/2; (* find the midpoint of the range *)
              READ-DIRECT(file,buffer,rec);
              (* compare given key with buffer *)
              IF givenkey=KEY(buffer) THEN (* a match has been found *)
                     found:=true
              ELSE IF givenkey > key(buffer) THEN
                     lo:=rec+1  (* all records of interest > rec *)
              ELSE IF (givenkey < key(buffer) THEN
                     hi:=rec-1;  (* all records of interest < rec *)
       END;
       BINSRCH:= found;  (* return true iff record found *)
```

   If found is true, the buffer will contain a record whose key matches the given key, and rec will contain the number of that record. If found is false, the given key is greater than the key of the record pointed to by hi, and less than the key of the record pointed to by lo, and hi + 1 = lo.

   It is possible that there are several records with keys that match the given key. In this case, any of the matching records may be the one in the buffer. If it is necessary to locate all of them, a sequential search must be made, both forward and backward from the found record, to locate all matching records.

   An important question to ask about this algorithm is the number of probes, or reads, of the file that are required before the search terminates. The answer depends on the size of the file, the number of matching records in the file, and the use of information theory. Each probe of the file gathers information about the location of the desired record. A read of an unordered file gives only information about the record read. However, a read of an ordered file gives information about all other records as well as the one read, since it can be determined if any other record will precede or follow the record read.

   The total amount of information required, on the average, is that required to satisfy the search. The simplest case occurs when there is exactly one record with a matching key in the file. By Shannon's information theory the amount of information needed to locate one specific record in a file of N records is $\log_2(N)$ bits. Determining that no record in the file matches the given key is equivalent to locating the position (between existing records, before the first record, or after the last record) where a record would be if it had that key. Since there are $N + 1$ such positions, the information required to determine that no such record exists is slightly higher as $\log_2(N + 1)$ bits. The third case occurs when there are K matching records ($K > 1$) in the file and it is only necessary to locate any one of the K records. In this situation less information is required and the amount is $\log_2(N/K)$ bits.

   A probe that fails to locate a matching record but succeeds in eliminating half of the records in the file from further consideration returns exactly 1 bit of information. Most probes will actually return slightly more than 1 bit of information since there is usually a small probability that the desired record will be located by the probe. This probability is highest near the end of the search when there are few records remaining in the records of interest. For example, the average information gained by probing the middle of three records remaining in the records of interest is $\log_2(3) = 1.585$ bits.

Thus we can equate the amount of information required [$\log_2(N)$ for a single matching record] to the amount of information gathered by the average probe (approximately 1 bit) to determine the average number of probes required to locate a record with a given key. Unfortunately, summation of a series is required for an exact solution and no simple formula is able to give an exact answer.

However, there are some approximate formulas that will give useful answers in most cases. First, consider some simple, limiting cases. There is a small but finite probability that a match will be found on the first probe. Thus the minimum number of accesses required is always one. In the case where no match exists, the search will proceed until all records have been eliminated. This requires $\log_2(N)$ (rounded up) probes. This will also be the number of probes required about half the time when a single matching record exists. Thus it is the worst case. The average case, where there is a single matching record, requires about $\log2(N) - 1$ (rounded up) probes. Where there are K matching records in a file of N records, the average search requires approximately $\log_2(N/K) - 1$ probes. These are approximations and are adequate for the estimates required for file design, but they do differ slightly from the exact solutions.

Blocking will improve the access statistics for the binary search. The worst-case search benefits the most, as the last records are close to each other. Since only half of the successful searches are worst-case searches, even this picture is overly optimistic for the average case. Blocking affects the binary search statistics by subtracting a few accesses from the $\log_2(N)$ formula. The values by which the search will be reduced from $\log_2(N)$ are shown in Figure 5.1 for the worst-case search and for searches that are one less than the worst case. The second row may be used to estimate the average case, although the average case will differ slightly from these figures.

	Blocking Factor									
	1	2	3	4	5	10	20	30	50	100
Worst-case search requires $\log2(N)$minus:	0.00	0.50	0.89	1.13	1.38	2.14	2.98	3.49	4.19	5.13
Search of one less than worst case requires $\log_2(N)$minus:	1.00	1.00	1.22	1.38	1.58	2.24	3.03	3.53	4.21	5.14

Figure 5.1 Reductions in physical accesses for binary search with blocking.

Read all records in key order (Algorithm 4.3).   Since the ordered file is required to be ordered by a key, a simple sequential read will suffice. Where it is necessary to read the records in order by a different key, the structure is of no help and Algorithm 3.7 would again be required.

5.4 SUMMARY

Ordered relative files are relative files constrained to being ordered by a key, having a valid key in each slot, and not using the record number for a key. This file type is appropriate for disk but not for tape and other sequential devices.

Ordered sequential files are sequential files constrained to being ordered by a key. Because they are used on sequential devices, records may not be updated or deleted.

Both types of ordered files require reorganization to physically add and delete records. A merge algorithm is used to build a new data file from the old file and a change file. Since the *merge algorithm* requires only one pass through each of the three files, it is very efficient.

The *binary search* algorithm may be used with an ordered relative file to locate a record with a given key. It operates in order $[\log(N)]$ time rather than order (N) time of the sequential searches.

Both types of ordered files produce all records in key order by a simple sequential read. The algorithms for the standard functions are shown in Figure 5.2.

5.5 THE STUDENT RECORDS PROBLEM

The binary search should be a great help in solving the student records problem as, for the first time, it is possible to retrieve records by a natural key without having to search sequentially for them. It remains to be seen whether the requirement of using the merge algorithm for adding and deleting records will offset this advantage.

The decision tree may again be pruned by some forethought. Variable-length records may not be used with the ordered relative file just as with the unordered relative file. This leaves the fixed-length student and course files and the enrollment file. To complicate matters, it is not obvious whether the key for the enrollment file should relate to the student entity or the course entity. Thus there are two versions of the enrollment file to consider. Both have the same record size and content, but one file is ordered by course, while the other will be ordered by student key. The space requirements will continue to be those shown in Figure 3.3.

| Function | Algorithm | Sequential Chronological File | | Rel. File | Ordered File | |
		Mag. Tape	Disk	Disk	Mag. Tape	Disk
Add a record	3.1 Append to file	×	×			
	4.1 Write direct			×		
	5.1 Merge				×	×
Delete a record	3.2 Flag as deleted		×	×		×
	5.1 Merge				×	×
Read all, any order	3.4 Sequential exhaustive read	×	×	×	×	×
Read all, key order	3.7 Iterative exhaustive search	×	×			
	4.3 Sequential ordered read			×	×	×
Read record by key	3.5 Limited sequential search	×	×	×	×	
	3.6 Exhaustive sequential search	×	×	×	×	
	4.2 Read direct			×		
	5.2 Binary search					×
Update current record	Update		×	×		×
Reorganize	3.3 Copy the valid records	×	×			
	5.1 Merge				×	×

Figure 5.2 Algorithms for the standard functions.

5.5.1 The Student Record File

The key for the student record file could be either the name or the identification number. Each has advantages. The identification number will always be unique and has only one form. If the name is used, it is feasible to produce both rosters and grade reports in alphabetic order. The choice will not affect the access statistics, and so can be made on these factors alone.

Whichever attribute is chosen as the key, we will assume that the student records are in place in the file before registration begins. Registration is done by using the binary search to access the student's record and updating that record with the added enrollments. Changes may be done by exactly the same process. The results, as shown in Figure 5.3, show the $N\log_2(N)$ statistics that are characteristic of tree searches. Although these statistics are not as good as those of order N, they are much better than those of order N^2, and numerically are much closer to N than to N^2. The factor J is dependent on the blocking factor and is derived from Figure 5.1.

Rosters will have to be produced by an exhaustive search of the file for each roster. Again, this results in statistics of order N^2. The rosters will be in alphabetic order if ''name'' was chosen for the key. Similarly, grades are entered by searching the file exhaustively for students enrolled in the given course.

Function	Algorithm	Physical Accesses per Record	Number of Records	Mult.	Total
Registration	5.2	$\log_2(N) - J$	1	N	$N \cdot \log_2(N) - NJ$
	Update	1	1	N	N
Change	5.2	$\log_2(N) - J$	1	N	$N \cdot \log_2(N) - NJ$
	Update	1	1	N	N
Rosters	3.4	$1/B$	N	$2N/5$	$2N^2/5B$
Grades in	3.4	$1/B$	N	$N/5$	$N^2/5B$
	Update	1	30	$N/5$	$6N$
Grades out	3.4	$1/B$	N	1	N/B

Total accesses	$0.6N^2/B + 2N\log_2(N) + N/B + 8N - 2NJ$

Note: For $N = 2000$, $B = 4$ ($J = 1.38$), accesses = 654,843; for $N = 10,000$, $B = 4$ ($J = 1.38$), accesses = 15,320,654 (N, number of students; B, blocking factor; J, reduction from Figure 5.1).

Figure 5.3 Function analysis for student record file.

The grade report can be produced by reading one pass through the file and printing each student's report in the order found. Again, if the key is "name," the report will be in alphabetic order.

The total statistics are only very slightly greater than those for the relative student record file of Chapter 4. The dominate N^2 term has exactly the same coefficient. The small increase in the lower-order terms is more than compensated for by the ability to use a natural key, such as name or identification number, rather than the artificial and arbitrary record number required with the relative file.

5.5.2 The Enrollment Record File Ordered by Student Key

Here again, there is a choice between name and identification number for the key. The advantages and disadvantages are the same as in the student record. Using the name will allow the rosters and grade reports to be in alphabetic order, but may also cause some confusion with similar names, and variations of names.

Registration is done by appending records as registration proceeds, using Algorithm 3.1. Clearly, this will result in an unordered file. This file will be regarded as a temporary file that collects the data but does not conform to the structure of the ordered relative file.

A sort is required after the registration has been completed and before any other functions are performed. The sort operation has been added to the table of functions, as shown in Figure 5.4. Once the sort has been done, the file will conform to the requirements of the ordered relative file.

Function	Algorithm	Physical Accesses per Record	Number of Records	Number of Mult.	Total
Registration	3.1	$1/B$	6	N	$6N/B$
	Sort				
Change	3.1	$1/B$	5	N	$5N/B$
	5.1	$1/B$	17	N	$17N/B$
Rosters	3.4	$1/B$	$6N$	$2N/5$	$2N^2/5B$
Grades in	3.4	$1/B$	$6N$	$N/5$	$6N^2/5B$
	Update	1	30	$N/5$	$6N$
Grades out	3.4	$1/B$	N	1	N/B
Total accesses					$3.6N^2/B + 29N/B + 6N$

Note: For $N = 2000$, $B = 20$, accesses $= 734,900$;   for $N = 10,000$, $B = 20$, accesses $= 18,074,500$ (N, number of students; B, blocking factor).

Figure 5.4 Function analysis for enrollment record file ordered by student key.

Notice that there are no statistics shown for the sort. This is because the sort is likely to be an **_external sort_**, meaning that it involves both file operations and internal sort operations. External sorts are very dependent on the sort algorithm used, the key size, the record size, the file size, and the amount of primary memory space available to work with. Consequently, it is difficult to provide specific statistics for file accesses until all of these factors are known. Suffice to say that most sort utilities commonly used will generate statistics of order $N\log(N)$. In problems where the total results are of order N^2, it is not likely that the sorts will figure heavily in the total results. Thus the sort statistics will be ignored in this example, making the totals shown somewhat short of the real totals but close enough for meaningful comparisons.

Changes are done in a similar manner to the registration. The changes are collected in a change file until the period for making changes has passed. The change file is then sorted into key order and merged with the old file, using Algorithm 5.1, to produce a new file. This sort is not shown in Figure 5.4, but would immediately precede the merge operation. This places a constraint on the system that none of the changes will affect the main file until all the changes are merged into it, or that multiple merges be done with a corresponding increase in accesses for the change function.

Rosters will require the sequential, exhaustive search of Algorithm 3.4. If "name" is the key, the rosters will be produced in alphabetic order. The "grades in" function is also done by a sequential, exhaustive search of the file. Each enrollment for the particular course is updated as it is found and the grade entered.

The grade report is very easy to produce, requiring only one sequential, exhaustive read of the file to produce all grades. Each student's enrollments are contiguous in the file since the file is ordered by student key. Again, the report will be in alphabetic order if "name" is used as the key.

Although the total statistics are of order N^2, the numbers are quite acceptable when compared to previous file designs. For example, the enrollment file solution using the sequential-chronological file required more than four times as many accesses. The exclusion of the sort statistics from the total here is not significant.

5.5.3 The Enrollment Record File Ordered by Course Key

The file is now ordered by course. It could also be ordered by a key consisting of course followed by student name. This would have the advantage of allowing rosters to be produced in alphabetic order by student name. Either way, where it is appropriate the binary search can be used as though course were the only key.

Registration is done by appending enrollment records in the order in which they are performed, as with the enrollment record file ordered by student. Again, an external sort is required but will not be counted in the statistics, as shown in Figure 5.5.

Changes are, again, done by entering all changes into a change file, sorting the change file, and then merging the change with the old file to create a new file. The only difference between the two forms of the enrollment record is the key used for the sorts.

Rosters are produced by first using the binary search of Algorithm 5.2 to find one of the enrollments for the course. There is no way of knowing, when the record is found, where it lies among all the enrollments for the course. However, the ordering guarantees that all enrollment records for one course are contiguous. Therefore, the remaining enrollment records may be located by searching sequentially, in both directions, from the record located by the binary search. This would best be done by using the READ-DIRECT operation and incrementing or decrementing the record number until all the enrollments for the course have been found.

Grades are entered by a very similar procedure. The only difference is that after an enrollment has been read, it is also updated to enter the grade.

To this point all the functions have been very efficient, being of order $N\log_2(N)$ at worst. However, the "grades out" function still has no good solution for this file design. It will be necessary to fall back on Algorithms 3.7 and 3.6 to group together all the enrollments for each student. Unfortunately, this will introduce statistics of order N^2.

Function	Algorithm	Physical Accesses per Record	Number of Records	Mult.	Total
Registration	3.1 Sort	$1/B$	6	N	$6N/B$
Change	3.1	$1/B$	5	N	$5N/B$
	5.1	$1/B$	17	N	$17N/B$
Rosters	5.2	$\log_2(N/30) - J$	1	$2N/5$	$0.4N(\log_2(N/30) - J)$
	Sequential search	$1/B$	29	$2N/5$	$58N/5B$
Grades in	5.2	$\log_2(N/30) - J$	1	$N/5$	$0.2N(\log_2(N/30) - J)$
	Sequential search	$1/B$	29	$N/5$	$29N/5B$
	Update	$1/B$	30	$N/5$	$6N/B$
Grades out	3.7	N/B	$6N$	1	$6N^2/B$
	3.6	N/B	$6N$	1	$6N^2/B$
Total accesses					$12N^2/B + 0.6N(\log_2(N/30) - J) + 51.4N/B$

Note: For $N = 2000$, $B = 20$ ($J = 3.03$), accesses = 2,405,140; for $N = 10,000$, $B = 20$ ($J = 3.03$), accesses = 60,025,700 (N, number of students; B, blocking factor; J, reduction from Figure 5.1).

Figure 5.5 Function analysis for enrollment record file ordered by course key.

5.5.4 The Course Record File

The key for the course record file is the course. The records are fixed in length and each will accommodate the maximum of 100 enrollments.

Registration is done by using the binary search to locate each course for which a student enrolls. After each course is read, it is updated by adding the student's enrollment to the record. Changes are performed in a very similar manner, by locating each course for which a student is making an enrollment change, and updating each course to reflect that change.

Rosters are, for this file design, one of the most efficient functions seen so far. The course is located by the binary search, and all enrollments for the course are produced from the one record.

"Grades in" is also very simple. It is done the same as the rosters except that the record is updated after the grades are entered.

Again, as with the enrollment file when ordered by course, there will be great difficulty producing the grade reports. Once more, Algorithms 3.7 and 3.6 will serve the purpose, but at a great price in efficiency. The analysis for the course records file is shown in Figure 5.6.

Function	Algorithm	Physical Accesses per Record	Number of Records	Number of Mult.	Total
Registration	5.2	$\log_2(N/5) - J$	6	N	$6N \cdot \log_2(N/5) - 6NJ$
	Update	1	6	N	$6N$
Change	5.2	$\log_2(N/5) - J$	5	N	$5N \cdot \log_2(N/5) - 5NJ$
	Update	1	5	N	$5N$
Rosters	5.2	$\log_2(N/5) - J$	1	$2N/5$	$0.4(N \cdot \log_2(N/5) - NJ)$
Grades in	5.2	$\log_2(N/5) - J$	1	$N/5$	$0.2(N \cdot \log_2(N/5) - NJ)$
	Update	1	1	$N/5$	$N/5$
Grades out	3.7	$N/5B$	$N/5$	1	$N^2/25B$
	3.6	$N/5B$	$N/5$	1	$N^2/25B$

$$0.08N^2/B + 11.6N \cdot \log_2(N/5) + 11.2N - 11.6NJ$$

Note: For $N = 2000$, $B = 1$ ($J = 1$), accesses = 319,300;   for $N = 10,000$, $B = 1$ ($J = 1$), accesses = 7,996,127 (N, number of students; B, blocking factor; J, reduction from Figure 5.1).

Figure 5.6 Function analysis for course record file.

5.5.5 Critique

These four files are compared in Figure 5.7. This scatter plot is similar to Figure 3.8 and is done to the same scale for comparison. While the space requirements shown in the two scatter plots are similar, the number of accesses has definitely decreased. However, the decreases have not been uniform. The course records file (4) is the most improved in Figure 5.7, but still uses the most space. Either the student record file (1) or the course record file (4) might be preferred, depending on whether file space or disk accesses were more critical.

Again, each file type has one or two functions that create most of the physical accesses. The files ordered by student key have difficulty with the rosters and "grades in" functions, while those ordered by course key are inefficient in producing the grade reports.

In comparing the results using the unordered relative file of Chapter 4 with the ordered relative file, it can be seen that the ordered student record file requires only slightly more accesses than the unordered version, but uses a natural instead of artificial key. The course record file requires slightly fewer accesses in the ordered version.

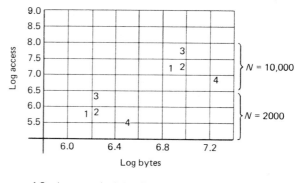

1 Student record;   2 Enrollment record, student key;
3 Enrollment record, course key;   4 Course record

Figure 5.7   Scatter plot of physical accesses versus storage space.

5.6 PROBLEMS

5.1. Why are the three constraints imposed on the ordered relative file more of a problem with disk files than with tape files?

5.2. Although the WRITE-DIRECT operation is possible with the ordered relative file, it is not needed. Explain why in the context of
(a) a disk file
(b) a magnetic tape file

5.3. Modify Algorithm 5.1 so that records with duplicate keys are not allowed, and an error message is produced if an attempt is made to add duplicates.

5.4. Modify Algorithm 5.1 to include a check to ensure that both the old file and change file are properly ordered.

5.5. Another form of tree search that is possible with the ordered relative file is a "trinary search." Instead of one record, midway between "hi" and "lo" being examined, two records are probed, one a third of the way from "hi" to "lo" and the other two-thirds of the way between them.
(a) Show that the trinary search requires fewer iterations than the binary search by calculating the number of iterations required for the worst case.
(b) Explain why the trinary search is not as efficient as the binary search in spite of the results of part (a).

5.6. Why is it necessary that records not be removed by flagging as empty if the binary search is to be used with a file?

5.7. Assume that an external sort requires $10N\log_2(N)$ accesses to sort a file of N records. Recalculate the results given in Figure 5.4 for the enrollment record file ordered by student with the sort added in.

5.8. Replace the "grades out" function algorithms in Section 5.5.3 by first sorting the enrollments into student order and then producing all the grade reports in one pass.

    (a)   Assuming the sort statistics of Problem 5.7, calculate the number of accesses as a function of N. What are the numeric results for N's of 2000 and 10,000?

    (b)   What is the most appropriate key to use for this sort? Why?

5.9. What is required to improve the "grades out" function in Section 5.5.4 by sorting? Why is this more difficult than the similar algorithm of Problem 5.8?

5.10. Explain why the relative positions of the four files in Figure 5.7 are unaffected by the value of N.

5.11. Solve the computer equipment problem described in Section B.2. Use the most effective file design for a single file. Any of the file types and algorithms studied so far may be used.

5.12. Solve the parts supply problem described in Section B.3. Use the most effective file design for a single file. Any of the file types and algorithms studied so far may be used.

6

Direct Access Files

6.1 DESCRIPTION AND ORGANIZATION

The *direct access* file is another variation of the relative file. The records are accessed by their record numbers as with the relative file, and the primitive operations are identical with those listed in Chapter 4.

The difference between the direct access file and the relative file is in the way the record numbers are assigned to the record and how the records are located. Instead of arbitrarily assigning a record number to a record, the record number is derived from a primary key by a function called a *hashing function*. The hashing function will be indicated here as H(key).

A good hashing function will have three attributes:

1. The record numbers it generates from the primary key will be uniformly and randomly distributed over the file [i.e., $0 \leq H(key) < N$]. This is essential to prevent records from clustering together in parts of the file.

2. Small variations in the value of the key will cause large variations in the value of H(key). This is necessary to distribute records with similar keys evenly about the file. All parts of the key must be used by the hashing function so that keys that are identical in all but a small part of the key will hash to different record numbers.

3. The hashing function must minimize the creation of synonyms. A *synonym* is defined as a key that hashes to the same record number as a different key. For example, if $H(X) = H(Y)$, then X and Y are synonyms. A good hashing function will have the property that the probability of any two keys being synonyms is equal to $1/N$. Synonyms are sometimes called *collisions*.

Methods of designing a good hashing algorithm, and methods for coping with synonyms will be discussed in detail in following sections of this chapter. It is vital to good efficiency that appropriate algorithms be employed for these functions.

6.2 PRIMITIVE OPERATIONS

The set of primitive operations for the direct access file is the same as that for the relative file. As with the relative file, attempts to read an empty slot, or to read or write to a slot outside the range of record numbers for the file will result in the VALID condition being set to false.

The primitive operations for the direct access file are:

OPEN   Sets the currency pointer to immediately before the first record and allows access to the file.

READ-NEXT   Sets the currency pointer to the next valid record in the file and returns that record to the user. An end-of-file condition is set if there is no next record.

READ-DIRECT   Sets the currency pointer to the slot specified and returns the record to the user if the slot is occupied. An invalid-record-number condition is set if the slot is not occupied or if the record number is outside the limits of the file.

WRITE-DIRECT   Sets the currency pointer to the slot specified and writes a record to that slot, whether or not the slot is already occupied. An invalid-record-number condition is set if the record number is outside the limits of the file.

UPDATE   Writes back the current record in the same location from which it was read. The currency pointer is unchanged. May be used to flag a record as deleted.

CLOSE   Terminates access to the file.

EOF   Returns a value of true if the currency pointer is beyond the last record of the file, otherwise, it is false.

VALID   Returns a value of true if the previous operation on the file was successful. False is returned if the operation failed for any reason or if a record was read which was empty. VALID will be false if an attempt is made to address a record that is outside the range of 0 to $N - 1$.

6.3 HASHING FUNCTIONS

The problem of finding a good hashing function is very closely related to the problem of finding a good generator of pseudorandom numbers. This is because the result of both should be a set of numbers that appears, by statistical tests, to be uniformly and randomly distributed over a given range. The difference is that the hashing function must be repeatable: given the same key, it must return the same record number every time. However, given a different key, no matter how slight the difference, it must return a record number that has no statistical relation to the first record number. Another way to think about the hashing function is that, given a set of valid keys, the function must return a set of numbers that appears to be random, as from a random number generator, even though the keys may be very unrandom in distribution.

The hashing function may also be viewed as a mapping from the address space of the key to the address space of the file. The file will have a finite number of addresses for records such as $0 \leq R < N$ for a file with N slots. Thus it has N distinct addresses. The key will have a larger address space. For example, the key might consist of a name represented by a string of 30 ASCII characters. Since, in general, each ASCII character can have any of 128 different values, the address space of the key is 128^{30}, which is roughly equal to 10^{63}, a very large space. It is obvious that there is no way to uniquely map so many possible values into the small address space of a file. Thus synonyms are inevitable. The most that is expected of a good hashing function is that synonyms appear no more often than would be expected in a similar set of random numbers.

Before operating on the key to produce a record number, the hashing function must be able to treat the key as though it were numeric. Often, the key will be numeric and can be directly used as such. At other times it may be of another form, as the name key just mentioned. A common practice is to treat such nonnumeric data types as though they were numeric. If the machine is told to add two 32-bit words together using the integer add operation, it does not really matter if the data of the words were previously interpreted as strings of alphanumeric characters; the addition will proceed. Clearly, the result cannot be interpreted as characters, but it could be interpreted as some kind of 32-bit integer.

Most machines have a small number of primitive data types for which there are arithmetic instructions. Frequently, the key to be used will not fit easily into one of these data types. It is not possible to discard the portion of the key that does not fit into such an arithmetic data type, as this would violate the second rule for hashing function that was set forth in Section 6.1. The solution is to combine the various parts of the key in such a way that all parts of the key affect the final result. Such an operation is termed *folding* of the key.

For example, consider a machine with a 32-bit integer data type and a 30-byte alphanumeric key. The key could be regarded as eight integers that are to be used by the hashing function to generate the record number. A simple function might add the eight integers together (using modulo 2^{32} addition), or perhaps combine them with the EXCLUSIVE OR operation. This is easy to do and usually effective enough. It does have the disadvantage that permutations of a key which involve interchanging characters that are separated by multiples of one-word length will result in the same folded key. For example, "BERT ADAMS" and "BART EDAMS" would fold to the same value.

These problems can be avoided by more elaborate folding schemes. These may include permuting the order in which the various bytes, or other components of the key, are ordered before folding according to the value of part of the key. Complicated folding schemes, however, should usually be avoided unless there is an obvious problem with the more straightforward methods. Some intelligent analysis of the likely values of the keys and their effect on the resulting record number distribution is required.

An alternative to folding is to retain the entire key and use routines that can handle multiple-word arithmetic operations. This will usually avoid the problems encountered with folding, but the improvement in record number distribution may not be worth the effort required.

Once the key has been put into a numeric form, there is a formula that is at once so simple and so effective that it is used nearly universally to map the key onto the record number space:

$$R = K \bmod N \tag{6.1}$$

where R = record number
K = numeric form of the key
N = number of slots in the file

Notice that this will always produce a record number such that $0 \leq R < N$. For good results K should be much larger (many orders of magnitude) than N. This will usually happen as a natural consequence of the difference in address space between the key and the file.

Although this formula has the advantage of being very simple, it can work very badly if N is not chosen with some care. For example, consider a nine (decimal) digit identification number used as a key. If $N = 1000$, the record number will simply consist of the three low-order digits of the key. The six high-order digits will have no influence on the record number. This violates the second principle that was stated in Section 6.1 for a good hashing function since a major part of the key is being ignored.

Suppose that the file size is changed so that $N = 1024$. If we analyze the situation in decimal, no problem is seen. However, if we look at it in binary, only the low-order 10 bits will affect the record number, and all the high-order bits are discarded without influencing the record number. Notice that this problem has nothing to do with the base that is used by the machine to represent the data. It will happen anytime that N is a small multiple of an integer raised to an integer power. In the neighborhood of any given number, there are many such numbers. Moreover, values of N that have many small factors will also produce a poor distribution when given similar keys.

A simple solution to this problem is to require that N always be a prime number. Since, by definition, a prime number can have no factors except itself and 1, there is never a danger that it will be a small multiple of an integer raised to an integer power. Extensive tests have shown that formula (6.1) works very well for a hashing function when N is prime. This is not a problem since there is always a prime number in the neighborhood of any desired file size. For example, 1009 is a prime near 1000. Many people who design files have either a table of prime numbers or a program to generate prime numbers in the neighborhood of a given number for this purpose.

As long as the folding, when needed, is done with some intelligent understanding of the nature of the key values, and N is a prime number, the algorithm of folding and applying formula (6.1) will usually give good results consistent with the requirements of Section 6.1. One exception to this rule is when values of K have consecutive values. This will lead to values of R having consecutive values, which violates the first attribute listed in Section 6.1 for hashing functions (i.e., that the record numbers be randomly and uniformly distributed).

For example, a college registrar once issued "pseudo social security numbers" to foreign students and others who did not have a number, or who did not care to have it used as an identification number. These numbers were of the form "999-99-XXXX", where the digits XXXX began with 0001, 0002, 0003. . . .. These identification numbers hashed to consecutive locations and resulted in a huge synonym chain (discussed in the next section) that caused very poor performance. The problem was solved by providing the registrar with a list of numbers to use of the form "999-YY-YYYY," where YYYYYY were digits supplied by a random number generator. By randomizing the numbers and providing a longer effective key, the corresponding record numbers were effectively disbursed over the file space. Changing the form of the number to "XXX-X9-9999" would also have had a similar effect.

There have been many other hashing functions used. Most are more complicated and few offer any advantages over formula (6.1). Where an advantage exists, it usually is due to knowledge of the values of the keys for a given application.

6.4 STRUCTURES AND ALGORITHMS FOR HANDLING SYNONYMS

As has been noted, it is inevitable that synonyms will be created by hashing. The probability that k records will hash to any slot is given by the formula:

$$P(k) = (M! \, (1 - 1/N)^{(M - k)}) \div (k! \, (M - k)! \, N^k) \qquad (6.2)$$

where $P(k)$ = probability of k records hashing to any one slot
M = number of records in the file
N = number of slots in the file

This formula can be nicely approximated for large values of N by the Poisson function as shown in formula (6.3). The **load factor**, f, is the ratio of records to slots in the file or $(M \div N)$.

$$P(k) = (f^k e^{-f}) / k! \tag{6.3}$$

where $P(k)$ = probability of k records hashing to any one slot
f = load factor of the file $(M \div N)$

A table of values calculated from formula (6.3) is shown in Figure 6.1.

Number of Records, k	Load Factor									
	20%	50%	70%	80%	85%	90%	95%	98%	99%	100%
0	.81873	.60653	.49659	.44933	.42741	.40657	.38674	.37531	.37158	.36788
1	.16375	.30327	.34761	.35946	.36330	.36591	.36740	.36780	.36786	.36788
2	.01637	.07582	.12166	.14379	.15440	.16466	.17452	.18022	.18209	.18394
3	.00109	.01264	.02839	.03834	.04375	.04940	.05526	.05887	.06009	.06131
4	.00005	.00158	.00497	.00767	.00930	.01111	.01313	.01442	.01487	.01533
5	.00000	.00016	.00070	.00123	.00158	.00200	.00249	.00283	.00294	.00307
6	.00000	.00001	.00008	.00016	.00022	.00030	.00039	.00046	.00049	.00051
7	.00000	.00000	.00001	.00002	.00003	.00004	.00005	.00006	.00007	.00007
8	.00000	.00000	.00000	.00000	.00000	.00000	.00001	.00001	.00001	.00001

Figure 6.1 Hashing probabilities with random distribution.

Notice that as the load factor approaches 100%, the fraction of slots to which no record has hashed approaches $1/e$ or approximately 0.368. Similarly, the fraction of slots to which exactly one record has hashed also approaches $1/e$, but from the other side. This means that for the remaining $(1 - 2/e)$ or approximately 26.4% of the slots, the remaining $(1 - 1/e)$ or 63.2% of the records have hashed. Thus there has been an average of 2.39 records hashed to each of these slots. Since only one record can be stored in each slot, some method must be devised to move the synonym records into the unused slots in such a way that they can be quickly retrieved when needed.

This section will explore five commonly used algorithms for handling this "synonym problem." These algorithms will also dictate the logical structure of the file, and thus the algorithms that are used for adding, deleting, and reading records in the file. Therefore, the algorithms for the basic functions will be treated separately for each method. In several cases there will be some variations of the algorithms as well. The solutions will progress from those that are usable, but not very efficient, to those that are more effective. However, this does not mean that the earlier algorithms should be ignored. There may be special situations where they will be the best choice. Also, the reader will gain a more mature perspective on the more effective methods by studying those that are less so.

6.4.1 Overflow File

A very simple solution to the synonym problem is to place all of the synonyms into another, or *overflow file*. If the load factor of the main file is low, the proportion of synonyms will be small, and the overflow file may not need much space. It may be organized in any way that the designer wishes.

One very simple way to organize the overflow file is to use it as a sequential-chronological file. As long as the number of records in it is small, the performance penalties may be acceptable.

It can also be organized as another, smaller, direct access file. Here again it will be necessary to have an overflow file for the overflow file. However, the second overflow file will be much smaller than the first, and much, much smaller than the main file.

There are two disadvantages of the overflow file. First, the main file cannot have a very high load factor or both the proportion and number of overflow records will become too high to manage efficiently. Second, because the main file has a low load factor, there will be considerable file space wasted in the form of empty slots. For a small file, this may be acceptable, but probably not for a large file. For these reasons, the overflow file is not recommended as a method of coping with synonyms and will not be analyzed in detail here.

6.4.2 Linear Probing

It would be much more convenient if all the records could be stored in one file instead of two or more files as when an overflow file is used. There are several ways this can be done. One method is to partition the file into a larger area used for hashed access, and a smaller overflow area. However, this does not allow the 37% of slots to which records have not hashed (at 100% load factor) ever to be used. It would be much more economical of storage space if some method were devised to store the synonyms in the (otherwise) unused slots. The remaining methods of this chapter concentrate on such methods.

A general method of relocating synonyms within the main file is open addressing. *Open addressing* means that some predictable sequence of slots is examined, or probed, until an empty one is found. The synonym is placed into this empty slot. Since the sequence of slots is predictable, it is repeatable. On retrieval, the same sequence is followed until the record is found. There are two methods of open addressing that will be examined in this section: linear probing and rehashing.

Linear probing simply means that when a synonym is identified, the file will be searched forward from the natural address of the record until an empty slot is found. The record is then inserted into the empty slot. The *natural address* of a record is the location which is given by the hashing function operating on the key of the record. Should the natural address be near the end of the file, or the file be nearly full, there might not be any empty slots before the end of the file. In this case, the search simply wraps around and continues at the front of the file with record number 0.

The algorithms for adding and retrieving records from a direct access file using linear probing are as follows:

Add (Algorithm 6.1)

```
procedure ALGOR6.1(file,newrecord,n);
k := FOLD(KEY(newrecord));    (* fold the key if necessary *)
r := k mod n;          (* calculate the natural address *)
READ–DIRECT(file,buffer,r);  (* get slot at natural address *)
WHILE VALID(file) DO BEGIN   (* search for empty slot *)
        r := (r+1) mod n;    (* go to next slot, wrap around
                if needed *)
        READ–DIRECT(file,buffer,r);
END;   (* empty slot is at r when loop exits *)
WRITE–DIRECT(file,newrecord,r);   (* write the new record *)
```

Read a record with a specific key value (Algorithm 6.2)

```
    logical function ALGOR6.2(file,buffer,givenkey,n);
    (* returns true iff matching record is found *)
    k := FOLD(givenkey);   (* fold the key if necessary *)
    r := k mod n;          (* calculate the natural address *)
    READ–DIRECT(file,buffer,r);  (* get slot at natural
        address *)
    WHILE VALID(file) and KEY(buffer) ≠ givenkey DO BEGIN
            r := (r+1) mod n;  (* calculate next address of
                linear probe *)
            READ–DIRECT(file,buffer,r);  (* get next
                record *)
    END;
    IF KEY(buffer) = givenkey THEN ALGOR6.2 := true
            (* record has been found *)
    ELSE ALGOR6.2 := false;  (* record does not exist *);
```

There are several difficulties with the linear probe method of handling synonyms. First, as the file approaches a load factor of 100%, it may become very congested in some areas with all slots filled for long stretches. Figure 6.2 shows the average number of accesses required to locate a given record with various load factors and blocking factors. Notice that at a 99% load factor, the **average** search extends to 25 records. The worst-case search at 99% will usually exceed 1000 records for large files. However, if the load factor is kept below some reasonable limit, say 85%, the performance is probably acceptable. Even at 85% load factor however, the worst-case search will usually be in the range 100 to 200 records.

Block-ing Factor	Load Factor												
	10%	20%	30%	40%	50%	60%	70%	80%	85%	90%	95%	98%	99%
1	1.05	1.11	1.20	1.34	1.50	1.73	2.1	2.9	3.9	5.9	10	18	25
2	1.03	1.06	1.10	1.16	1.26	1.38	1.56	1.95	2.3	3.1	5.5	11	15
3	1.02	1.05	1.07	1.11	1.16	1.23	1.37	1.65	1.9	2.5	4.1	7.3	9.6
5	1.015	1.03	1.04	1.07	1.09	1.14	1.21	1.37	1.58	1.94	3.1	4.9	6.2
10	1.010	1.015	1.02	1.03	1.05	1.08	1.13	1.23	1.31	1.47	1.77	2.4	2.9
20	1.001	1.004	1.011	1.016	1.02	1.03	1.06	1.10	1.14	1.23	1.42	1.81	2.5
50	1.000	1.002	1.005	1.009	1.013	1.02	1.03	1.05	1.07	1.10	1.3	1.4	1.5

Figure 6.2 Average physical search lengths for linear probing: successful search.

Since the linear probe does a sequential search from the slot of the natural address, blocking will greatly reduce the number of physical accesses as shown in Figure 6.2. Unfortunately, there is no simple, direct method to calculate effects of blocking or the combined effects of adding and deleting records. Consequently, the numbers shown in Figure 6.2, and subsequent similar figures in this chapter, were derived empirically. Actual files may deviate from these figures. However, the average values for many large files will be very close to those shown.

A second problem with linear probing is that a record cannot easily be deleted. Algorithm 6.2 regards an empty slot in the probe sequence as an indication that the record it is seeking is not present in the file. As long as records are never deleted, this is a valid assumption. If, however, records are deleted, an empty slot is no longer a reliable signal that the search can be terminated. How, then, can the algorithm know when to terminate an unsuccessful search?

A simple but costly approach is to continue the search until the record is found or until the search has passed through the entire file and returned to the natural address of the key. This would work but would require a sequential read of the entire file every time an unsuccessful search was made. Such an algorithm would be feasible only where the probability of an unsuccessful search was very small.

Another approach would be not to actually delete a record, but to flag it as "abandoned." Algorithm 6.2 would not terminate upon finding an abandoned record, however, such a record could be replaced by a new record by making an appropriate modification of Algorithm 6.1. Records that have been abandoned, but not replaced, would have to be included in calculating the load factor. Using this approach, the following algorithm could be used to logically remove records without leaving the corresponding slots empty. The function REMOVE is used to set a flag in the record contained in the buffer to indicate that the record is abandoned.

Delete (Algorithm 6.3)

```
logical function ALGOR6.3(file,givenkey,n);
(* returns true iff matching record found and deleted *)
k := FOLD(givenkey);   (* fold the key if necessary *)
r := k mod n;          (* calculate the natural address *)
READ-DIRECT(file,buffer,r);  (* get slot at natural
      address *)
WHILE VALID(file) and KEY(buffer) ≠ givenkey DO BEGIN
        r := (r+1) mod n;  (* calculate next address of
            linear probe *)
        READ-DIRECT(file,buffer,r);  (* get next
            record *)
END;
IF KEY(buffer) = givenkey THEN BEGIN   (* record has been
      found *)
        REMOVE(buffer);  (* set flag as abandoned *)
        UPDATE(file,buffer);  (* write back flagged
            record *)
        ALGOR6.3 := true  (* record found and deleted *)
ELSE ALGOR6.3 := false;  (* record does not exist *);
```

Read all records in any order.   This function differs from Algorithm 3.4 only in that abandoned records must be skipped over. It is still a sequential read of the entire file.

Read all records in key order.   Since one of the basic requirements of the hashing function is that the record numbers be random in appearance, there can be no physical ordering of the file that relates to any key value. Consequently, it is again necessary to rely on the inefficiencies of Algorithm 3.7 if this function must be done with a direct access file.

6.4.3 Rehashing

Rehashing is a different method of open addressing for finding an alternate location within the main file for a synonym. It requires two hashing functions. The main hashing function is first applied to the folded key: $R = K \bmod N$. If record R is already occupied, a synonym exists, and the second hashing function $D = (K \bmod J) + 1$ is applied to the folded key. J is a different prime number, less than N. D is used as a displacement from the original record number R. Since $R + D$ could be larger than N, the addition is done modulo N. This causes the sequence of record numbers to wrap around the file and begin again near the front of the file.

Because each synonym will usually search along a different sequence of slots for a place to locate, rehashing tends to avoid the congestion that can result in some neighborhoods with linear probing. This, in turn, results in fewer records being examined during a search. However, since the displacement D will nearly always be greater than the blocking factor, the advantages of blocking are lost.

The problem of knowing when to terminate an unsuccessful search is very similar to that for linear probing. The only difference is in the sequence of records examined by the search. As with linear probing, the best solution is probably to flag those records that have been logically deleted as abandoned rather than empty. With this variation, the algorithms for the basic functions using a direct access file with rehashing are as follows.

Add (Algorithm 6.4).   The first hashed address, R, is examined. If it is empty or abandoned, the record is inserted and the function is complete. If it is occupied, the displacement D is calculated and the slot at $(R + D)$ mod N is examined. Again, the record is inserted if the slot is free. The process is repeated at $(R + 2D)$ mod N, $(R + 3D)$ mod N, and so on, until a vacancy is found. In the following algorithms the function AB is true if the record in the buffer has been flagged as abandoned; otherwise, it is false.

```
procedure ALGOR6.4(file,newrecord,n);
k := FOLD(KEY(newrecord));  (* fold the key if necessary *)
r := k mod n;       (* calculate both hash functions *)
d := (k mod j)+1;
DO BEGIN             (* iterate until a vacant slot is found
     for record *)
        READ-DIRECT(file,buffer,r);
        IF VALID(file) and NOT AB(buffer) THEN r := (r+d) mod n;
END UNTIL not VALID(file) or AB(buffer);  (* empty or
    abandoned *)
(* Now we have a vacant slot, write the record *)
WRITE-DIRECT(file,newbuffer,r); (* write record *)
```

There are several potential problems with this method of finding an alternate location. First, for a given pair of keys that are synonyms with the first hashing function, it is highly undesirable that they also be synonyms with the second algorithm, as they would then be competing for the same set of slots. By using different constants in the hashing function, this possibility is reduced to one in $N*J$. Second, D must be greater than zero or the procedure will loop forever. This is assured by the +1 term used in the calculation of D. Third, the procedure will also loop forever if it never finds a vacant slot. If the same small set of slots is examined repeatedly, this could happen even though there were still empty slots elsewhere. However since N is prime, and D is less than N, this cannot happen. R will be forced to take on all possible values before any are repeated.

Read a record with a specific key value (Algorithm 6.5)

```
logical procedure ALGOR6.5(file,buffer,givenkey,n);
k := FOLD(givenkey);  (* fold the key if necessary *)
r := k mod n;         (* calculate both hash functions *)
d := (k mod j)+1;
READ-DIRECT(file,buffer,r);  (* get record at natural address *)
WHILE VALID(file) AND KEY(buffer) ≠ givenkey DO BEGIN
        (* iterate until a vacant slot or the record is found *)
        r := (r+d) mod n;
        READ-DIRECT(file,buffer,r);
        END;
        IF VALID(file) and not AB(buffer) THEN ALGOR6.5:=true
            (*record ok*)
        ELSE ALGOR6.5:= false;  (* search is unsuccessful *);
```

Delete (Algorithm 6.6).   This is similar to Algorithm 6.3, differing only in the manner the file is probed:

```
logical function ALGOR6.6(file,givenkey,n);
(* returns true iff matching record is found and
    deleted *)
k := FOLD(givenkey);   (* fold the key if necessary *)
r := k mod n;          (* calculate both hash functions *)
d := (k mod j) + 1;
READ-DIRECT(file,buffer,r);  (* get record at natural
    address *)
WHILE VALID(file) AND KEY(buffer) ≠ givenkey DO BEGIN
        r := (r+d) mod n;  (* calculate next address of
            probe *)
        READ-DIRECT(file,buffer,r);  (* get next
            record *)
END;
IF VALID(file) THEN BEGIN  (* record has been found *)
        REMOVE(buffer);  (* set flag as abandoned *)
        UPDATE(file,buffer);  (* write back flagged
            record *)
        ALGOR6.6 := true  (* matching record found
            and deleted *)
ELSE ALGOR6.6 := false;  (* record does not exist *);
```

Read all records in any order, and read all records in key order.   Both of these functions are identical to the direct access with linear probing. Algorithms 3.4 and 3.7 will be required if they have to be performed on this file type.

6.4.4 Chaining Without Replacement

Both the linear probe and rehashing algorithms require long average searches at higher load factors, because the sequence of records that are probed will include many records that are neither synonyms nor are they associated in any other way with the record for which the search is done. Thus the search path will include many times more records than the number of synonyms.

Chaining without replacement is a method that avoids having to examine such a large number of nonsynonym records. It requires the use of pointers to build a series of linked lists in the file. When a record is being added and its natural address is occupied, it is added to a linked list whose head is the record at the natural address. Upon retrieval, it is only necessary to search the linked list to examine all the possible candidates for synonyms.

The problem of where to put the synonyms remains and is a separate problem from the question of finding the synonyms. While rehashing could be used to determine an alternate location for the synonym, linear probing is usually used. It has the advantage of allowing the blocking to reduce the number of physical accesses. Later in this section, a modification of linear probing will be examined that causes the advantages of blocking to be even more important.

This method of adding records will cause chains that originate at different natural addresses to *coalesce*, which will make searches longer than they otherwise would be. Figure 6.3 illustrates the process. As the sequence begins, all occupied slots in the range of record numbers 1236 to 1244 have been filled with records that are at their natural addresses. The next record to be added hashes to record 1236, which is already occupied. A linear probe locates a vacant slot at 1238, where the new record is placed. A pointer in the record at 1236 links the natural address to the new record.

Record Number	Natural Address	Forward Pointer		Record Number	Natural Address	Forward Pointer
1236	1236			1236	1236	1238
1237	1237			1237	1237	
1238				1238	1236	1242
1239	1239			1239	1239	
1240	1240			1240	1240	
1241	1241			1241	1241	
1242				1242	1238	1244
1243	1243			1243	1243	
1244				1244	1236	

(a)	(b)

Figure 6.3 Coalescing synonym chains. (a) Before additions. (b) After additions.

The next record added hashes to 1238, which is now occupied with the synonym from 1236. The linear probe locates a slot at 1242 into which this second new record is placed, and the chain is extended.

The third new record hashes to 1236, which is still occupied. The linear probe locates a slot at 1244 into which the record is placed. The chain, beginning at 1236, is followed until its end (1242) and then linked to 1244, which becomes the new end of chain. The end of chain can be recognized because the forward pointer has a null value (such as –1).

After the three records in the example have been added, we have two chains that have coalesced. One begins at 1236, the other at 1238. Synonyms from both addresses will be found intermixed along the chain. As the load factor becomes high, the chains tend to become very tangled. This will require a periodic reorganization of the file or efficiency will suffer after many adds and deletes.

Although it is quite possible to add and retrieve records if the chains are built using only a forward pointer, it is customary to use a backward pointer also, making the chains doubly linked. This is because some operations done in deleting records are greatly simplified if the list is doubly linked.

The space required in each record for the synonym chain pointers can be a consideration. However, it is usually a profitable trade for the improved performance as seen in Figure 6.4. The values in this table contrast very favorably with those shown in Figure 6.2 for the linear probing method, especially at the higher load factors.

Block-ing Factor	Load Factor												
	10%	20%	30%	40%	50%	60%	70%	80%	85%	90%	95%	98%	99%
1	1.05	1.10	1.15	1.22	1.29	1.37	1.46	1.55	1.60	1.67	1.73	1.76	1.77
2	1.03	1.06	1.09	1.13	1.19	1.25	1.33	1.41	1.46	1.51	1.57	1.60	1.61
3	1.018	1.04	1.08	1.11	1.15	1.20	1.26	1.33	1.38	1.43	1.48	1.51	1.52
5	1.008	1.021	1.03	1.06	1.09	1.13	1.18	1.24	1.28	1.33	1.38	1.42	1.43
10	1.004	1.010	1.019	1.03	1.05	1.07	1.10	1.15	1.18	1.22	1.27	1.30	1.31
20	1.002	1.006	1.015	1.018	1.025	1.04	1.06	1.9	1.11	1.14	1.18	1.21	1.22
50	1.000	1.000	1.004	1.005	1.009	1.017	1.026	1.04	1.06	1.08	1.11	1.14	1.15

Figure 6.4 Average physical search lengths for chaining without replacement using linear search: successful search.

The problem of the unsuccessful search is much simplified with this method. As noted earlier, the search may be terminated when the end of the synonym chain is reached, and that can be determined by finding a forward pointer with a null value. For this reason it is important that all records be initialized with null values in the pointer fields. Figure 6.5 shows the lengths that can be expected for unsuccessful searches. The lengths are greater since each chain must be searched to its end.

Block-ing Factor	Load Factor												
	10%	20%	30%	40%	50%	60%	70%	80%	85%	90%	95%	98%	99%
1	1.11	1.22	1.33	1.47	1.63	1.81	2.01	2.27	2.39	2.55	2.70	2.79	2.82
2	1.05	1.11	1.21	1.29	1.41	1.55	1.74	1.95	2.08	2.22	2.37	2.44	2.48
3	1.04	1.10	1.17	1.23	1.32	1.45	1.60	1.79	1.91	2.05	2.19	2.29	2.32
5	1.017	1.04	1.07	1.13	1.20	1.30	1.43	1.59	1.70	1.83	1.99	2.08	2.12
10	1.014	1.019	1.04	1.07	1.11	1.16	1.26	1.38	1.48	1.60	1.72	1.82	1.85
20	1.011	1.017	1.03	1.04	1.06	1.10	1.15	1.25	1.30	1.39	1.50	1.61	1.64
50	1.000	1.000	1.008	1.011	1.021	1.04	1.06	1.11	1.15	1.21	1.30	1.39	1.42

Figure 6.5 Average physical search lengths for chaining without replacement using linear search: unsuccessful search.

The algorithms for the basic file functions, using chaining without replacement and linear probing, follow. The functions FWD(buffer) and BKWD(buffer) allow access to the forward and backward pointers of the record contained in the buffer. The function GETNEWSLOT(R) returns the record number of a vacant slot in the neighborhood of record number R. This function is shown in Algorithm 6.7.

Add (Algorithm 6.7)

```
procedure ALGOR6.7(file,newbuffer,n);
k := FOLD(KEY(newbuffer));   (* fold the key if
   necessary *)
r := k mod n;   (* calculate the natural address *)
READ-DIRECT(file,buffer,r);   (* get slot at natural
   address *)
IF not VALID(file) THEN UPDATE(file,newbuffer)
   (* write rec *)
ELSE BEGIN (* find end of chain and add new record
      to end *)
      WHILE FWD(buffer) ≠ null DO BEGIN (* get
         next rec *)
            r := FWD(buffer);
            READ-DIRECT(file,buffer,r);
      END;  (* last record of chain is now in buffer, r
         points to it *)
      j := GETNEWSLOT(r);   (* returns record nbr of
         vacant slot *)
      FWD(buffer) := j;   (* link new slot into
```

```
              chain *)
         UPDATE(file,buffer);
         BKWD(newbuffer) := r;  (* set pointers for new
              record *)
         FWD(newbuffer) := null;
         WRITE-DIRECT(file,newbuffer,j);  (* write new
              record *)
    END;
    integer function GETNEWSLOT(r);  (* returns address
         of empty *)
    j := r;  (* initialize to given slot *)
    DO BEGIN
         j := (j+1) mod n;  (* address of next slot with
              wraparound *)
         READ-DIRECT(file,localbuffer,j);  (* test next
              slot *)
    END UNTIL not VALID(file);  (* empty slot has been
         found *)
    GETNEWSLOT := j;  (* return the record number *)
```

Delete.   Again it is the delete function that complicates a method that is otherwise very satisfactory. There are two problems, a minor one and a major one. The minor problem is that when deleting records, care must be exercised not to break a chain. This can be done by locating the records that precede and follow the record being deleted and causing their pointers to point to each other. This requires a few extra reads and writes, but the algorithm is straightforward.

The major problem is that a record that has a valid forward pointer may be the chain head for one or more records on down the chain. Should it be deleted, the search algorithm would find an empty record at the natural address and conclude that no such record exists. Even if it were known to exist, there would be no method of locating it except for a sequential search.

It might seem possible to replace the record being deleted with the next one on the chain. However, this would move the problem down the chain only one step. It would also introduce another difficulty. The next record on the chain might be at its natural address. Moving it up the chain would make it impossible to locate by a forward search of the chain from the natural address.

Clearly, there is no simple way to remove a record when chaining without replacement is used, just as with linear probing and rehashing. As with those methods, it is possible to flag a record as having been abandoned rather than empty. The pointers will continue to link the record into the chain. It may be replaced by a new record only if it has a null backward pointer or is found during an insert operation while searching for the end of the synonym chain.

As with the linear probing and rehashing, abandoned records must be included in the load factor calculations. Consequently, the file will require periodic reorganizations. The best method of reorganizing is to read each active record of the file in an order that is related neither to the order the records appear in the file, nor to the order in which they were added to the file. As each record is read, it is added to a new file by Algorithm 6.7. When the process is completed, the old file is purged.

Read a record with a specific key value (Algorithm 6.8). This function will normally be one of the most frequently used in a system, and it is for the ability to use it that this structure has been developed.

```
logical function ALGOR6.8(file,givenkey,n);
(* returns true iff matching record is found *)
k := FOLD(givenkey);
r := k mod n;  (* hash to natural address *)
READ-DIRECT(file,buffer,r);  (* get slot at natural
    address *)
WHILE VALID(file) and givenkey ≠ KEY(buffer) and
      FWD(buffer) ≠ null DO BEGIN (* find next record
          on chain *)
        r := FWD(buffer);  (* get pointer for next record
            in chain *)
        READ-DIRECT(file,buffer,r);  (* read it *)
END;  (* either record is found or it does not exist *)
IF givenkey = KEY(buffer) THEN ALGOR6.8 := true(*rec
    is found *)
ELSE ALGOR6.8 := false; (*  search is unsuccessful *)
```

Read all records in any order, and read all records in key order. Again, direct access files do not offer any algorithms for these functions beyond those of Algorithms 3.4 and 3.7. Since Algorithm 3.7 is very inefficient, it should be avoided whenever possible.

Before leaving the chaining without replacement method of organizing direct access files, it is worth reconsidering the best use of blocking to reduce the number of physical accesses in a search. This can be done by adopting a better strategy for locating an empty slot than the simple forward search used in Algorithm 6.7. A better strategy would be to locate the synonym within the same block as the end of chain whenever possible. The only time that a synonym would be allowed to locate in another block would be when the block containing the end of chain was full.

This change can be implemented by a minor modification to the GET-NEWSLOT function of Algorithm 6.7. Instead of beginning the linear search at the record following the end of chain, it is begun with the first record of the block containing the end of chain. In the following revision of GETNEWSLOT, the variable b represents the blocking factor.

```
integer function GETNEWSLOT(r); (* returns address
    of empty *)
(* following calculation is done with integer divide *)
j := b * (r/b) - 1;   (* calculate the first record in
```

```
           block - 1 *)
   DO BEGIN
           j := (j+1) mod n;   (* address of next slot with
              wraparound *)
           READ-DIRECT(file,localbuffer,j);   (* test next
              slot *)
   END UNTIL NOT VALID(file);   (* empty slot has been
      found *)
   GETNEWSLOT := j;   (* return record number *)
```

The result of this minor modification is shown in Figure 6.6 for successful searches and Figure 6.7 for unsuccessful searches. These figures may be compared with Figures 6.4 and 6.5, respectively, to see the improvement caused by this minor change.

Block-ing Factor	Load Factor												
	10%	20%	30%	40%	50%	60%	70%	80%	85%	90%	95%	98%	99%
1	1.05	1.10	1.15	1.22	1.29	1.37	1.46	1.55	1.60	1.67	1.72	1.76	1.77
2	1.006	1.019	1.04	1.08	1.12	1.18	1.24	1.32	1.38	1.44	1.50	1.54	1.55
3	1.000	1.004	1.018	1.04	1.08	1.12	1.18	1.26	1.30	1.35	1.41	1.45	1.46
5	1.000	1.001	1.003	1.009	1.023	1.05	1.09	1.13	1.17	1.21	1.26	1.30	1.31
10	1.000	1.000	1.000	1.001	1.004	1.008	1.022	1.05	1.08	1.11	1.16	1.19	1.21
20	1.000	1.000	1.000	1.000	1.000	1.002	1.006	1.02	1.04	1.08	1.11	1.14	1.15
50	1.000	1.000	1.000	1.000	1.000	1.000	1.002	1.009	1.02	1.04	1.07	1.10	1.11

Figure 6.6 Average physical search lengths for chaining without replacement using block preference search: successful search.

Block-ing Factor	Load Factor												
	10%	20%	30%	40%	50%	60%	70%	80%	85%	90%	95%	98%	99%
1	1.11	1.22	1.33	1.47	1.63	1.81	2.01	2.27	2.39	2.55	2.70	2.79	2.82
2	1.016	1.05	1.10	1.19	1.30	1.43	1.59	1.80	1.93	2.11	2.26	2.36	2.39
3	1.000	1.018	1.05	1.10	1.22	1.32	1.47	1.68	1.79	1.93	2.09	2.18	2.21
5	1.000	1.004	1.008	1.03	1.07	1.14	1.25	1.38	1.50	1.62	1.76	1.86	1.89
10	1.000	1.000	1.000	1.001	1.010	1.03	1.08	1.17	1.23	1.34	1.49	1.60	1.64
20	1.000	1.000	1.000	1.000	1.000	1.006	1.018	1.08	1.15	1.24	1.35	1.44	1.47
50	1.000	1.000	1.000	1.000	1.000	1.000	1.007	1.03	1.07	1.13	1.23	1.32	1.35

Figure 6.7 Average physical search lengths for chaining without replacement using block preference search: unsuccessful search.

6.4.5 Chaining with Replacement

Although chaining without replacement was successful in greatly reducing the length of the search path, the problem of deleting records continued, as with the earlier methods of coping with synonyms. A variation on this method will not only solve the deletion problem, but will cause a further reduction in the average search length as well.

Chaining with replacement differs from chaining without replacement in that when inserting a new record, if the slot at the natural address is occupied by a record for which it is not the natural address, that record will be relocated to another empty slot so that the new record may be placed at its natural address. This simple change has two very salutary effects.

First, the probability that a record will be located at its natural address is considerably increased. All synonyms must be located in slots to which no record has hashed. This will clearly work to reduce the length of the average search.

Second, the synonym chains cannot coalesce as they did when chaining without replacement was used. This is because all records on a chain are synonyms with the record at the head of chain. Thus none of them can be another chain head. Consequently, it is possible to delete records without fear of leaving some records unlinked to their chain head. Another benefit derived from the absence of coalescence is that the chains will be shorter, resulting in shorter searches, both successful and unsuccessful.

Figure 6.8 illustrates the process. This is the same example as that of Figure 6.3 except that chaining with replacement is used instead of chaining without replacement. As before, the initial state of the file shows all occupied slots in the range of record numbers 1236 to 1244 filled by records that are at their natural addresses. The next record to be added hashes to record 1236, which is already occupied with a record for which it is the natural address. A linear probe locates a vacant slot at 1238, where the new record is placed.

The next record to be added hashes to 1238, which is now occupied with the synonym from 1236. Since this record is not at its natural address, it is moved. The probe locates another empty slot at 1242, the record at 1238 is moved there, and the chain pointers linking the synonym chain that begins at 1236 are updated. Finally, the record that hashed to 1238 is placed at its natural address, which is now vacant.

The third new record hashes to 1236, which is still occupied with a record for which it is the natural address. The chain is followed to its end at 1242, from where the probe locates a vacant slot at 1244. This third record is then placed at this location and linked to the end of the chain. In comparing Figure 6.8 with Figure 6.3, notice that while all three records that hashed to 1236 are still chained together, the record that hashed to 1238 is no longer linked with them.

Record Number	Natural Address	Forward Pointer
1236	1236	
1237	1237	
1238		
1239	1239	
1240	1240	
1241	1241	
1242		
1243	1243	
1244		

Record Number	Natural Address	Forward Pointer
1236	1236	1242
1237	1237	
1238	1238	
1239	1239	
1240	1240	
1241	1241	
1242	1236	1244
1243	1243	
1244	1236	

(a)   (b)

Figure 6.8 Synonym chains when chaining with replacement.
(a) Before additions. (b) After additions.

The benefits of these improvements may be seen in Figure 6.9, which gives the average number of physical accesses required in a successful search. While the numbers are still greater than the ideal of 1.000, they are getting much closer for most cases. A separate table for unsuccessful searches is not needed. Since chains cannot coalesce, it is an easy matter to calculate the average unsuccessful search length from the average successful search length.

Block-ing Factor	Load Factor												
	10%	20%	30%	40%	50%	60%	70%	80%	85%	90%	95%	98%	99%
1	1.04	1.09	1.14	1.19	1.24	1.30	1.35	1.40	1.42	1.45	1.47	1.48	1.49
2	1.014	1.05	1.08	1.13	1.17	1.23	1.28	1.34	1.36	1.39	1.42	1.43	1.44
3	1.013	1.04	1.06	1.10	1.14	1.18	1.22	1.28	1.31	1.34	1.38	1.40	1.41
5	1.012	1.025	1.04	1.06	1.10	1.13	1.18	1.24	1.26	1.30	1.33	1.35	1.36
10	1.009	1.013	1.023	1.04	1.05	1.07	1.10	1.14	1.17	1.20	1.23	1.25	1.26
20	1.003	1.005	1.008	1.013	1.022	1.03	1.06	1.09	1.11	1.13	1.16	1.19	1.20
50	1.000	1.001	1.005	1.007	1.008	1.010	1.017	1.03	1.05	1.07	1.09	1.11	1.12

Figure 6.9 Average physical search lengths for chaining with replacement using linear search: successful search.

Consider each synonym chain to be a small sequential file of length N and each successful search to be a sequential search of that file by Algorithm 3.5. The average successful search will require the reading of L records, where $L = (N + 1)/2$. Solving this function for N yields $N = 2L - 1$. Thus the values for unsuccessful searches may be calculated from the table of successful searches by doubling the number of accesses and subtracting one. For example, a file with a load factor of 90% and a blocking factor of 10 requires an average of 1.20 physical accesses for a successful search. An unsuccessful search will then require $(2 \times 1.20 - 1)$ or 1.40 physical accesses.

The algorithms for chaining with replacement are straightforward except for the relocation required when moving a record.

Add (Algorithm 6.9). There are two ways to find a new location for a record that is being displaced to allow a new record to be located at its natural address. A simple method would be to use the GETNEWSLOT function to locate a slot, beginning with the old slot. This has the disadvantage that the record gets progressively farther and farther from its natural address. If deletions are rare, this may not be a problem; on the other hand, if they are frequent, it will cause the chains to be stretched out across the file with time.

A second method is to use the add function to reinsert the record into the file, just as though it were being added for the first time. This requires a recursive call to the add function.

```
integer function ADD(file,newbuffer,n);
(*returns address of record added *)
k := FOLD(KEY(newbuffer));  (* fold key and hash *)
r := k mod n;
READ-DIRECT(file,buffer,r);  (* read from natural
      address *)
IF not VALID(file) THEN BEGIN
        (* write it to its natural address *)
        UPDATE(file,newbuffer);
        ADD := r;  (* return the natural address *)
END ELSE IF H(KEY(newbuffer)) ≠ H(KEY(buffer)) THEN BEGIN
        (* record not at natural address, move it out *)
        j := ADD(file,buffer,n);  (* recursive call, returns
            new address *)
        (* patch up synonym chain for record just
            moved *)
        IF BKWD(buffer) ≠ null THEN BEGIN
                (* update forward pointer of previous
                    record *)
                READ-DIRECT(file,buffer2,BKWD(buffer));
                FWD(buffer2) := j; (* previous record
                    points to new addr *)
                UPDATE(file,buffer2);
        END;
        IF FWD(buffer) ≠ null THEN BEGIN
                (* update backward pointer of next
                    record *)
                READ-DIRECT(file,buffer2,FWD(buffer));
                BKWD(buffer2) := j;(* next record points
```

```
                          to new address *)
                     UPDATE(file,buffer2);
             END;
             (* now insert new record at natural address in
                 vacated slot *)
             WRITE-DIRECT(file,newbuffer,r);
             ADD := r;  (* return address of new record *)
    END ELSE BEGIN (* natural address is occupied by
          synonym *)
             (* find end of synonym chain *)
             WHILE FWD(buffer) ≠ null DO BEGIN  (* get
                 next link *)
                     r:=FWD(buffer);  (* address of next
                         record in chain *)
                     READ-DIRECT(file,buffer,r);
             END;  (* r now points to end of chain, record
                in buffer *)
             j := GETNEWSLOT(r);  (* find empty slot *)
             BKWD(newbuffer) := r;  (* set back pointer of new
                 record *)
             FWD(buffer) := j;(* set forward pointer of old
                 end of chain *)
             (* write old end-of-chain record back *)
             WRITE-DIRECT(file,buffer,r);
             (* write out the new record *)
             WRITE-DIRECT(file,newbuffer,j);
             ADD := j;  (* return address of new record *)
    END;
```

Delete (Algorithm 6.10).   There are two complications when deleting a record. The first occurs when the record being deleted is the chain head for a synonym chain. By definition, it is at the natural address for all the synonyms. Another synonym must replace the deleted record, or the chain will not have a head, and thus would be lost. The second problem is to patch up the synonym chain so that it remains unbroken whether the deleted record is a chain head or not. Notice the use of "double buffering" in this algorithm so that the previous record is available as well as the current record, when following down the chain.

```
logical function ALGOR6.10(file,givenkey,n);
(* returns true iff matching record found and deleted *)
k := FOLD(givenkey);  (* hash the given key *)
r := k mod n;
READ-DIRECT(file,buffer1,r);  (* read record at natural
    addr *)
WHILE VALID(file) and KEY(buffer1) ≠ givenkey and
        FWD(buffer1) ≠ null DO BEGIN
        (* search until key matches, or end of chain
```

```
                    found *)
            buffer2:= buffer1;  (* save previous record *)
            r:= FWD(buffer1);   (* address of next link in
                chain *)
            READ-DIRECT(file,buffer1,r);  (* read next
                record *)
    END;
    IF VALID(file) and BKWD(buffer1) = null and
            FWD(buffer1) ≠ null and KEY(buffer1) = givenkey
            THEN BEGIN
            (* chain head is being deleted, must be replaced
                with next rec *)
            buffer2:= buffer1;  (* save copy of deleted
                record *)
            READ-DIRECT(file,buffer1,FWD(buffer2));  (* get
                next rec *)
            WRITE-DIRECT(file,buffer1,r);  (* put it in
                vacated slot *)
            buffer3:= null;  (* make old slot of 2nd
                record empty *)

            WRITE-DIRECT(file,buffer3,FWD(buffer2));
            IF FWD(buffer1) ≠ null THEN BEGIN
                    (* update bkwd pointer of third record
                        in chain *)
                    buffer2:= buffer1;  (* save old
                        second record *)

                    READ-DIRECT(file,buffer1,FWD(buffer2));
                        (* get rec *)
                    BKWD(buffer1) := r;  (* point to new
                        chain head *)
                    WRITE-DIRECT(file,buffer1,FWD(buffer2));
            END;
            ALGOR6.10:= true;  (* record found and
                deleted *)
    END ELSE IF VALID(file) AND KEY(buffer1) = givenkey
            THEN BEGIN  (* found record, now patch
                up chain *)
            IF BKWD(buffer1) ≠ null THEN BEGIN
                    (* fix pointer in previous record which
                        is still in buffer2 *)
                    FWD(buffer2) := FWD(buffer1);
                    WRITE-DIRECT(file,buffer2,BKWD(buffer1));
            END;
            IF FWD(buffer1) ≠ null THEN BEGIN
                    (* fix pointer in next record *)
                    READ-DIRECT(file,buffer2,FWD(buffer1));
```

```
                    BKWD(buffer2):= BKWD(buffer1);
                    WRITE-DIRECT(file,buffer2,FWD(buffer1));
          END;
          buffer1:= null;   (* put null record into
             buffer *)
          WRITE-DIRECT(file,buffer1,r);   (* write out
             empty record *)
          ALGOR6.10 := true;   (* record found
             and deleted *)
     END ELSE ALGOR6.10 := false;   (* record not found *);
```

Read all records in key order, and read all records in any order. Again, the method of chaining with replacement does not alter these functions. Algorithms 3.4 and 3.7 must be used.

Read a record with a specific key value (Algorithm 6.11). This algorithm is really the culmination of the study of direct access files. It will allow a record with a given key to be retrieved quickly and efficiently. All the benefits of this file type are realized in this one algorithm. Of course, it is not possible to use this algorithm unless the structure implied in Algorithms 6.9 and 6.10 is used.

```
     logical function ALGOR6.11(file,buffer,givenkey,n);
     (* returns true iff matching record is found and in
        buffer *)
     k:=FOLD(givenkey);   (* hash the given key *)
     r:=k mod n;
     READ-DIRECT(file,buffer,r);   (* read record at
        natural address *)
     WHILE VALID(file) and KEY(buffer) ≠ givenkey and
              FWD(buffer) ≠ null DO BEGIN
              (* search until key matches, or end of
                 chain found *)
              r:=FWD(buffer);   (* address of next link
                 in chain *)

              READ-DIRECT(file,buffer,r);   (* read
                 next record *)

     END;
     IF VALID(file) and KEY(buffer) = givenkey THEN
              ALGOR6.11 := true   (* record found*)
     ELSE ALGOR6.11 := false;   (* record not found *);
```

Before we leave the direct access file using chaining with replacement, the effect of using block preference in locating an empty slot for a new record should be noted. As with chaining without replacement, starting the search at the beginning of the current block makes a significant difference, especially for the larger block sizes. The statistics are shown in Figure 6.10. The change is effected by making the same change in the procedure GETNEWSLOT as was done for chaining without replacement. Here again, the average search lengths for unsuccessful searches can be calculated by doubling the numbers for the successful search and subtracting one.

Block- ing Factor	Load Factor												
	10%	20%	30%	40%	50%	60%	70%	80%	85%	90%	95%	98%	99%
1	1.04	1.09	1.14	1.19	1.24	1.30	1.35	1.40	1.42	1.45	1.47	1.48	1.49
2	1.006	1.022	1.05	1.07	1.12	1.16	1.21	1.27	1.30	1.33	1.36	1.37	1.38
3	1.000	1.002	1.018	1.03	1.07	1.10	1.14	1.20	1.23	1.26	1.29	1.31	1.32
5	1.000	1.000	1.005	1.011	1.023	1.05	1.09	1.14	1.17	1.20	1.23	1.25	1.26
10	1.000	1.000	1.000	1.001	1.010	1.014	1.04	1.07	1.09	1.12	1.15	1.17	1.18
20	1.000	1.000	1.000	1.000	1.000	1.000	1.002	1.014	1.03	1.05	1.08	1.10	1.11
50	1.000	1.000	1.000	1.000	1.000	1.000	1.000	1.002	1.010	1.026	1.05	1.07	1.08

Figure 6.10 Average physical search lengths for chaining with replacement using block preference search: unsuccessful search.

6.5 SUMMARY

The *direct access file* is a very effective method for retrieving a record, given the value of the primary key for the record. The *hashing function* can be both simple and effective if a little thought is given to the parameters of the function. Problems can result if the *folding* is done without regard to the likely values of the keys, or if the number of slots in the file, N, is not prime.

The most troublesome aspect of the direct access file is the management of *synonyms* or *collisions*. Many clever methods have been developed to solve this problem, some more successfully than others. The overflow file method causes a high proportion of the file space to be wasted and, rather than solving the synonym problem, defers it to a smaller file.

Open addressing with *linear probing* has the advantage of being simple to understand and program. For these reasons it is commonly used. However, at the higher load factors, it can yield very long searches which raise the average search length to values that may be unacceptable, as seen in Figure 6.11. In addition, there is the problem of deleting records. Records may not be reset to the empty condition, but can be flagged as "abandoned." Over a period of time, as records are added and deleted, these records that are abandoned, but not empty, will cause an unacceptable level of congestion. As a result, the file will need to be reorganized. Because of these problems, the apparent simplicity of linear probing is more than offset by the need to manage and reorganize the file in most applications.

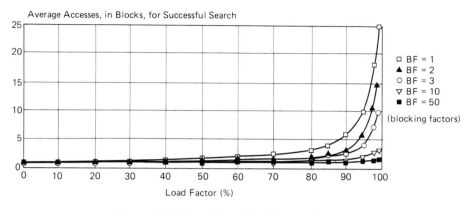

Figure 6.11 Search length for linear probing.

Rehashing is another variation of open addressing. The advantage of rehashing is that synonyms are not competing for the same sequence of slots in which to locate. The disadvantage is that consecutive locations will nearly always be too far apart for blocking to contribute to a reduction in physical accesses. Rehashing may be seen as a method for managing a file where the occurrence of synonyms is unusually high. Here, however, it is a more productive course to improve the folding function to reduce the number of synonyms.

Chaining without replacement is also commonly used. It has the advantage of greatly reducing both the worst case and average searches from those found in the earlier methods as seen in Figure 6.12. (Notice the difference in the vertical scale between Figures 6.11 and 6.12.) However, the problem of deletions remains due to the ***coalescing of chains***.

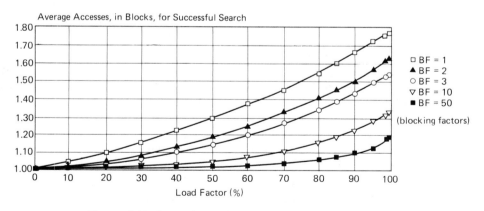

Figure 6.12 Search length for chaining without replacement.

Chaining with replacement solves the problem of deletions as well as causing a further reduction in search lengths. While the basic algorithms for chaining with replacement are more complex than the others, the overall problem of file management is made simpler. This may not always be obvious at the start of a file project where the designer may see the immediate problems as looming large while the more distant problems of file management, including the need for periodic restructuring, seem less important. Figure 6.13 summarizes the average chain lengths for chaining with replacement using block preference.

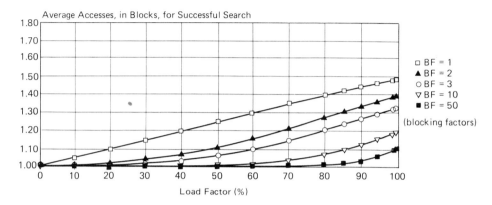

Figure 6.13 Search length for chaining with replacement.

Clearly, chaining with replacement is the best general method for using direct access files. There may be an occasional application where foreknowledge of the rate and nature of adds and deletes would give the advantage to one of the simpler methods. Whether or not such an occasional application would have enough advantage to warrant using different sets of algorithms is questionable. Thus, in the summary figure of algorithms for the standard functions (Figure 6.14), those shown for the direct access file are those for chaining with replacement, using block preference.

The direct access file does not perform well where records are retrieved by anything other than the primary key. Where multiple keys are used, it may be combined with indexes as seen in Chapter 10. Where there is a need to read the file in order by any key, an external index is needed to perform the function efficiently with a direct access file.

However, direct access requires fewer physical accesses than most other methods when retrieving a record by a natural key. For example, the binary search, as applied to the ordered relative file, requires an average of 12.3 accesses to locate a record in a file of 10,000 records, while direct access, with a reasonable blocking factor, requires only slightly more than one access. Where this type of access dominates an application, direct access is clearly the design of choice.

Direct access files must be carefully monitored for *load factor*, regardless of the method used to manage synonyms. All methods will show an accelerat-

Function	Algorithm	Sequential Chronological File Mag. Tape	Disk	Rel. File Disk	Ordered File Mag. Tape	Disk	Direct Accesses File
Add a record	3.1 Append to file	×	×				
	4.1 Write direct			×			
	5.1 Merge				×	×	
	6.9 Chain with replacement						×
Delete a record	3.2 Flag as deleted		×	×		×	
	5.1 Merge				×	×	
	6.10 Delete from chain						×
Read all, any order	3.4 Sequential exhaustive read	×	×	×	×	×	×
Read all, key order	3.7 Iterative exhaustive search	×	×	×	×	×	×
	4.3 Sequential ordered read			×	×	×	
Read record by key	3.5 Limited sequential search	×	×	×	×		
	3.6 Exhaustive sequential search	×	×	×	×		
	4.2 Read direct			×			
	5.2 Binary search					×	
	6.11 Direct access						×
Update current record	Update		×	×		×	×
Reorganize	3.3 Copy the valid records	×	×				
	5.1 Merge				×	×	

Figure 6.14 Algorithms for the standard functions.

ing degradation of performance as the load factor approaches 100%. Only the overflow file method can function at load factors exceeding 100%. Other methods, such as linear probing, should not be used with load factors greater than 80 or 85%.

The algorithms presented in this chapter have not provided for tests for a file that is overly full. Most of the "add" algorithms will loop endlessly if an attempt is made to add records beyond the file capacity. While the algorithms could be modified to detect this condition, or even searches of excessive length, it is a better strategy for the library procedures that add and delete records to keep statistics on the number of active records. These can be kept in a file header or other reserved area.

Two limits on load factors can be set. Whenever a record is added, such that the resulting load factor would exceed the first limit, a warning message can be sent. Attempts to make additions beyond the second limit would result in an error condition. For example, the limits might be set for 85% and 95% load factors. All additions that result in a load factor greater than 85% would cause an exceptional condition to be returned and/or a message to be sent. Additions that would cause the load factor to exceed 95% would be rejected as an error.

Expanding a direct access file requires a complete reorganization. This is because the hashing function depends strongly on the value, N, of the file size and all records would need to be rehashed when the value of N is changed. With some advance warning, the reorganization can be scheduled for a time when the impact on normal operations is minimized. A type of file organization that avoids this problem will be studied in Chapter 7.

6.6 THE STUDENT RECORDS PROBLEM

Direct access, like the binary search, is a method for retrieving a single record by a primary key. Unlike the ordered relative file, however, the direct access file does not allow records to be retrieved in order by a key. This will cause some significant differences in the way the functions of the student record problem are done. Improved statistics are expected when retrieving a record by key, but a degradation of performance can be anticipated for other modes of access.

Another difference is found in the space requirements. When chaining is used, it is necessary to add space in each record for the forward and backward pointers. Since the largest space requirement anticipated is for 10,000 students, it is safe to assume that the pointers can be contained within a 16-bit integer. Thus two bytes will be allowed for each pointer, or a total of four bytes for both pointers. The revised space requirements are shown in Figure 6.15.

File	Record Length	Number of Records	Total Space of Active Records
Student record	$85 + 10 (60 + 5) + 4 = 739$	M	$739M$
Enrollment record	$5 + 60 + 85 + 4 = 154$	$6M$	$924M$
Course record	$60 + 100 (85 + 5) + 4 = 9064$	$M / 5$	$1813M$

Figure 6.15 Three record types with space requirements.

Since the number of records in the student file can no longer equal the number of students (to avoid too high a low factor), the letter M will be used to indicate the number of students, and the letter N will be used for the number of slots in the file.

Blocking will be important in determining the number of accesses. Unlike previous solutions of the student records problem, it will be necessary to know the blocking factor immediately in order to look up the number of accesses expected. Thus B must be set before the functional analysis table can be filled in. At 256 bytes per sector, the course record will require 36 sectors for one record ($B = 1$). If the other record types are allowed to have blocks this large, the blocking factors could be as large as 12 for the student record file, and 59 for the enrollment record file. The total amount of space required will have to include the unused slots in the files as well as any space wasted in blocking.

6.6.1 The Student Record File

The student record file will use the student identification number (SSN) as the primary key. A blocking factor of 9 has a blocking efficiency of 99.92%, while a blocking factor of 12 has a blocking efficiency of 98.97%. Both are close enough to 10 to use the statistics for a blocking factor of 10 from Figure 6.10 in calculating physical accesses.

A load factor of 90% is a reasonable compromise between space wasted and access time. A higher load factor, such as 95%, could be used if there were assurances that no students would be added beyond the design goals. Since the penalty for running out of slots is very high, it is better to be safe and waste a little space.

The number of slots in the file will be the next prime number above the calculated file size. For $M = 2000$ this will be $2000 \div 90\% = 2222.2$. The next prime is 2237. For $M = 10,000$, the next prime above $10,000 \div 90\% = 11,111.1$ is $11,113$.

The total storage space required for $M = 2000$ is approximately $(2237 \div 99.92\%) \cdot 739 = 1,654,467$ bytes, or 827 bytes per student. The difference between 739 and 827 bytes per student is accounted for in having only 90% of the slots used, space lost in blocking, and "rounding up" to the next prime number. The 90% load factor accounts for all but six of the excess bytes per student. Similar figures will result for other values of M.

Registration is done by using direct access to read each student's record. The record is then updated with the courses for which the student registers. Changes are done by exactly the same process, with the same statistical results.

Rosters will again have to be produced by an exhaustive search of the entire file. Since the order in which the students appear in the file depends on the hash of their identification numbers, the order of the rosters will have no sensible meaning. Grades are also input by the process of an exhaustive, sequential search, with each student's record being updated as the grades are entered. Again the order in which the students' records are found is essentially random.

The grade report is produced in one sequential pass through the file. There is no order to the report. The only way to force the report to be read in alphabetic order by student name would be to resort to Algorithm 3.7. An external sort would be much faster.

The functional analysis for the student records file is shown in Figure 6.16. Although the term M^2 (or N^2) does not appear in the statistics, it is implied, in that N is always slightly larger than M and the product $M \cdot N$ appears in one term. This term is of order N^2 and is the dominate term in the expression.

Function	Algorithm	Physical Accesses per Record	Number of Records	Mult.	Total
Registration	6.11	1.12	1	M	$1.12M$
	Update	1	1	M	$1.00M$
Change	6.11	1.12	1	M	$1.12M$
	Update	1	1	M	$1.00M$
Rosters	3.4	$1/B$	N	$2M/5$	$2N \cdot M/5B$
Grades in	3.4	$1/B$	N	$M/5$	$N \cdot M/5B$
	Update	1	30	$M/5$	$6M$
Grades out	3.4	$1/B$	N	1	N/B
Total accesses					$0.6N \cdot M/B + 10.24M + N/B$

Note: For $M = 2000$, $N = 2237$, $B = 9$, accesses = 318,995; for $M = 10,000$, $N = 11,113$, $B = 9$, accesses = 7,512,301. (M, number of students; N number of slots; B, blocking factor).

Figure 6.16 Function analysis for student record file.

Care should be exercised when comparing the results here with those in Section 5.5.1. The total number of accesses is smaller, but the reduction is due almost entirely to a difference in blocking factors. The dominant term has the same coefficient in both total expressions. Moreover, the rosters and grade reports cannot be produced in alphabetic order here as they were with the ordered sequential file.

6.6.2 The Enrollment Record File

The enrollment record file is not feasible with direct access. The reason is that the key is required to be a primary, or unique, key. Any unique key for the enrollment record would require a combination of student and course keys. Therefore, it would be necessary to know both keys, at the same time, to retrieve any records. An examination of the functions shows that for most functions, one key or the other is available, but not both. Thus exhaustive sequential searches would be required for most functions and this would not be an effective design.

6.6.3 The Course Record File

The key for the course records is, again, the course. Since the record is so large, a blocking factor of 1 is probably as large as is feasible. Each record has space for 100 enrollments. The number of slots in this file will be the next prime number above the calculated file size. For $M = 2000$ there will be 2000 ÷ 5 = 400 courses. Allowing for a 90% load factor yields 400 ÷ 90% =

444.4; the next prime number is 449. For $M = 10,000$, the appropriate value is $(10,000 \div 5) \div 90\% = 2222.2$, giving a prime of 2237. These prime values are used for N, the number of slots, in Figure 6.17.

Registration is performed by accessing each course record for which a student wishes to enroll and adding that student's enrollment to the record. The record is then written back to the file. Changes of schedule are performed in a similar manner, adding or deleting enrollments as required.

Rosters are done very simply by reading the record for the course required, which contains all the roster information for that course. Similarly, grades are entered by reading the one record for the course, updating all the grades, and writing the course record back to the file.

The problem, once again, occurs when the grade report is to be produced. The only algorithms available that will group together all the enrollments for each student is the combination of Algorithms 3.7 (to identify the next student in alphabetic order) and 3.6 (to find all the enrollments for that student). As before, these algorithms result in statistics of order N^2 which dominate the totals. The results are summarized in Figure 6.17.

These statistics are somewhat worse than those derived in Chapter 5 for the ordered relative file using course records. The dominant N^2 term has a slightly greater coefficient when the ratio of the two different N's is taken into account. This is due to the 10% of free slots that must still be read in sequential processing. However, all functions except the grades out are now of order M, which is a decided improvement over the order $N\log(N)$ of the relative file.

Function	Algorithm	Physical Accesses per Record	Number of Records	Mult.	Total
Registration	6.11	1.45	6	$M/5$	$1.74M$
	Update	1	6	$M/5$	$1.20M$
Change	6.11	1.45	5	$M/5$	$1.45M$
	Update	1	5	$M/5$	$1.00M$
Rosters	6.11	1.45	1	$2M/5$	$0.58M$
Grades in	6.11	1.45	1	$M/5$	$0.29M$
	Update	1	1	$M/5$	$0.20M$
Grades out	3.7	N/B	N	1	N^2/B
	3.6	N/B	N	1	N^2/B
Total accesses					$2N^2/B + 6.46M$

Note: For $M = 2000$, $N = 449$, $B = 1$, accesses = 416,122; for $M = 10,000$, $N = 2237$, $B = 1$, accesses = 10,072,938, M, number of students; N number of slots; B, blocking factor.

Figure 6.17 Function analysis for course record file.

6.6.4 Critique

The best of the two solutions studied here is clearly the student record file. It requires less than half the space of the course record file, and fewer accesses. Unfortunately, the statistics are still dominated by sequential algorithms so that the advantages of the direct access structure are hidden in the totals.

Although the student record has an advantage in accesses, it must be realized that the difference in blocking factors accounts for all of that difference and more. With the same blocking factor, the course record file would require fewer accesses. The point is moot since the very large size of the course record makes similar blocking factors impractical.

It is instructive to compare the results with those obtained using the ordered relative file. These are the only two methods studied so far that allow a record to be retrieved directly using the value of a natural key. In the case of the student record file, there are two places where a record is retrieved in this manner: once in registration, and again in change of schedule. The algorithms compared are the binary search (Algorithm 5.2) and direct access using chaining with replacement (Algorithm 6.11).

The binary search requires $\log_2(N) - J$ physical accesses, which calculates out to values of 9.59 and 11.91 for 2000 and 10,000 students, respectively. By contrast, the direct access file requires 1.12 accesses, regardless of file size. Thus the two methods differ in this example by a factor of about 10, which is very significant.

6.7 PROBLEMS

6.1. Calculate the number of records that can be expected in the overflow file described in Section 6.4.1 with the following parameters. There have been 2000 records inserted and the main file has the capacities (slots) as shown below. Use the data given in Figure 6.4. Also calculate the total space (in slots) required for both the main and overflow files, assuming that the overflow file is filled to 70% of its capacity in each case.
  (a) Main file capacity = 2000 ÷ 0.2 (20% load factor)
  (b) Main file capacity = 2000 ÷ 0.5
  (c) Main file capacity = 2000 ÷ 0.7
  (d) Main file capacity = 2000 ÷ 0.9
  (e) Main file capacity = 2000 ÷ 1.0

6.2. Modify Algorithm 6.1 to permit the new record to be inserted into the first slot found that is either empty or abandoned. Use the function AB(buffer), which will be true if and only if the record contained in the buffer has been abandoned.

6.3. When calculating the load factor for a direct access file with linear probing, why is it necessary to include the abandoned records?

6.4. Why, in Algorithm 6.7, is it better to find an empty slot in the neighborhood of the last record in the chain instead of in the neighborhood of the natural address?

6.5. Modify Algorithm 6.7 to allow abandoned records to be reused. Use function AB as described in Problem 6.2. Does the function GETNEWSLOT need to be changed?

6.6. A file has a blocking factor of 3 and uses chaining without replacement to manage synonyms. It is initially empty in the range of slots 0 to 8. Records are added in sequence that hash to the following addresses: 2, 4, 2, 3, 5, 3, 6, 2. Draw a diagram, similar to Figure 6.3, to show the chains when chaining without replacement is used and empty slots are found using

    (a)   a linear search.

    (b)   block preference.

6.7 Repeat Problem 6.6 using chaining with replacement.

6.8. Rewrite Algorithm 6.10 so that when a record is deleted and there are synonyms that follow it on the chain, each of the following synonyms is physically moved up the chain to replace the one above it. Why is this algorithm superior to Algorithm 6.10?

6.9. Write a set of procedures to add, delete, and retrieve records for a direct access file. In each case there are three formal parameters for the procedure: the file identifier, the buffer, and the parameter N, which gives the capacity of the file. To support these three procedures, write a fourth procedure "hash" which has two formal parameters: the buffer and N. Hash will perform the hashing, including extracting the key from the buffer, folding, and calculating the natural address. The add procedure has a functional return of the actual address where the new record was written, the retrieve procedure returns the address where the record was found, and hash returns the natural address. Write these procedures for one of the following methods.

    (a)   Linear probing

    (b)   Chaining without replacement using linear searching

    (c)   Chaining with replacement using block preference

6.10. Solve the computer equipment problem described in Section B.2. Use the most effective file design for a single file. Any of the file types and algorithms studied so far may be used.

6.11. Solve the parts supply problem described in Section B.3. Use the most effective file design for a single file. Any of the file types and algorithms studied so far may be used.

7

Extendible Hash Files

7.1 DESCRIPTION AND ORGANIZATION

Although the direct access file is one of the most efficient structures known for retrieving a record by key, it suffers a major deficiency—it is fixed in size. Because of this **static structure**, it is poorly suited for applications where the number of records is not well known in advance or where the number of records fluctuates widely.

That it must be fixed in size is clear from the operation of the hashing function. The first requirement of a hashing function is that its values are distributed uniformly and randomly over the address space of the file as shown in Figure 7.1. If the file were to change in size, a different hashing function would be required. All records previously hashed into the file would have to be moved to new locations as specified by the new hashing function. This, of course, is equivalent to reorganizing the file and simply moves the data from one static file to another static file.

It would be much more convenient to have a **dynamic file structure** which expands and contracts automatically as dictated by the number of records in the file. Specifically, a dynamic file structure ideally should have three properties:

1. The file will automatically expand as necessary to accommodate new records. The expansion will not require a reorganization of the file or the relocation of more than a small fraction of the records in the file.

2. The file will automatically contract so that the probability of the load factor dropping below 50% is negligibly small. As with the expansion, the contraction will not require a reorganization of the file or the relocation of a significant number of records.

116

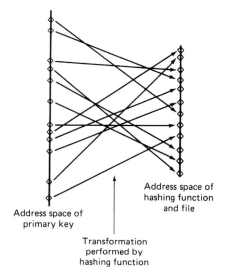

Address space of
hashing function
and file

Address space of
primary key

Transformation
performed by
hashing function

Figure 7.1 Hashing in a direct access file.

3. The file structure will allow retrieval of a record by primary key with one access to the file.

The last of these properties is the only one possessed by the direct access file.

Extendible hashing is a method of organizing a file so that it has the three properties listed above. Instead of using one transformation on the key, the hashing function, there is a series of three transformations performed to convert the key to a file pointer.

7.1.1 Key Transformations

The sequence of transformations is shown in Figure 7.2. The first transformation is a hashing function that maps the keys randomly onto some fixed address space represented by the range of the hashing function. The first few digits of this result are then extracted for use as an index into a directory. The directory contains pointers that point to the file.

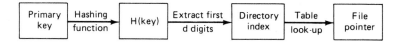

Figure 7.2 Key transformations in extendible hashing.

The file pointers do not point to individual records, but rather to blocks of records called buckets. A **bucket** is a large block of records all of which are read with one physical read operation. The method of placing and locating records within the bucket is not important since no additional physical I/O operations are required. Buckets may be added to and deleted from the file at any time.

The first transformation used with extendible hashing is similar to the hashing function employed in the direct access file. The same three properties for a hashing function that were stated in Section 6.1 are required here: (1) uniform and random distribution of keys over the range of the function; (2) small variations in the key will cause large variations in the value of the function; and (3) synonyms occur no more often than random probabilities would allow. A fourth requirement is added to require the range or address space of the hashing function be close to a power of 2. The reason for this will be seen shortly.

The hashing functions discussed in Chapter 6 are fully applicable here. Particularly, the requirement that the address space of the hashing function be a prime number of integers should be observed. Since the hashing function will not map directly into record numbers, the selection of the range of the hashing function is somewhat arbitrary and is not tied to the number of records in the file. It will be convenient to choose a range equal to the first prime number smaller than a "round" binary number such as 2^{16}. For example, the largest prime number less than 2^{16} is 65,521.

The second transformation extracts a relatively small integer from H(key) by using the first few digits of the hashing function. There are several arbitrary choices in the selection of digits. The base of the number system in which the digits are chosen will have a significant effect on the way the file expands and contracts. It is advantageous to use as small a base as possible; hence binary will be used as the base and bits will be the digits. Another choice is which digits to use. Conventionally, the high-order digits are selected, but the low-order digits or some other set of digits would serve equally well.

The digits extracted from H(key) are then used as an index into a one-dimensional array of file pointers. This array is called the **directory** and contains 2^d entries, one for each combination of d digits extracted from H(key). The complete sequence of transformations is illustrated in Figure 7.3.

The number of digits extracted from the hashing function value, the number of entries in the directory, and the number of buckets in the file all will change automatically as the file expands and contracts. Consequently, it is necessary to store some parameters to indicate the current state of the file. Specifically, the number of digits, d, used to index into the directory are stored with the directory as seen in Figure 7.4.

The transformations shown in Figure 7.4 have used the first three binary digits from the hashing function to partition the address space of the hashing function into eight equal segments. These eight segments correspond to eight

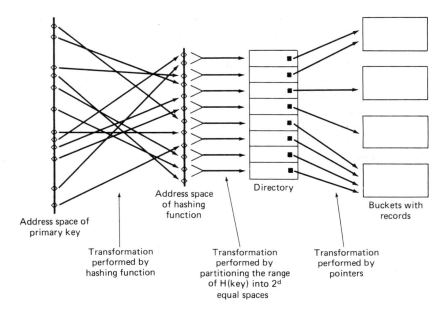

Figure 7.3 Extendible hashing.

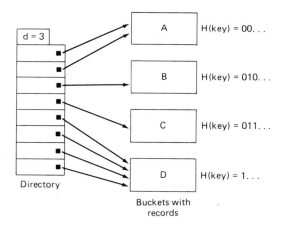

Figure 7.4 Directory of order $d = 3$ with four buckets.

entries in the directory. For example, suppose that H(key) = 0110100101100101 in binary. The first three digits, 011, have a value of 3. By using 3 as an index into the directory, we find a pointer that points to bucket C. (The first element in the directory has an index of zero.)

The complete sequence of retrieving a record from the extendible hash file consists of five steps. First the key is hashed to produce H(key). Second, the first d digits (bits) are extracted from H(key) to form an index into the directory. Third, the index is used to locate the appropriate bucket pointer in the directory. Fourth, the pointer is used to read the bucket into primary memory. Fifth, the desired record is located within the bucket.

7.1.2 File Expansion and Contraction

The reason for the complicated organization of the extendible hash file is to allow the file to expand and contract gracefully as the number of records varies. A rule is imposed on the buckets that sets a minimum and maximum load factor for each bucket. Typically, these are 50% and 100%, respectively, although other figures are sometimes used. A change in the file structure is triggered whenever these limits are violated by the addition or deletion of a record.

Consider the small file of Figure 7.4. Suppose that a record is to be added which maps into bucket D. If bucket D is already full, there is no room for the new record. This triggers an expansion of the file. A new bucket, E, is added to the file. Half of the pointers that point to bucket D are changed to point to bucket E. The records in bucket D that are reached through the pointers that were changed must be moved to bucket E. This will be approximately half of the records that were in bucket D. This leaves both buckets approximately half full and there is ample room for the new record.

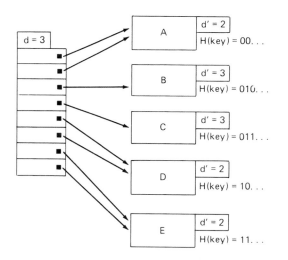

Figure 7.5 Distribution of keys among buckets after splitting bucket D.

The result of this split is shown in Figure 7.5. Notice that before the split, all records for which H(key) = 1... were in bucket D. Now those where H(key) = 10... are in bucket D and those where H(key) = 11... are in bucket E. The parameter d' shown with each bucket in Figure 7.5 indicates the number of digits of H(key) whose value is common to all records in the bucket. This must always be equal to or less than the number of digits, d, used to index into the directory. The number of pointers that point to a given bucket will always be $2^{(d - d')}$.

Bucket splitting can continue as the file grows as long as there are at least two pointers pointing to the bucket that must be split. If a bucket for which there is only one pointer in the directory ($d = d'$) overflows, the directory must be enlarged before the bucket can be split.

For example, if bucket C in Figure 7.5 overflows, a new bucket, F, can be allocated to enlarge the file. However, there is no place in the directory for separate pointers to both buckets C and F. Hence the directory must be enlarged to allow for more pointers.

The directory is enlarged by doubling the number of entries when binary digits are used for the index. Each pointer in the original directory is duplicated and occupies two consecutive positions in the new directory. The directory in Figure 7.5 would contain the following pointer values: A, A, B, C, D, D, E, E. After the directory is expanded it would contain values A, A, A, A, B, B, C, C, D, D, D, D, E, E, E, E.

Once the directory has been expanded, bucket C has two pointers and so can be split. The second C pointer is changed to F and the records originally in C are divided between C and F according to the value of the fourth digit of H(key). The resulting file is shown in Figure 7.6.

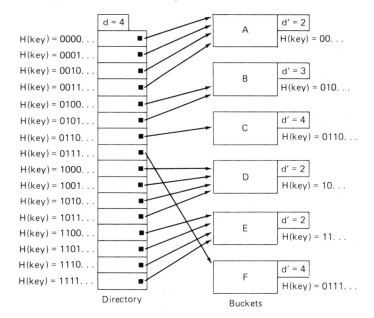

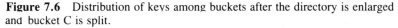

Figure 7.6   Distribution of keys among buckets after the directory is enlarged and bucket C is split.

The process for contracting the file is the reverse of enlarging it. Buckets must be combined if three conditions are true. First the average load factor for the two buckets cannot exceed 50%. Otherwise, there would not be room in the combined bucket for all the records. Second, the buckets to be combined must have the same value of d'. Third, the keys of the records in both buckets must share a common value of the first $(d' - 1)$ digits of H(key). These last two conditions are necessary so that all of the records of the combined bucket will share a common value of the first d' digits of H(key).

For example, assuming that the first condition is met, buckets A and B in Figure 7.6 still cannot be combined because they have different values of d'. Buckets A and D cannot be combined because their records do not share a common value of the first $(d' - 1)$ digits of H(key). However, buckets D and E could meet all conditions and thus be combined.

The directory must be contracted whenever all pairs of pointers have the same value. For example, a directory with pointer values A, A, A, A, B, B, C, C, D, D, D, D, E, E, F, F must be contracted by producing a new directory with half as many entries. The value of each pair of pointers in the old directory is used as one value in the new directory. Thus the new directory constructed from the values above would have the values A, A, B, C, D, D, E, F. However, a directory with pointer values A, A, A, B, B, B, C, C, D, D, D, D, E, E, F, F cannot be contracted because there is a pair of values (A, B) that are not equal.

Because there may not be another bucket available for combining when a bucket's load factor drops below 50%, it is not possible to guarantee that the load factor for a bucket, or the entire file, will not fall below 50%. However, if the hashing function is able to randomize the keys well, the probability of the load factor of the file dropping below 50% is negligibly small. As shown below, it will normally be about 69%.

The average number of buckets and directory entries after many random insertions and deletions is given by the following formulas:

$$\text{number of buckets} = N \div (B\ln(2)) \qquad (7.1)$$
$$\text{number of directory entries} = N \div (B\ln^2(2)) \qquad (7.2)$$

where N = number of records in the file
B = number of records that can be fit into a bucket

Note that formula (7.2) represents an average value. The actual number of entries at any given time will always be a power of 2.

The directory will nearly always contain more pointers than the number of buckets because some buckets will have more than one pointer. The average ratio of pointers to buckets is $1 \div \ln(2)$ or 1.44. Since the average load factor, as derived from formula 7.1, is 69%, the average number of pointers will be about $2.08N \div B$.

7.1.3 Bucket Structure

All of the prior description has been concerned with locating the bucket in which the desired record is stored. Nothing has been said about how to locate the record within the bucket. There are two reasons for this. First, whatever method is used to organize the bucket internally will not affect the number of physical I/O operations and so will not have a significant impact on most file operations. Second, there are many feasible solutions, with no clear preference between them.

Structures as simple as a sequential-chronological organization with a bit map are feasible. To find the desired record, each record in the bucket is examined in sequence and its key is compared to the given key until a match is found or the end of the bucket is reached. More sophisticated structures can be employed with a reduction in the CPU time required and a modest increase in complexity.

The ordered relative file could be used for the internal bucket structure and would permit a binary search to be used to find the desired record. The problem of insertions and deletions is solved by moving blocks of records as necessary to make room for a new record or close up a gap when an old record is removed. Thus the reorganization is continuous and can be done entirely within primary memory.

Direct access is frequently used and would involve fewer moves of records. Each key would be hashed again, using a separate hashing algorithm from that used to locate the bucket. Here synonyms would have to handled by one of the methods of Chapter 6.

7.1.4 Similar Structures and Analysis

The extendible hash file is a specific instance of a large class of structures that use a tree search to find the desired item. More specifically, it employs a radix tree or a trie. When the radix is 2, the radix tree becomes a binary tree. Figure 7.7 shows the directory of Figure 7.6 redrawn as a balanced binary tree. Such a tree could replace the directory and serve the same function. The only difference is the method used to locate the file pointer.

The duplicate pointers in the tree of Figure 7.7 can be eliminated by pruning back the tree. When this is done, the tree of Figure 7.8 results. This has the advantage of being smaller since there is just one leaf node per bucket. It is not forced to be balanced as is the tree implicit in extendible hashing. When the directory of extendible hashing is replaced by a tree similar to that of Figure 7.8, the technique is called *dynamic hashing*.

The tree of Figure 7.8 is poorly balanced. Some dynamic hashing techniques include rotation algorithms to keep the tree balanced. This is not really necessary in most cases, however. If the hashing function is able to randomize the keys well, H(key) will be uniformly distributed over its range and the result-

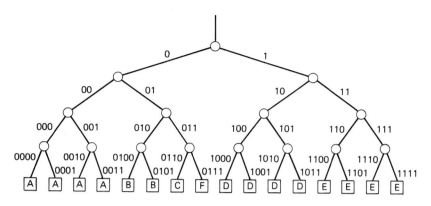

Figure 7.7 Directory of Figure 7.6 restructured as a binary tree.

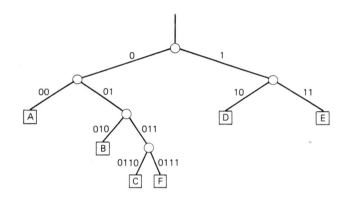

Figure 7.8 Binary tree directory used in dynamic hashing.

ing tree will be nearly balanced. The only exception will occur when the total number of records in the file is small and the bucket size is small. Then the "sample" size is too small for the randomness of the distribution to be apparent. This same uniformity of distribution will tend to keep the buckets at about the same load factor. This means that when records are being added to the file, all the buckets will tend to overflow at about the same time. Thus the load factor will tend to fluctuate periodically between more than 50% and less than 100% as the number of records increases.

Besides dynamic hashing there have been several other similar schemes developed, such as *expandable hashing* and *virtual hashing*, all of which seek to meet the objectives of a dynamic file structure with rapid access.

Several design factors should be noted in extendible hashing. First, the synonym problem has been solved almost incidentally to solving the problem of expansion of the file. If synonyms should occur, they will be placed into the same bucket. Because the internal organization of the bucket is independent of the structure outside the bucket, synonyms do not need to be treated any differently than any other pair of records in the same bucket. In addition, since the range of the hashing function can be arbitrarily large, the probability of synonyms can be made arbitrarily small.

While the range of the hashing function may be arbitrarily large, there is a lower limit that must be observed. There must be a sufficient number of digits in the range of the hashing function to index the directory at its maximum size. In other words, there must be at least d digits in the value of the hashing function for the largest d that can exist for the file. For example, a range of 16 bits will be adequate for a file of over 6 million records with a bucket capacity of 50. Since there is no upper limit, it is wise to select a range that is much more than sufficient for the file.

7.2 PRIMITIVE AND SUPPLEMENTARY OPERATIONS

The set of primitive operations for the extendible hash file is similar to that used for previous file types with the exception that the read and write operations reference an entire bucket instead of a single record. In addition, it is necessary to have operations to allocate new buckets to the file and remove buckets that are not needed from the file. There are many methods for managing the allocation and deallocation of buckets within a file system. The details are not important to the method. Therefore, for this file type only, we will introduce two new primitives for managing the bucket allocation and deallocation.

The primitive operations for the extendible hash file are:

OPEN Sets the currency pointer to immediately before the first bucket and allows access to the file.

READ-DIRECT Sets the currency pointer to the bucket specified and returns that bucket to the user. An invalid condition is set if the bucket does not exist in the file.

WRITE-DIRECT Sets the currency pointer to the bucket specified and writes to that position. An invalid condition is set if the bucket number does not exist in the file.

UPDATE Writes back the current bucket to the file. The currency pointer is unchanged.

CLOSE Terminates access to the file.

VALID Returns a value of true if the previous operation on the file was successful. False is returned if the operation failed for any reason. VALID will be false if an attempt is made to address a bucket that is not part of the file.

ALLOCATE Allocates a new bucket to the file from the free-space pool of the file system. The bucket number is returned by the function (See Section A.1).

DEALLOCATE Removes a bucket from the file and returns the space to the free space pool of the file system (See Section A.1).

In addition to the file primitives, it will be helpful to use several procedures to manipulate the components of the extendible hash file. The external specifications are given here without algorithms, as many of the implementation details will be system dependent.

integer function H(key): a hashing function as described in Section 6.3. The range of the function is from 0 to $(N - 1)$, where N is a prime number slightly smaller than a convenient power of 2.

integer function EXTRACT(j,d): extracts the first d high-order bits from j and returns them as an integer.

function KEY(recordbuffer): returns the key value associated with the record in recordbuffer.

procedure GET(bucketbuffer,key,recordbuffer): copies a record whose key value equals "key" from the bucket in bucketbuffer to recordbuffer. VALID is set to false if there is no record in the bucket whose key value matches "key."

procedure GET-NEXT(bucketbuffer,recordbuffer): copies the next valid record in bucketbuffer to recordbuffer. The first call after bucketbuffer has been loaded returns the first valid record. The EOF condition is set to true if GET-NEXT is called after the last valid record in bucketbuffer has been read.

procedure PUT(bucketbuffer,recordbuffer): copies the record from recordbuffer into the bucket in bucketbuffer. VALID is set to false if there is not room for the record in the buffer.

procedure DELETE(bucketbuffer,key,load): deletes a record from the bucket in bucketbuffer whose key value equals "key." "Load" is set to a value equal to the load factor of the bucket after the deletion is done. VALID is set to false if a record with a matching key value cannot be found.

procedure PARAM(filename,bucket,dp,load): returns the local order (dp) and the load factor (load) of the given bucket.

Four other procedures will be needed to split and combine buckets and to expand and contract the directory. The algorithms for these are described in the next section.

7.3 ALGORITHMS

Of the six standard file functions described in Section 3.3, five can be used on the extendible hash file. As with the direct access file, there is no direct way to read all the records in order by key.

The algorithms for this file are divided into two groups. The first are those for the supplementary operations previously mentioned. They will be given first so that their use will be understood when they appear in the algorithms for the standard file functions.

7.3.1 Supplementary Algorithms

The first supplementary algorithm expands the directory when it is determined that this is necessary. It has two parameters, the array containing the directory and the order of the directory, d. The present directory must have 2^d entries, and the new directory will have twice as many entries. The directory array must be large enough to contain all the entries after expansion. Both the array and d are passed by reference and the value of d is increased to reflect the new order of the directory. The algorithm expands the directory in place rather than copying the pointers to a new array.

```
procedure EXPAND(directory,d);
(* doubles the size of the directory and increases the order
     by 1 *)
(* original directory has 2^d entries numbered 0 to 2^d - 1 *)
FOR i := (2^d - 1) DOWNTO 0 DO BEGIN (* duplicate each entry *)
        directory(2*i + 1) := directory(i);
        directory(2*i) := directory(i);
END;
d := d + 1;
```

Similarly, the procedure CONTRACT reduces the size of the directory by half and decrements *d* by 1. Because of the requirement that both members of each pair of pointers have the same value before the directory can be contracted, it is necessary to check each pair for compliance. If any pair fails this test, the error parameter is set to true and the directory is left unchanged. If the directory is successfully contracted, the error parameter is set to false.

```
procedure CONTRACT(directory,d,error);
(* halves the size of the directory and decreases the order by 1
     iff each pair of pointers has the same value *)
(* original directory has 2^d entries numbered 0 to 2^d - 1  *)
(* first check pair values *)
i := 0;
error := false;
WHILE i < 2^d and not error DO BEGIN   (* check each pair *)
        IF directory(i) ≠ directory(i + 1) THEN error := true;
        i := i + 2;
END;
(* now remove the odd entries and contract *)
IF not error THEN BEGIN
        d := d - 1;
```

FOR i := 1 to (2^d − 1) **DO** directory(i) := directory(2*i);
END;

A pair of procedures is also needed to split and combine buckets. The first of these, SPLIT, requires three parameters. Oldbucket is a pointer to the original bucket. Newbucket is a pointer for the new bucket. Both are passed by reference. The local order of the oldbucket is passed as dp (d prime). This value is increased by 1 and returned by the procedure.

```
procedure SPLIT(filename,oldbucket,newbucket,dp);
(* gets new bucket and divides the records in oldbucket between
    the two buckets,  increments dp by 1 *)
ALLOCATE(filename, newbucket);  (* first get a new bucket *)
READ-DIRECT(filename,oldbucketbuf,oldbucket); (* read
    oldbucket *)
WHILE not EOF(oldbucketbuf) DO BEGIN
        (* loop once for each record in the oldbucket *)
        GET-NEXT(oldbucketbuf,recbuf); (* get one record from
            bucket *)
        IF (EXTRACT(H(KEY(recbuf)),(dp + 1))) mod 2 = 1 THEN BEGIN
                (* for this record the next bit of H(key) after
                    the first dp bits is a 1; this record
                    must be moved to the new bucket *)
                DELETE(oldbucketbuf,KEY(recbuf));
                        (* deletes current record in buffer of
                            the old bucket *)
                PUT(newbucketbuf,recbuf);
                        (* insert current record in buffer of the
                            new bucket *)
        END; (* of testing one record *)
END;   (* all records have been moved to the buffer of
    the new bucket *)
WRITE-DIRECT(filename,oldbucketbuf,oldbucket);
        (* write back the old bucket from its buffer *)
WRITE-DIRECT(filename,newbucketbuf,newbucket);
        (* write out the new bucket from its buffer *)
dp := dp + 1;  (* increase the local order by 1 *)
```

The procedure JOIN combines the records from two buckets into one bucket and deletes the other bucket from the file. If there are too many records to fit into one bucket, error is set to true and the file is not changed. Otherwise, error is false and d' is reduced in value by 1.

```
procedure JOIN(bucket1,bucket2,dp,error);
(* combines records from both buckets into bucket1 and
    deletes bucket2 *)
(* first load the bucket buffers from the file *)
READ-DIRECT(filename,bucketbuf1,bucket1);
READ-DIRECT(filename,bucketbuf2,bucket2);
```

```
error := false;   (* initialize error flag *)
(* now copy the records from bucket2 to bucket1 *)
WHILE not EOF(bucket2) and not error DO BEGIN
        (* loop once for each record moved *)
        GET-NEXT(bucketbuf2,recbuf);
        IF not EOF(bucketbuf2) THEN BEGIN
                PUT(bucketbuf1,recbuf);   (* move the
                        record to bucket1 *)
                IF not VALID(bucketbuf1) THEN error := true;
                        (* overflow in bucket1 *)
        END;
END;   (* all records copied *)
IF not error THEN BEGIN   (* put the file in order *)
        WRITE-DIRECT(filename,bucketbuf1,bucket1);
                (* write out the new bucket1 with all
                        the records *)
        DEALLOCATE(filename,bucket2);   (* delete empty bucket *)
        dp := dp - 1;   (* decrement the local order *)
END;
```

We have now defined a dozen procedures upon which the standard file function for the extendible hash file can be built. Although this may seem like a large number of procedures, the algorithms for the standard functions would be very complicated without them. This proliferation of procedures illustrates the wisdom of building libraries of procedures for accessing files of various types. Without the libraries, the task of using files becomes very complicated and error prone.

7.3.2 Algorithms for the Standard Functions

Add is done by hashing the key of the new record, extracting the high-order *d* bits from the hashing function, indexing into the directory for the bucket pointer, reading the bucket, inserting the new record into the bucket, and writing the bucket out. Thus adding is usually a sequence of simple operations.

The complexity is greatly increased, however, because of the possibility of overflowing the bucket. When this happens, the bucket must be split. The split, in turn, may require that the directory be enlarged. Thus the instructions needed to handle the possible exceptions will exceed those needed for the simple add. *Algorithm 7.1* includes the exception-handling code.

```
procedure ADD(filename,directory,d,recbuf);
(* recbuf holds the new record to be added *)
h := H(KEY(recbuf));   (* hash the key of the new record *)
index := EXTRACT(h, d);   (* get the high-order bits for
        the index *)
bucket := directory(index);   (* find the bucket pointer *)
READ-DIRECT(filename,bucketbuf,bucket);   (* read the bucket *)
```

```
PUT(bucketbuf,recbuf);   (* insert record into the bucket *)
IF not VALID(bucketbuf) THEN BEGIN   (* overflow:
    must split bucket *)
        IF dp = d THEN   EXPAND(directory,d);   (* expand
            the directory *)
        (* calculate the indexes for the first and last pointers
            to the current bucket *)
        first := 2^(d - dp) * EXTRACT(h,dp);
        last := first + 2^(d - dp) - 1;
        (* now split the bucket *)
        SPLIT(filename,bucket,newbucket,dp);
        (* insert pointer(s) in the directory for the
            new bucket *)
        (* calculate the index of the first pointer to be changed *)
        first := first + (first - last + 1)/2;
        FOR index := first TO last DO directory(index) :=
            newbucket;
        (* all expansion is done, call ADD recursively to insert
            record *)
        ADD(filename,recbuf);   (* guaranteed to work the second
            time *)
END ELSE (* write the updated bucket back to the file *)
        WRITE-DIRECT(filename,bucketbuf,bucket);
```

The ***delete*** function is similar to ADD in that the basic operation can be done in a few simple steps. However, the deletion will occasionally cause a bucket to underflow, in which case an attempt must be made to join the bucket with another one. The attempt will not always be successful due to the constraints for combining buckets discussed in Section 7.1.2. ***Algorithm 7.2*** performs the delete function. This algorithm has two procedures; the main procedure DELETE calls a second procedure TEST to determine if a given pair of buckets can be combined.

```
procedure DELETE(filename,key);
(* key is key of record to be deleted *)
h := H(key);   (* hash the key for future use *)
index := EXTRACT(h,d);   (* calculate index *)
bucket := directory(index);   (* get bucket pointer from
    directory *)
READ-DIRECT(filename,bucketbuf,bucket);   (* read the bucket *)
DELETE(bucketbuf,key,load);   (* delete the record *)
IF VALID(bucketbuf) THEN BEGIN   (* record deleted ok, continue *)
        (* write the bucket back to the file *)
        WRITE-DIRECT(filename,bucketbuf,bucket);
        IF load < 0.5 THEN BEGIN (* bucket underflow *)
        (* three conditions are necessary for two buckets to be
            combined
                1. Their average load factor ≤ 50%
```

  2. Their local orders are the same

  3. All keys in both buckets share a common value
   of the first (dp-1) bits of H(key)   *)

(* assertion: only the two buckets whose pointers are
 adjacent in the directory to those of the current
 bucket can meet the third condition *)

  (* calculate the indexes for the first and last
  pointers in the directory for the current
  bucket *)

first := $2^{(d - dp)}$*EXTRACT(h,dp);
last := first + $2^{(d - dp)}$-1;
(* check the previous bucket *)
p := first - 1;
IF. p $\geq$ 0 **THEN** TEST(filename,p,ok);
IF not ok **and** last < $(2^d - 1)$ **THEN BEGIN**
  (* check next bucket *)
  p := last;
  TEST(filename,p,ok);
  p := p + 1; (* set this index to the
   other bucket *)
END;
IF ok **THEN BEGIN** (* join the qualified
  buckets *)
  JOIN(bucket, directory(p),dp,error);
  (* reflect the change in the directory
   pointers *)
  IF not error **THEN** directory(p) := bucket;
  (* attempt to contract the directory *)
  CONTRACT(directory,d,error);
END;
  END;
END;
procedure TEST(filename,p,ok);
(* tests the bucket whose pointer is at directory(p) with the
 bucket whose pointer is at directory(p+1) to see if the
 three necessary conditions are all met for combining the
 buckets. ok is set to true if all conditions are met,
 otherwise it is false *)
(* get the parameters of both buckets *)
PARAM(filename, directory(p),dp1,load1);
PARAM(filename, directory(p+1),dp2,load2);
ok := true; (* until proven false *)
IF ((load1 + load2)/2) > 0.5 **THEN** ok := false
  (* first condition *)
ELSE IF dp1 $\neq$ dp2 **THEN** ok := false (* second condition *)
ELSE IF EXTRACT(p,dp1) $\neq$ EXTRACT((p+1),dp2) **THEN** ok := false;
  (* third condition *)

Algorithm 7.3, for reading all the records in any order, uses the directory to point to the current set of buckets. The entire directory is read sequentially and each new bucket is read into the buffer. Each record in the bucket is then read in turn.

```
READ-ALL(filename);
(* reads and processes all records in the file *)
oldbucket := null;
FOR i := 0 TO 2^d - 1 DO BEGIN  (* read each directory entry *)
        bucket := directory(i);  (* get the next
           bucket pointer *)
        IF bucket ≠ oldbucket THEN BEGIN
                (* this is a new bucket,process it *)
                READ-DIRECT(filename,bucketbuf,bucket);
                WHILE not EOF(bucketbuf) DO BEGIN
                        (* process each record in the bucket *)
                        GET-NEXT(bucketbuf,recordbuf);
                        PROCESS-RECORD(recbuf);
                END;
      END;
```

Algorithm 7.4 reads a record with a specific key value. This is the simplest of the algorithms and requires a minimum of disk accesses. Since the directory for even a large file can be left in primary memory while the file is open, the only access required is the read of the bucket containing the record. Thus the number of physical reads will be exactly one.

```
READ-BY-KEY(filename,key,recbuf);
(* this procedure returns the desired record in recbuf.  If
    a record whose key value matches "key" cannot be found,
    a null value is placed in recbuf. *)
h := H(key);  (* hash the key *)
bucket := directory(EXTRACT(h,d));  (* look up the
        bucket number *)
READ-DIRECT(filename,bucketbuf,bucket);  (* read the bucket *)
GET(bucketbuf,key,recbuf);  (* copy the record to the buffer *)
IF not VALID(bucketbuf) THEN recbuf := null;  (* record
    not found *)
```

The final operation of updating does not require any new algorithms. Whether a record has been read by Algorithm 7.3 or 7.4, the modified version may simply be rewritten to the bucketbuffer and the bucket updated from the buffer. Of course, updates may not include the key value. If it is necessary to change the key for a record, it must be deleted and added to the file with its new value.

All of the algorithms for the standard file functions are unique to the extendible hash file due to its unique structure. Moreover, no algorithms applicable to other files are suitable for the extendible hash file for the same reason. This will be true of most files that have a complex structure, particularly when auxiliary structures such as directories or indexes are used.

7.4 THE STUDENT RECORDS PROBLEM

Because the size of the files used for the student records problem can be known in advance, there is no significant advantage in using the extendible hash file over the direct access file. While the disk accesses will be slightly fewer, the order remains unchanged and the complexity is considerably greater.

However, it is instructive to see how some of the files used for the student records problem might be designed using extendible hashing. Because this is a familiar problem to the reader, there will be a good basis for comparison.

The fixed-length student, enrollment, and course records will be used in three file designs. The records will be the same as those described in Section 3.6 and summarized in Figure 3.3. These records have lengths of 735, 150, and 9060 bytes, respectively. So as to have all the buckets about the same size, we will choose 9000 bytes as a target size for our buckets. Also, to simplify the analysis, we will use a population of 10,000 students in all the examples.

The student record file with a record length of 735 bytes will have 12 records in a bucket of 8820 bytes. When the file is fully populated there will need to be about $10,000 \div 12 \div 0.69 = 1208$ buckets if the load factor is 69%, as given by formula (7.1). This number of buckets will require a directory of about 1750 pointers by formula (7.2). The next higher power of 2 is $2^{11} = 2048$. Thus we would expect that a directory of order 11 and a hashing function with a range of 16 bits will be sufficient. The hashing function could use the prime number of 65,521 as the divisor.

The fixed-length enrollment file is smaller at 150 bytes. A bucket of 9000 bytes can accommodate 60 of these records; however, there will be 60,000 records all together. When fully populated at a load factor of 69%, the file will require $60,000 \div 60 \div 0.69 = 1450$ buckets.

The directory size expected will be about 2101 entries. This is just slightly greater than 2^{11} and the directory may be either of order 11 or order 12. Even at the larger size there would be only 4096 entries. At 2 bytes per pointer, the directory would still be smaller than the size of one bucket. The same hashing parameters as the student record file would be suitable for the enrollment file.

The course file presents a new problem. Can the extendible hash file function when there is only one record per bucket, or even a small number of records per bucket? There are several problems.

Bucket splitting and combining will look very different. Since buckets are either empty or full and the empty ones can usually be combined, they will be relatively few. However, whenever a record is added to the file, a bucket will always have to be split, sometimes more than once to separate the new record from the old.

A more serious problem is that of synonyms. Two records that are synonyms will always have to be placed in the same bucket, regardless of the local order. If only one record can fit in a bucket, synonyms cannot be tolerated. While making the range of the hash function large will reduce the probability of synonyms, there can be no absolute guarantee that they will not occur. The probability that there is no pair of synonyms in a file is given by

$$P_{(\text{of no synonyms})} = (1 - 1/R)^K \qquad (7.3)$$

where R = range of the hashing function
       K = number of pairs which can be shown as $N(N - 1)/2$ for a file of N records

This expression can be simplified where $R \gg 1$ by using a series expansion. When this is done and N is substituted in, the probability of no synonyms becomes

$$P = e^{(N(1 - N)/(2R))} \qquad (7.4)$$

Substitution of the parameters of the course file into formula (7.4) with 2000 records and a hash function range of 2^{16} gives $e^{-30.5}$ or essentially zero probability of no synonyms. If a hash function with a range of 2^{32} is used, the probability of no synonyms becomes 0.999535, meaning that about 1 file in 2000 will have a synonym. This is marginally acceptable, but it would be better to increase the range of the hashing function a few more bits.

Thus we can conclude that it is feasible to use the extendible hash file with a bucket capacity of one record if the range of the hash function is sufficiently large. Some empty buckets will be inevitable, but the average load factor for the file will be reasonable.

It must be noted that there is never an absolute guarantee that there will not be a synonym problem with the extendible hash file. The probability may be made arbitrarily small, but never zero. Where even a very small probability cannot be tolerated, it may be wise to reserve one bucket for synonyms. This will, however, create extra accesses for unsuccessful searches.

7.5 SUMMARY

An *extendible hash file* is a *dynamic file structure* that allows automatic expansion and contraction while maintaining an average load factor of 69%. Records are stored in large blocks or *buckets*. A record with a given primary key value is found by processing the key through a hashing function. The high-order bits of the result are used as an index into a *directory* array where a pointer to the bucket containing the desired record is found. The internal organization of each bucket is independent of the basic file structure and any convenient method may be used.

The file will automatically expand as necessary to accommodate new records. Similarly, it will automatically contract to maintain a high load factor. Buckets are *split* when the file expands and *combined* when it contracts. The expansions and contractions are done by allocating and deallocating buckets from the file system free-space pool. The directory will also automatically *expand* and *contract* as the file size changes. For all but the largest files, the entire directory can be left in primary memory, making it possible to read records with one disk access.

The *range of the hashing function* is independent of the number of records in the file and should be made much larger than the number of records. This is essential when the number of records per bucket is one or a small number. As before, the hashing function should include division by a *prime number* to yield a random distribution of values.

Both the number of buckets and the number of entries in the directory may be estimated for the average case. However, any file at a particular time may deviate significantly from the averages.

The directory of the extendible hash file is equivalent to a radix tree (also called a digital tree) or a trie. When the directory is explicitly structured as a binary radix tree, the file structure is called a *dynamic hash file*. *Expandable hashing* and *virtual hashing* use related techniques.

7.6 PROBLEMS

7.1. Show that there will always be at least two pointers in the directory that point to a given bucket if $d' < d$ for that bucket.

7.2. Show that the directory would have to be expanded by multiples of 10 instead of 2 if decimal digits were extracted instead of binary digits for the index of the directory.

7.3. Redraw the file of Figure 7.6 after buckets A, B, D, and E have split because of added records. What is the order of the directory?

7.4. Continue the expansion begun in Problem 7.3 by splitting bucket C. What is the order of the directory?

7.5. List all the pairs of buckets that could be combined in Figure 7.5.

7.6. Each of the following lists shows the pointer values in a directory at a particular time. For each list, determine if the directory can be contracted, and if it can, make a list showing the contents of the contracted directory.
(a) A, A, A, A, B, B, C, C, C, C, D, D, E, E, E, E
(b) A, A, A, A, A, B, B, B, B, C, C, D, D, D, E, E
(c) A, A, B, B, B, B, C, D, D, D, D, D, E, E, E, E

7.7. Show that the average number of pointers is $2.08(N \div B)$ by using formulas (7.1) and (7.2).

7.8. For each of the following files, determine the minimum number of bits required in the range of the hashing function so that each entry in the directory can be uniquely indexed.   Use formula (7.2) to find the average number of directory entries.   Allow for deviations from the average value.   Remember that the directory will always have 2d entries.

(a)   10,000 records with 25 records per bucket
(b)   100,000 records with 10 records per bucket
(c)   1,000,000 records with 8 records per bucket

7.9. Repeat Problem 7.8 if decimal digits are used to index the directory instead of binary digits.

7.10. Show that the directory indexes for the pointer(s) to a given bucket will always be inclusively bounded by the indexes "first" and "last", where

$$\text{first} = 2^{(d - d')} \cdot \text{EXTRACT}(h,dp),$$
$$\text{last} = \text{first} + 2^{(d - d')} - 1,$$

d is the order of the directory, d' is the local order of the bucket, and h is the hash function result for any key in the bucket.

7.11. Prove the assertion in Algorithm 7.2 that all buckets whose keys share a common value of the first $d' - 1$ bits of H(key) must have adjacent pointers in the directory.

7.12. What is the probability that no synonyms exist in a file of 10,000 records when the hashing function has a range of

(a) 2^{16}?
(b) 2^{20}?
(c) 2^{24}?
(d) 2^{28}?
(e) 2^{32}?
(f) 2^{36}?
(g) 2^{40}?

7.13. What feature of formula (7.4) accounts for the sudden switch from probabilities very near zero to probabilities very close to 1 in Problem 7.12?

7.14. Derive formula (7.4) from formula (7.3).   The Maclaurin expansion

$$\ln(1 + X) = X - X^2/2 + X^3/3 - X^4/4 + \cdots$$

may be useful.

8

Indexed Sequential Files

8.1 DESCRIPTION AND ORGANIZATION

The *indexed sequential file* can be thought of as a variant of the ordered relative file. Like the ordered relative file, it is ordered on a key. Unlike the ordered relative file, it can be accessed by means of an index. The *index* is a structure that contains information on where a record with a given key is located. Just as there are many ways of structuring files, there are many ways of structuring indexes. The term "indexed sequential" usually refers to ordered relative files in which the blocks of the index are intermingled with blocks of records in such a manner as to minimize the access time.

The primary advantage of the indexed sequential file is that the binary search of the ordered relative file can be replaced with a *tree search* of the index. While tree searches, like binary searches, are of order $\log(N)$, they are generally faster than binary searches. This is because the binary search requires approximately $\log_2(N)$ accesses while a tree search requires approximately $\log_b(N)$ accesses, where b is the number of branches per node. Thus the binary search is equivalent to a worst-case tree search. For example, $\log_2(10,000) = 13.29$ while $\log_{50}(10,000) = 2.35$.

8.1.1 Index Structure

The index for an indexed sequential file is mixed with the data for the file. Typically, most blocks are used for data, but some are used for the index. This presents a problem when reading or writing the file in that most file systems do not have the ability to distinguish between two different types of fixed-length records within the same file. There are two ways to work around this problem. The first is to define the file to the file system as having one large record per block. The details of determining which kind of block is being processed, and of locating a logical record within the block are left to the library routines or the application program. This method is simple and can be used with any file system. A second method is available with some file systems that allow an entire block to be transferred to the user's buffer instead of a single record. This engenders the same complications as the first method, but permits the file description to more nearly correspond to the true structure. For the purposes of describing algorithms in this chapter, we will assume that the former method is being used and that the reads and writes performed will transfer an entire block to or from our buffer area.

The motivation for mingling the data and index is to place each of the index nodes near the data being indexed. A good analogy is found in a large, unabridged dictionary. Such dictionaries frequently are published in several volumes. Each volume is indexed on its binding according to the range of the alphabet it contains; for example, A-D, E-M, N-R, and S-Z. Within each volume, there may be a thumb index that locates the starting point for all words beginning with a given letter. Within the section containing all words beginning with one letter, there is an index in the form of "guide words" printed at the top of each page, showing the limits of the alphabetic sequence for words on that page. A search for a given word is made by working through this hierarchy of indexes until the page containing the given word is located. Only then is it necessary to search a page for the matching word and, since the last level of the index is on the same page, there is no need to look elsewhere for the data.

This method of mingling the index and data seems strange at first. However, consider how useful a dictionary might be if the only indexing available was a conventional, sequential index located in another volume giving the page number for each word. By mixing the index with the data, faster access is possible.

Just as with the dictionary, it is frequently true of disk files that the structure of the index is intimately tied to the physical structure of the medium. For example, it is common practice for the root, or master, node of the index to index the first key found on each cylinder of the disk over which the file is spread. At the beginning of each cylinder is another node of the index that indexes the first key found on each track of that cylinder, and at the beginning of each track is an index node showing the key of the first record in each block on that track. This index has three levels. To locate the block containing a given key it is necessary to examine one node at each of three levels. Since there is only one node at the root level, and all searches begin at the root node, it is common practice to leave the root node in memory at all times that the file is open. This saves one physical read for each access.

Such a hardware-dependent index is illustrated in Figure 8.1. Each track is divided into four blocks. A block may contain 10 data records or an index node.

The file begins with the first track of cylinder 201. Each block is numbered starting with zero. The end of the file is in cylinder 225.

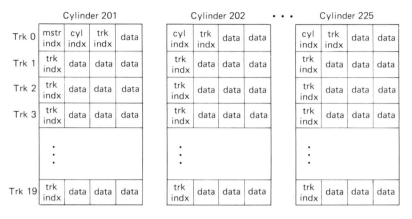

Figure 8.1 Hardware-dependent indexed sequential file.

The first block (block 0) is used for the root, or master, index node. Block 1 contains the cylinder index for cylinder 201, and block 2 contains the track index for the remainder of this track. Each of the remaining tracks on cylinder 201 contain one index block and three data blocks. The first track on each of the following cylinders contains one cylinder index node, one track index node, and two data blocks. All of the remaining tracks have one track index node and three data blocks.

A more detailed look at each kind of node is shown in Figure 8.2. The records are being indexed on names, and the master index begins with the key of the very first record (Aaron). It continues with the keys of the first data record in each of the following cylinders. There will be 25 entries in the master index since there are 25 cylinders in the file. Each key of the index is followed by a pointer that contains the block number of the corresponding cylinder index. Thus the key value ''Biffy'' is associated with the value ''80,'' which is the block number of the cylinder index for the cylinder in which the first record has the key ''Biffy.''

The cylinder index in block 80 contains the key of the first data record in each of the tracks of this cylinder. The corresponding pointers point to the blocks that contain the track index for each track. Thus the key value ''Bill'' is associated with the value ''84,'' which is the block number of the track index for track 1 on cylinder 202. This track index contains the keys for the first record in each of the three remaining blocks.

To retrieve a record with a given key, a node at each of the three levels is examined in turn. For example, suppose we wish to find the record with the key value ''Birt.'' The master index shows that this key falls between ''Biffy'' and ''Delbert.'' The pointer from ''Biffy'' is followed to block 80. This index node

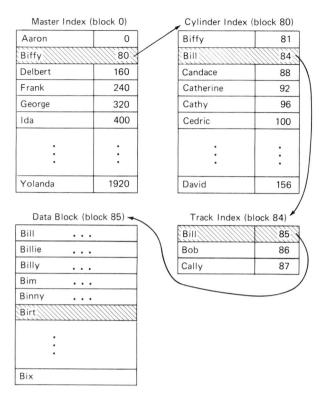

Figure 8.2 Retrieval example.

shows that "Birt" must be on the track that begins with block 84. The track index at block 84 is read and indicates that "Birt" must be in block 85 since it falls between "Bill" and "Bob." Block 85 is then read, and the records are searched sequentially until "Birt" is located.

The advantage of this method of searching lies in the fact that most of the time required for an average disk access is taken by the arm movement time. If the number of times the arm must be moved can be reduced, the access will be faster. If we assume that no other processes are using the same disk drive, and this may not be valid with a multiprogramming system, the search described above will require only that the arm be moved to cylinder 202. Thereafter, all index and data blocks needed can be read without repositioning the arm. Indexed sequential files in which the structure of the index is determined by the physical organization of the disk are said to be tightly bound to the medium.

There is no significant advantage in having a separate index for each track. This is a vestige of methods of handling disk I/O that are no longer common. If the disk drive is being shared by many processes, there is also little advantage to indexing cylinders since it is likely that the arm will have been moved by other processes between reads. However, the general structure of mingling the index and data in one file is still widely used. It has the advantage of requiring only one file for both functions. Where disk caching or virtual memory management systems are used, there is always the possibility of reducing the number of accesses when consecutive reads are close together on the disk. Indexed sequential files in which the structure of the index is independent of the physical organization of the disk are said to unbound to the medium.

Whether the file design is intimately bound to the hardware constraints or not, the question of designing the file is not simple. There are two important design choices that must be made.

The first is to choose an appropriate blocking factor. The factors mentioned in Chapter 2 are just as important as always. In addition, because the index nodes will be contained within the same-sized blocks, the index nodes must be considered.

The second is to design the index. The number of entries that can fit into a block will depend on block size, the key length, and the pointer length. These are related as follows:

$$b \leq L \div (K + P) \tag{8.1}$$

where b = number of index entries per node (index blocking factor)
L = total size of each block
K = length of one key field
P = length of one pointer field

The number of entries per node, b, will determine the number of levels of the index that are required. It is important to keep the number of levels to a minimum since each additional level will require another physical read from the file. Three reads are required to retrieve a record from the file in the example above: one to read the cylinder index, one for the track index, and one for the data block (the master index is kept in primary memory). If the index had four levels, four reads would have been necessary.

The number of levels of the index, k, depends on b and the number of records or blocks in the file as follows:

$$k \geq \log_b(M) \tag{8.2}$$

where M is the number of indexed items in the file. The same relationship can also be stated as:

$$M \leq b^k \tag{8.3}$$

These are very important relationships that must be considered when designing an indexed sequential file, or any other tree structure.

It may not be possible to balance all of these factors in a highly efficient manner, especially if the index structure is tied to the medium structure. The best compromise is usually to waste some space in the index nodes, since these are much fewer than the data nodes. The following two examples will illustrate the process.

8.1.2 Example Using Tight Binding between File and Medium

Consider a file of $N = 10,000$ records, each record requiring 160 bytes. The key field is 16 bytes in length and pointers are 4 bytes long. The file is to be stored on an HP 7925 disk which has 256 bytes per sector, 64 sectors per track, 9 tracks per cylinder, and a total of 815 cylinders.

A blocking factor of 6 yields a storage efficiency of 93.8% and a modestly sized block of four sectors or 1024 bytes. Larger blocking factors will not reduce the number of levels of the index, so there is little advantage in using them. The capacity of each node may be calculated by formula (8.1) as $(4 \times 256) \div (16 + 4) = 51$ entries. This will be more than adequate for a three-level index.

Each track has room for $64 \div 4 = 16$ blocks. Thus the track indexes will need a capacity of 15 entries, well below the 51 maximum. Each cylinder index will require 9 entries, again well below the limit. The space occupied by the entire file is that required for the data blocks plus that required by the index blocks. The data will require one block for every six records, or 1667 blocks. Allowing for 10 blocks per cylinder for indexes (nine track indexes and one cylinder index), the number of cylinders can be calculated by

$$CYL = BLKS \div (BPT \times TPC - IBPC) \tag{8.4}$$

Where $BLKS$ = number of data blocks in the file
BPT = number of blocks per track
TPC = number of tracks per cylinder
$IBPC$ = number of index blocks per cylinder

Plugging the parameters of the problem into formula (8.4) gives 12.44 cylinders for the file. This is an approximation since the master index node is not included; it will bring the total to 12.5 cylinders. Thus the master index will require 13 entries.

The file requires 13 cylinders of total space or $13 \times 9 \times 64 \times 256 = 1,916,928$ bytes, of which $160 \times 10,000 = 1,600,000$ are used for data records. The difference is either used for index space or wasted. The overall efficiency is 83.5%.

The master index requires 13 entries of 20 bytes each and is easily kept in primary memory while the file is open. The cylinder indexes require nine entries each, while the track indexes require 15 entries each. Each disk access will require three reads, all from the same cylinder: one for the cylinder index, one for the track index, and one for the data block.

8.1.3 Example Using No Binding between the File and the Medium

In this example, the same parameters will be used that were stated for the previous problem. Since there is no consideration of the physical design of the disk, it is possible to proceed directly by calculating the number of levels of index required. Formula (8.2) gives $k \geq \log_{51}(1667) = 1.89$. Thus a two-level index can be built using blocks of 1024 bytes. The product of number of index entries per node, and the number of index nodes at a given level must equal or exceed the total number of items indexed by that level. If all nodes carry about the same number of entries, 41 could be used since $41^2 = 1681$. However, the total space required for index nodes will be reduced if the lower levels are loaded to capacity since there will then be fewer low-level nodes. In this case, a master node of 33 entries and second-level nodes of 51 entries will yield a capacity of $51 \times 33 = 1683$, which is sufficient.

The total number of blocks required for the file will be 1667 data blocks, plus 33 second-level index blocks, plus one master block or a total 1701 blocks. The total file space is $1701 \times 1024 = 1,741,824$, which gives a gross storage efficiency of 91.9%, a considerable improvement over the previous example.

The file will begin with the master index block, followed by an index for the first 51 data blocks (Figure 8.3). After those data blocks, there will be another index block followed by 51 more data blocks, and so on. A retrieval will require two physical accesses, one for the second-level index block, and one for the data block (the master index node is again memory resident). This compares favorably with the three accesses required in the first example.

Mstr Indx Blk	2nd level Indx	51 data blks. . .	2nd level Indx	51 data blks. . .	2nd level Indx	51 data blks. . .	2nd level Indx	et cetera

Figure 8.3 Indexed sequential file with two-level index and no physical binding.

By divorcing the index structure from the physical structure of the disk, it is possible to design a more efficient index. This will not always be true, but more often than not it will be possible to save accesses by this design strategy. The disadvantage is that the efficiency that might be gained by having all accesses at the same cylinder cannot be guaranteed, since there is no constraint that the lowest-level index nodes will be in the same cylinder as the data they index. However, in this example and many other cases, there is a high probability of the index and data being in the same cylinder anyway. Here the lowest-level index and the corresponding data span 52 blocks, while a cylinder contains 144 blocks.

It is worth considering what might happen if there were more records in the file. For example, if there were 100,000 records, the same block size would yield $100,000 \div 6 = 16,667$ blocks. By formula (8.2), the number of levels of the index would become $\log_{51}(16,667) = 2.47$, or three levels. This would require an additional physical access for each retrieval. However, if the block size were doubled to 2048 bytes, there would be two benefits. First, there would be only half as many blocks (8334) to index, and second, there would be room for twice as many entries (102) in each index node. The result by formula (8.2) is $\log_{102}(8334) = 1.95$, so that a two-level index is again possible. Because the block size has such a powerful influence on the index structure, the two must always be considered together.

8.2 PRIMITIVE OPERATIONS

The same basic set of primitive operations that were used for the direct access file are appropriate here. A difference is that whole blocks will be read or written at one time instead of single records. The blocking and unblocking will have to be done outside the file system. For that purpose, several functions will be defined here. The primitive operations are:

OPEN Sets the currency pointer to immediately before the first record and allows access to the file.

READ-NEXT Sets the currency pointer to the next valid record in the file and returns that record to the user. An end-of-file condition is set if there is no next record.

READ-DIRECT Sets the currency pointer to the slot specified and returns the record to the user if the slot is occupied. An invalid-record-number condition is set if the slot is not occupied or if the record number is outside the limits of the file.

WRITE-DIRECT Sets the currency pointer to the slot specified and writes a record to that slot, whether or not the slot is already occupied. An invalid-record-number condition is set if the record number is outside the limits of the file.

UPDATE Writes back the current record in the same location from which it was read. The currency pointer is unchanged. May be used to flag a record as deleted.

CLOSE Terminates access to the file.

EOF Returns a value of true if the currency pointer is beyond the last record of the file; otherwise, it is false.

VALID Returns a value of true if the previous operation on the file was successful. False is returned if the operation failed for any reason.

To this set of file system primitives, it will be helpful to add a set of library procedures to access individual records and index entries. These procedures will need to have knowledge of the block size, record size, key size, and pointer size. These parameters can be passed as formal parameters, as global variables, or coded into the procedures. While the first method is preferred, the parameters needed will not be defined here to simplify the examples. The six procedures are:

logical function GET-REC(blockbuf,recbuf,k)

Functions: 1. Copies the data record at slot k in the block buffer to the record buffer.

2. Returns a value of true unless slot k does not exist or is empty, in which case a value of false is returned.

Parameters:

1. blockbuf—location into which a data block has been stored.

2. recbuf—location into which a data record is copied.

3. k—number of the slot in the block (first slot is number 0).

logical function PUT-REC(blockbuf,recbuf,k)

Functions: 1. Inserts the data record found in recbuf into slot k in block-buf.

2. Returns a value of true unless slot k does not exist, in which case false is returned.

Parameters:

1. blockbuf—location of a data block.

2. recbuf—location from which a data record is transferred.

3. k—number of the slot in the block.

function GET-KEY(blockbuf,k)

Function: 1. Returns the value of the key at slot k from the block buffer. If there is not a valid key at slot k, a null value is returned.

Parameters:

1. blockbuf—location into which an index block has been stored.

2. k—number of the slot in the block.

logical function PUT-KEY(blockbuf,key,k)

Functions: 1. Inserts the key into slot k in the index block found in blockbuf.

2. Returns a value of true unless slot k does not exist, in which case a value of false is returned.

Parameters:

    1. blockbuf—location of an index block.

    2. key—value of a key to be inserted into the index.

    3. k—number of the slot in the block.

integer function GET-POINTER(blockbuf,k)

Function: 1. Returns the pointer associated with key k in the current index block. A null value is returned if no key is at that location.

Parameters:

    1. blockbuf—location into which an index block has been stored.

    2. k—number of the slot in the block.

logical function PUT-POINTER(blockbuf,ptr,k)

Functions: 1. Inserts the pointer value into the current index block at slot k.

    2. Returns a value of true unless slot k does not exist.

Parameters:

    1. blockbuf—location of an index block.

    2. ptr—value of pointer to be inserted.

    3. k—number of the slot in the block.

Notice that a type has not been specified here for the functional return of GET-KEY. This is because keys can be of many different types. This procedure will be treated as though it returns a value of the appropriate type. These procedures will be used in this chapter to develop algorithms.

8.3 ALGORITHMS

The indexed sequential file, in its simplest form, is just like the ordered relative file except that there are index blocks scattered throughout the length of the file. The index allows records to be retrieved by key value more quickly than was possible with the binary search. In this simple form, the indexed sequential file can be used in much the same manner as the ordered relative file, except that the retrieval and reorganization algorithms are different. Later in this section we consider alternatives to reorganizing the file to make additions.

8.3.1 Algorithms for Simple Indexed Sequential Files

Add is not allowed in the simple form of the file. Like the ordered relative file, there is no place to insert a new record. Records may be added only by merging them into the file during a reorganization.

Reorganization (Algorithm 8.1).   Algorithm 8.1 is similar to Algorithm 5.1 in that the old file is combined with an ordered change file to create a new file. The only difference is that the index must also be created at the same time as the new file. A plan, similar to those in the examples of Section 8.1, must be developed to determine which blocks will be used for the index. As the file is written to the data blocks, the lowest index blocks are developed simultaneously by inserting the key of the first record in each block into the index block, with its pointer. When the index block is filled, it is written out and a new one is begun.

After all the data and lowest-level index blocks have been written, the next-level index blocks can be filled by scanning the lower level-index blocks. This process continues until the master index block has been written.

Delete (Algorithms 3.2 and 5.1).   Delete can be done either by putting the deleted records into the change file, or by flagging the records as empty. Since it is blocks and not records that are indexed, there is no harm done in flagging a record empty. All records in a block could be flagged empty without causing problems. In this respect, the indexed sequential file differs from the ordered sequential file, where records may not be deleted.

Read a record with a specific key value (Algorithm 8.2).   This is the principal reason for having the index, and hence the indexed sequential file. A tree search is done on the index to locate the block containing the required record. That block is then read and searched for the record. While a binary search could be used for finding the matching record, a sequential search will be very fast since no I/O is required. This is usually done for the sake of simplicity. The master index node is read once, when the file is opened, and is passed as a parameter to the search procedure.

```
logical function ALGOR8.2(file,givenkey,recbuf,masbuf,lev);
(* returns true only if record found and in recbuf. Masbuf has
    master index node, lev is the number of levels in the index *)
j := 1;  (* initialize the level counter *)
buf := masbuf;  (* move the root node for first call to
    NEXT-POINTER *)
DO BEGIN  (* loop once for each level of index *)
        p := NEXT-POINTER(buf,givenkey);  (* pointer to
            next level *)
        IF p > 0 THEN READ-DIRECT(file,buf,p);  (* get block
            at next level *)
        j := j+1;  (* increment level counter *)
END UNTIL j = lev or p = 0 or not VALID(file);  (* normal exit
        and two error condx *)
IF p = 0 or not VALID(file) THEN ALGOR8.2 := false  (* error
    exit *)
ELSE BEGIN  (* now search the data block for the
    required record *)
```

```
                    k := 0;

                    WHILE GET-REC(buffer,recbuf,k) and KEY(recbuf) <
                        givenkey DO k := k+1;
                    IF KEY(recbuf) = givenkey THEN ALGOR8.2 := true ELSE
                        ALGOR8.2 :=false;
END;
```

The procedure NEXT-POINTER reads the index node in the buffer and returns the pointer to the next block, which is either another index node at the next level or the data block. It also does an error check to see if the value of the given key is less than that of the first key in the index node. This can happen if the given key is less than the first key in the file. In this situation, NEXT-POINTER returns a value of zero to indicate the error.

```
integer procedure NEXT-POINTER(buffer,givenkey);
(* buffer must contain a node of the index.  The procedure
    returns the pointer that corresponds to the next index level
    or data block. *)
k := 0;  (initialize to the start of the index block *)
WHILE GET-KEY(buffer,k) < givenkey DO k := k+1;
IF GET-KEY(buffer,k) > givenkey THEN k := k - 1; (* correct
    the overshoot *)
IF k < 0 THEN NEXT-POINTER = 0;  (* error:  givenkey less than
    first key *)
ELSE NEXT-POINTER := GET-POINTER(buffer,k);  (* return pointer *)
```

Read all records in key order (Algorithm 8.3).   Since the file is ordered by a key, it is a simple matter to read it in key order. This algorithm is a slight variant of Algorithm 4.3. There are two differences. First, it is necessary to skip over the blocks containing index nodes. This requires a knowledge of the index design. Because it is not necessary to read the index nodes, the READ-DIRECT primitive should be used instead of the READ-NEXT function. The second difference is that the GET-REC procedure will be needed to extract each record from the block.

Read all records in any order (Algorithm 8.3).   Although this function does not have as many constraints as the read in key order, there is really no easier way to do this function than Algorithm 8.3.

8.3.2 Algorithms for Expandable Indexed Sequential Files

The simple file, described in Section 8.3.1, does not allow records to be added without reorganizing the file. This problem can be mitigated by leaving spaces in the file where new records can be inserted. This is not a total replacement for reorganization, but it can greatly reduce its frequency.

There are three places where space can be made for new records to be inserted. The simplest is within each block. Some fraction of the slots in each block can be left empty at the time the file is reorganized, as shown in Figure 8.4. The larger the fraction, the longer will be the time between reorganizations, and the greater will be the wasted space. Because it is the block, not the record, that is indexed, new records can be inserted into the appropriate block without changing the index or any other block of the file. At such time as a block overflows, it is necessary to reorganize. This strategy permits the following algorithm.

Add (Algorithm 8.4).   Algorithm 8.4 adds by using overflow records within the block. This procedure is similar to Algorithm 8.2 in its beginning since both must locate the block appropriate for the given key.

```
logical function ALGOR8.4(file,recbuf,masbuf,lev);
            (* recbuf has record to be added, returns true if record
                added, false if no space left or key is less than
                key of first record. *)
j := 1;  (* initialize the level counter *)
buf := masbuf;  (* move the root node for first call to
     NEXT-POINTER *)
DO BEGIN  (* loop once for each level of index *)
        p := NEXT-POINTER(buf,givenkey);  (* pointer to next
            level *)
        IF p > 0 THEN READ-DIRECT(file,buf,p);  (* get block at
            next level *)
        j := j + 1;  (* increment level counter *)
END UNTIL j = lev or p = 0 or not VALID(file);  (* normal exit
     and two error condx *)
IF p = 0 or not VALID(file) THEN ALGOR8.4 := false   (* error
     exit *)
ELSE BEGIN  (* now search the data block for empty slot *)
        k := 0;
        WHILE GET-REC(buffer,recbuf,k) DO k := k + 1;
        IF PUT-REC(buffer,recbuf,k) THEN BEGIN
                UPDATE(file,buffer);  (* write out updated
                    block *)
                ALGOR8.4 := true;
        ELSE ALGOR8.4 := false;
END;
```

This procedure uses the function NEXT-POINTER described earlier. All the other algorithms developed for the simple file will work for this method as well, with minor modifications to skip over empty slots. A minor problem with this algorithm is that it may leave new records slightly out of order. A solution is to find the boundary between the two records where the new record belongs. All records below this boundary are moved down one slot and the new record is inserted in order. This could be done by a procedure that replaces the search for an empty slot in Algorithm 8.4. This is left as an exercise.

Data Blk	Data Blk	Data Blk	Data Blk	Indx Blk	Data Blk	Data Blk	Data Blk	Data Blk	Data Blk	Data Blk	Data Blk	Data Blk	Data Blk	Data Blk

Figure 8.4 Space for new records in each data block (shading represents space left empty at reorganization).

The second place where space can be left for new records is at the end of a group of blocks that are indexed by the same index node. One or more blocks are left empty at the end of such a block group, as seen in Figure 8.5. When a record is to be added, it is inserted sequentially into the overflow area for the group of blocks in which it belongs. This has the advantage that less space is wasted than when overflow space is provided in each block. This is because new records are seldom distributed uniformly over the file space, but will tend to cluster in some blocks. By pooling the overflow space for a large number of blocks, the space can be used more effectively.

Data Blk	Data Blk	Data Blk	Data Blk	Data Blk	Data Blk	Data Blk	Data Blk	Data Blk	Data Blk	Data Blk	Data Blk	Data Blk	O' fl Data Blk	Indx Blk

Figure 8.5 Space for new records at end of group of blocks.

This strategy has disadvantages too. When a retrieval is being done, it will be necessary to read and search the overflow area any time a matching record cannot be located in its indexed block. This is true not only for records that have been added to the overflow area, but also for unsuccessful searches. Depending on the proportion of unsuccessful searches, this could add a significant number of physical accesses. In addition, it becomes difficult to read all the records in order by key, since those records added to the overflow area will be slightly out of order.

The third place new records can be placed is in an overflow area at the end of the file (see Figure 8.6). This concept is similar to the overflow file sometimes used with direct access files. This method has the same advantages and disadvantages as the previous, except that both are intensified.

Indx Blk	Data Blk	Data Blk	Data Blk	Data Blk	Data Blk	Data Blk	Data Blk	Data Blk	Data Blk	Data Blk	Data Blk	O' fl Data Blk	O' fl Data Blk	O' fl Data Blk	O' fl Data Blk

Figure 8.6 Space for new records at end of files.

All three of these methods are used, both singly and in combination. For example, it is possible to leave empty slots in each block and to leave empty blocks at the end of each group of blocks. The first choice for inserting a new record is within its indexed block. If that is full, an overflow block is used. File systems that support indexed sequential files will usually provide for one or more of these overflow methods.

Regardless of the overflow method used, eventually the file will need to be reorganized. This is due not only to a limited space for overflow records, but also to two other factors. First, the performance of most methods is degraded as a higher proportion of the records fall into the overflow areas. Additional accesses and time are required to search these areas. Second, the index will have to be reorganized as the distribution of keys shifts with the adds and deletes.

8.4 SUMMARY

The *indexed sequential file* allows rapid access to a record with a given key value by using an *index* that is intermingled with the data blocks in the file. Where data access is usually by the key value of a single attribute, or sequential by order of the same key, this can be a very effective file organization. It shares many properties with the ordered relative file: Both are ordered by the value of a key; both can be processed sequentially by key order; and both use a tree search to locate a record with a given key value.

There are two important differences. First, the tree search is much faster with the indexed sequential file. This is because the binary search is searching a binary tree that requires $\log_2(N) - 1$ logical accesses. (Figure 5.1 shows the physical accesses required for various blocking factors.) The indexed sequential file requires approximately $\log_b(N/B)$ (rounded up) access, where b is usually much larger than 2. For example, the file described in Section 8.1.3 requires $\log_{51}(1667)$, or two accesses to reach a record, while a binary search would require an average of $\log_2(10,000) - 1.8$, or 11.5 physical accesses.

The second difference is in the way records may be added to the files. Both methods will eventually require a complete reorganization, but it is possible to add a limited number of records to the indexed sequential file without reorganizing it. While the methods of adding, and subsequently finding, new records complicate the algorithms, they can be done so that the number of accesses is not significantly increased, at the expense of wasted storage space.

The algorithms now available for the standard file functions are shown in Figure 8.7.

8.5 THE STUDENT RECORDS PROBLEM

The decision tree for the student records problem can be pruned very effectively since the problem has already been solved for the ordered relative files. There are only a few differences in the factors that need to be considered between the two file types: the addition of the index and the differences in algorithms. The latter are not great differences since those functions that require accesses of order N^2 will still dominate.

Function	Algorithm	Seq. Chronological File		Rel. File	Ordered File		Direct Access File	Indexed Seq. File
		Mag. Tape	Disk	Disk	Mag. Tape	Disk		
Add a record	3.1 Append to file	×	×					
	4.1 Write direct			×				
	5.1 Merge				×	×		×
	6.9 Chain with replacement						×	
	8.4 Block overflow							×
Delete a record	3.2 Flag as deleted			×		×	×	×
	5.1 Merge				×	×		×
	6.10 Delete from chain						×	
Read all, any order	3.4 Sequential exhaustive read	×	×	×	×	×	×	×
Read all, key order	3.7 Iterative exhaustive search	×	×	×	×	×	×	
	4.3 Sequential ordered read				×	×		×
Read record by key	3.5 Limited sequential search	×	×	×	×			
	3.6 Exhaustive sequential search	×	×	×	×			
	4.2 Read direct			×				
	5.2 Binary search					×		
	6.11 Direct access						×	
	8.2 Indexed sequential tree search							×
Update current record	Update		×	×		×	×	×
Reorganize	3.3 Copy the valid records	×	×					
	5.1 Merge				×	×		×

Figure 8.7 Algorithms for the standard functions.

The student record file was found to be the best solution for the ordered relative file in Chapter 5. We can safely assume that it will also be the best solution for the indexed sequential file.

8.5.1 The Student Record File

The index design is simple. If we assume the blocking factor of 4 that was used in Chapter 5 for the student record file, we find a block size of at least $4 \times 735 = 2940$ bytes. Again, there is a choice of name or SSN for the student record key. Name has the advantage of allowing the rosters and grades to be processed alphabetically and so will be used for this solution. It must be noted, however, that since the name key is significantly longer, it will cause the number of levels of the index to increase at lower values of N than would be true for the SSN key. This will turn out to be of no consequence for this problem, but could be significant for larger values of N. The number of entries that may be placed in one block is found from formula (8.1) to be $b \leq 2940 \div (32 + 2) \geq 91$.

By applying formula (8.2), it is possible to determine the number of levels of the index for a given N. For $N = 2000$ and $B = 4$, k is found to be $k \geq \log_{91}(2000/4) = 1.38 \leq 2$. For an N of 10,000, $k \geq \log_{91}(10,000/4) = 1.73 \leq 2$. Thus a two-level index is both necessary and sufficient for all capacities from 2000 to 10,000.

If the lowest-level index nodes are filled to capacity, there will be a need for $(2000 \div 4) \div 91 = 5.49 \leq 6$ index blocks for 2000 students, and $(10,000 \div 4) \div 91 = 27.5 \leq 28$ index blocks for 10,000 students. There will also be one master index block. The index will cause only a very modest increase of about 1% in the file size.

The registration function can be done efficiently by finding each student's record with Algorithm 8.2 and updating it with the courses for which he registers. The $\log_b(N/B)$ term cannot be used as an exact term, but must be rounded up to the next integer value per formula (8.2). Change of schedule is done in exactly the same manner as the registration. The function summary for the student record file is shown in Figure 8.8.

Function	Algorithm	Physical Accesses per Record	Number of Records	Mult.	Total
Registration	8.2	$\log_b(N/B)$	1	N	$N \cdot \log_b(N/B)$
	Update	1	1	N	N
Change	8.2	$\log_b(N/B)$	1	N	$N \cdot \log_b(N/B)$
	Update	1	1	N	N
Rosters	8.3	$1/B$	N	$2N/5$	$2N^2/5B$
Grades in	8.3	$1/B$	N	$N/5$	$N^2/5B$
	Update	1	30	$N/5$	$6N$
Grades out	8.3	$1/B$	N	1	N/B
Total accesses					$0.6N^2/B + 2N(\log_b(N/B) + N/B + 2N$

Note: For $N = 2000$, $B = 4$ $b = 91$, accesses $= 612,500$; for $N = 10,000$, $B = 4$ $b = 91$, accesses $= 15,030,500$ (N, number of students; B, blocking factor; b, index blocking factor).

Figure 8.8 Function analysis for student record file.

The remaining functions are done much as they were for the ordered relative file, except that the slightly modified sequential search algorithm

(Algorithm 8.3) is substituted for Algorithm 3.4. Again, it is these exhaustive sequential searches that generate the order N^2 statistics that will dominate the results.

8.5.2 Critique

The indexed sequential file solution may be compared most appropriately with the ordered relative file solution of Chapter 5. Both solutions share a common set of statistics for the last three functions because they share a common set of algorithms. When all functions are included, there seems to be little difference between the solutions. However, if the functions of rosters and grades in are subtracted from the totals, there is a very significant difference. For $N = 10,000$, the remaining functions require 320,654 for the ordered relative file, but only 30,500 for the indexed sequential file, a considerable reduction.

As with the previous solutions, the indexed sequential file suffers from having only one key by which efficient retrievals can be done. This results in very inefficient retrievals being necessary when other keys are used. This problem will be addressed in Chapters 9 through 11.

The problem of reorganizing the file has been sidestepped here by assuming that the file has already been organized before registration starts, and that it is not necessary to add students thereafter. This is not quite realistic. However, by allowing some space for expansion, as detailed in Section 8.3.2, a reasonable number of students could be added and deleted without requiring reorganization.

8.6 PROBLEMS

8.1. How many index levels are required for indexed sequential files with the following parameters? Assume no binding between the file and the medium. All sizes are in bytes.

	Record Size	Block Size	Key Size	Pointer Size	Number of Records
(a)	100	1000	38	4	100,000
(b)	100	1000	48	4	100,000
(c)	400	1200	30	2	4,000
(d)	400	1200	30	2	6,000
(e)	400	400	30	2	6,000

8.2. For each of the files in Problem 8.1, calculate the number of physical accesses required for
(a)   a binary search.

(b)   a search by Algorithm 8.2.

8.3.   Recalculate the example of Section 8.1.2 for a disk drive with the following characteristics: sector size = 1000 bytes; track size = 24 sectors; cylinder size = 12 tracks.

8.4.   Recalculate the example of Section 8.1.3 for the disk described in Problem 8.3.

8.5.   Modify Algorithm 8.4 to insert new records exactly in order.   (*Hint*: Use double buffering for the records.)

8.6.   Calculate the minimum value of N for which the index in the example of Section 8.5.1 will require three levels when the pointer requires four bytes and
(a)   name is used as the key
(b)   SSN is used as the key.

8.7.   Recalculate the example of Section 8.5.1 if the blocking factor of the data is 2.

8.8.   Write a program that will copy an ordered relative file into an indexed sequential file, and build the index.   What parameters are needed by the program?

8.9.   Solve the computer equipment problem described in Section B.2.   Use an indexed sequential file.

8.10. Solve the parts supply problem described in Section B.3.   Use an indexed sequential file.

9

Indexes

9.1 INDEX CONCEPTS

An *index* can be defined as a data structure containing a function, where the argument of the function is a key and the value of the function is a record number. In other words, with an index it is possible to find the record number associated with a given key value. The hashing function of the direct access file is a different method for finding a function that translates a key value into a record number. It does not require a data structure like an index, but suffers from the inevitable synonym problem. Moreover, the hashing function determines the record number, while the index permits the key value and the record number to be specified independently.

While the file itself could be considered an index, it would be a very inefficient index if algorithms such as 3.5, 3.6, or 3.7 were required to find the record number. Thus an index is usually a separate structure from the file—not only logically separate, as with the indexed sequential file, but physically separate, as when the index is located in a file of its own, as seen in Figure 9.1.

The cost of obtaining the record number from the index must be as low as possible, and certainly much less than the cost of finding the desired record(s) by searching the file. For this reason, many structures that could meet the functional definition of an index will not be considered. We consider only those structures that are efficient enough to be feasible in some applications.

The key for an index may be a single attribute, a part of an attribute, or some combination of several attributes. Keys may or may not be unique in value. There may be one index for a data file, as with the indexed sequential file, or there may be multiple indexes for a data file, each with a different key.

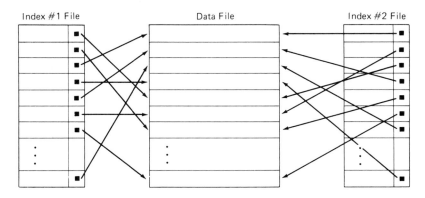

Figure 9.1 Data file with two indexes in separate files.

The length of an index record must be kept as small as possible. In simple indexes, each index entry will consist of the key value and a data record pointer, as shown in Figure 9.1. More complex indexes will have other fields as well as these. Short index records permit a large blocking factor, which is especially advantageous in indexes.

Since the file cannot be ordered by more than one key, it is generally not possible to index blocks, as was the case with the indexed sequential file. Instead, each record must be indexed separately. This results in considerably more index entries, but permits the data file to be ordered in any manner that is convenient.

Each index structure will have a set of algorithms appropriate to that structure. In some cases these will be identical with file algorithms already studied. In other cases, new algorithms will be needed to use the indexes.

9.2 LINEAR INDEXES

The simplest type of index is a linear index. This is similar to the indexes found at the back of books. A *linear index* is one in which the index records are ordered by key value as an ordered relative file, with no additional structure. Such an index shares many of the properties of the ordered relative file, both good and bad.

Like the ordered relative file, the best algorithm for finding a record with a given key value is the binary search of Algorithm 5.2. This search will be somewhat faster for the index than for the corresponding file since the blocking factor will usually be significantly larger for the index. All records of the data file may be accessed in key order, by reading the index file in sequence (Algorithm 4.3) and accessing each data record as its pointer is found in the index.

A combination of these two algorithms may be used to read some subset of the file where the subset is based on a range of values of the key. For example, suppose that there is a payroll file that has an index, among others, by salary. A list is needed of all employees earning between $20,000 and $25,000 per year. A binary search of the salary index could locate either the index entry of an employee now making $20,000, or locate the place in the index immediately preceding the first employee making more than $20,000. In either case, a short sequential search of the immediate neighborhood will locate the index entry for the first employee whose salary equals or exceeds $20,000. From this point in the index, a sequential read of the index may proceed until the first salary greater than $25,000 is found. As each index entry is read, the pointer is used to access and read the corresponding payroll record. This ability to locate efficiently all data records having a range of key values can be very helpful in some applications.

Also like the ordered relative file, the linear index is very difficult to update. Deleted records can be flagged in the index by replacing the pointer with a null value. However, there is no place to insert a new index entry in the required order. There are compromise solutions, similar to those used with the indexed sequential file, that permit a limited number of entries to be added before a reorganization is necessary. For example, if 20% of the index record slots in each block are left empty, new records could be added by rearranging the older records. When some block fills up, it will be necessary to reorganize the index.

The reorganization is similar to that required for the ordered relative file in that a totally new index is built. It differs in that the data file is the source for the new index instead of using the old index and a change file. The old index is discarded and a new one is built in three steps. First, the data file is read, and the key value and pointer are extracted for each valid record. These are appended to a temporary file. Second, the temporary file is sorted by the key. Third, the values from the sorted temporary file are copied into an index file, adding whatever structure is needed.

This need to reorganize the index is a major reason for not using linear indexes. The fact that the binary search represents a worst-case tree search is another reason for preferring other index structures. However, in applications where the rate at which records are added is low, the simplicity of the linear index may be valued over more complicated index structures.

9.3 TREE INDEXES

A *tree index* is one in which there is a hierarchy of indexes. The root or first level of the index points to the second level of the index. Each level of the index points to lower levels until the lowest or leaf nodes are reached. The leaf nodes have pointers only to the data file. The index used with the indexed sequential file is a tree index.

9.3.1 Heterogeneous Trees and Homogeneous Trees

Tree indexes may be classified as either homogeneous trees or heterogeneous trees. *Heterogeneous trees* are those where each node of the tree contains only one kind of pointer but the pointers are different for the leaf nodes than for the higher-level nodes. The leaf node pointers point to records in the data file, while the pointers in higher-level nodes point to lower-level nodes of the index. Because the two kinds of nodes are structurally different, the tree is called heterogeneous. Such a tree is shown in Figure 9.2.

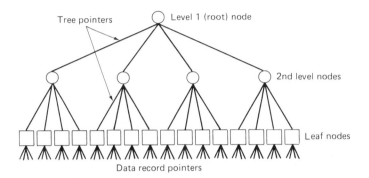

Figure 9.2 A heterogeneous tree index.

Heterogeneous tree indexes are the simplest type because there is only one pointer associated with each key value. Thus the index records have the same simple form seen in the linear index.

Homogeneous trees are those where each node contains two types of pointers, data pointers and tree pointers. All nodes are identical in form. The leaf nodes have empty tree pointers but active data pointers. Both kinds of pointers are active in the higher levels of the tree. To maintain the tree structure most effectively, it is necessary that a node in a homogeneous tree have as many data pointers as keys, but have one more tree pointer than the number of keys. This causes the internal structure of each node to be somewhat irregular, as seen in Figure 9.3.

Each tree pointer points to a node whose key values are bounded by the key values on each side of the pointer. The first tree pointer in a node points to a node whose keys are all less than or equal in value to the first key in the node of the pointer. Figure 9.4 shows a small homogeneous tree. To avoid confusion between pointers, the tree pointers are shown as being between the keys, while the data pointers are shown below the keys. The values have been replaced by arrows for the tree pointers and are omitted for the data pointers. We will follow this convention when diagramming homogeneous tree indexes.

An entry is located in such a tree by first searching the root node. Comparison of the given key with the key values in the node will result either in

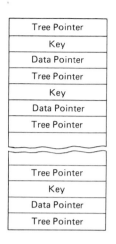

| Tree Pointer |
| Key |
| Data Pointer |
| Tree Pointer |
| Key |
| Data Pointer |
| Tree Pointer |
| Tree Pointer |
| Key |
| Data Pointer |
| Tree Pointer |

Figure 9.3 Structure of one node of a homogeneous tree index.

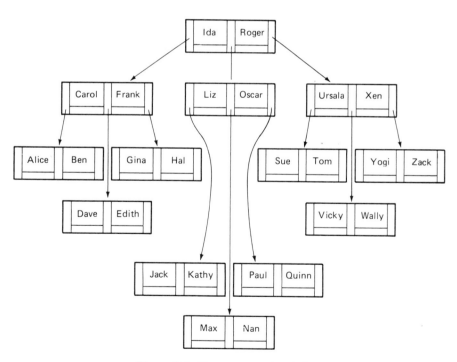

Figure 9.4 Homogeneous tree index.

finding a match, or finding that the value lies between two keys, before the first key, or after the last key. In the former case, the data pointer is used to retrieve the data record. In the latter case, the corresponding tree pointer is used to find another node of the index and the process is repeated.

For example, to retrieve the data record for which the key value is "Paul," we examine the keys in the root node and find that the value of "Paul" lies between "Ida" and "Roger." The middle pointer is followed to the next node of the search, where we find that the value "Paul" is greater than the last key. The rightmost pointer is then followed to the node containing the entry for Paul. Had Paul not been found here, the search would terminate as unsuccessful since the tree pointers in this leaf node are empty.

There is one important difference between homogeneous and heterogeneous tree indexes that results from the different internal structure: tree height and average search length. The average search length will be longer for the heterogeneous tree than for the homogeneous tree. This is because the search must always extend to a leaf node, while searches of the homogeneous tree may be concluded at any node where a match is found. The price paid for this advantage is in the form of added space for the double set of pointers, and slightly more complex algorithms.

9.3.2 Tree Height and Fan-Out

Let us define the number of tree pointers, b, that exist at any node of an index tree as the *fan-out factor*. Each node may have b son nodes. Figure 9.2 shows a three-level index with a fan-out factor of 4. This heterogeneous index has capacity to index 4^3 or 64 data records. A homogeneous index with the same fan-out factor and number of levels could index 63 records. (The number is smaller because there would be only three keys per node instead of four.)

Since the indexed sequential file uses a heterogeneous tree index, the equations developed in Section 8.1.1 are equally valid for all heterogeneous tree indexes. The number of levels, k, required for an index is given by formula (8.2), which is repeated here:

$$k \geq \log_b(M) \tag{8.2}$$

where M is the number of data records being indexed.

In the limiting case where $b = 2$, the tree search becomes a binary search. To state it another way, tree searches are generalizations of the binary search, allowing for more than a two-way split at each node.

The homogeneous tree index is slightly more complicated to analyze since the number of data pointers in each node is one less than b, and data pointers exist at all levels of the tree. For a tree of k levels and fan-out factor b, there will be $(b - 1)$ keys at the root level, $b(b - 1)$ at the second level, $b^2(b - 1)$ at the third level, up to $b^{(k - 1)} (b - 1)$ at the leaf level. The total number of data records indexed will be given by the series $(b^0 + b^1 + b^2 + \ldots + b^{(k-1)}) \cdot (b - 1) = b^k - 1$. Just as formulas (8.2) and (8.3) give the height and capacity for heterogeneous trees, formulas (9.1) and (9.2) give the relations for homogeneous trees:

$$M \leq b^k - 1 \qquad (9.1)$$

where k = number of levels of the tree
M = number of data records indexed

and

$$k \geq \log_b(M + 1) \qquad (9.2)$$

Thus it can be seen that the difference between the capacity of homogeneous and heterogeneous trees having the same fan-out and height is insignificant. This is due to the homogeneous tree having one less key per node than a heterogeneous tree with the same fan-out factor.

9.3.3 Adding and Deleting Tree Entries

The most difficult part of managing an index tree is adding and deleting tree entries without totally reorganizing the index. There are numerous algorithms for solving this problem, most of which are applicable only to specific tree structures. The methods deal with two aspects of the problem: adds and deletes that can be done entirely within one node, and adds and deletes that affect more than one node.

A simple method of managing changes within one node was seen in Chapter 8 where extra space was left in each leaf node of the heterogeneous tree, so that entries could be added. As long as space remained in the node for a new entry, this worked well. The method fails when there is not room for another entry. By the reverse process, entries may be removed from leaf nodes without limit, although this could leave empty nodes.

The method can be extended for heterogeneous trees by leaving empty slots in all levels of the tree. When a leaf node becomes full, the entries in that node are divided between the original node and a new leaf node. The new node requires an entry in the next higher level of the index. This can be added, since there was extra space left in all nodes. When, after many additions, the node immediately above the leaf becomes full, the process of splitting and adding an entry to the next level can be repeated at higher levels of the tree. Ultimately it will be necessary to split the root node, at which time a new root node must be created. The old root node is now at the second level and the tree becomes another level higher. This method can be used without leaving extra slots in the nodes, but the node splitting will begin with the first addition.

This method will cause the tree to have more levels than are necessary after many additions and deletions. This is because the population in many of the nodes will be much less than 100% and even less than 50% in some nodes. This reduces the effective fan-out factor for the tree, causing it to become taller.

Additions and deletions for homogeneous trees may be done in the same manner as with heterogeneous trees when they are performed in leaf nodes. However, these operations are more complicated if they are done in a nonleaf node. Simply deleting an entry in a nonleaf node would cause the pointer to a lower-level node to be deleted, thereby cutting off a branch of the tree. To prevent this, it is necessary to replace the deleted entry with one from a lower node of the tree. This can be done effectively by replacing the deleted key with an appropriate entry from a leaf node. The appropriate leaf entry can be either the rightmost entry from the subtree to the left of the deleted entry, or the leftmost entry from the subtree to the right of the deleted entry.

For example, it is necessary to remove the key "Ida" from the index of Figure 9.4. The rightmost entry of the left subtree is "Hal," which is deleted from the leaf node and moved into the root node (with its data pointer) to replace "Ida." If the leftmost entry of the right subtree had been chosen, "Jack" would replace "Ida." Both versions work equally well.

Creating new nodes when one overflows is also more complicated in the homogeneous tree. If the overflowing node were to be split into two nodes, with the entries divided between them, there would also have to be a new key entry in the father node to separate the two nodes. We cannot just create a new entry as was done with the higher levels of the heterogeneous tree; it must be the key for a bona fide data record. The answer is to "promote" the middle key from the overflowing node to the next higher level of the tree. Thus, when a node is to be split, it is a three-way split. The middle key is promoted up the tree. All keys to the left of the middle entry are left in the original node, while those to the right of the middle are placed into a new node. The tree pointers for the next-higher node must be adjusted to include the new node.

Should the next-higher node be full, the process is repeated until, in the worst case, the root is split and the tree grows by one level. This will happen rarely, but it will happen if all the nodes from the root to the leaf are full. For example, consider again the tree of Figure 9.4. It is necessary to add the key "Dan" to the tree. Clearly, it belongs before "Dave" in the "Dave–Edith" node. Since this node is full, it is split. The (now) middle entry, "Dave," is promoted to the next node up the tree, and two leaf nodes replace the old leaf node; one with the single entry "Dan," the other with "Edith."

The problem is only partly solved. "Dave" must now be inserted into the "Carol–Frank" node, where there also is no room. Again, the node is split three ways, with the middle key, which is again "Dave," being promoted. The process is repeated with the "Ida–Roger" node being split and a new root node being created with the single value "Ida." The resulting tree is seen in Figure 9.5.

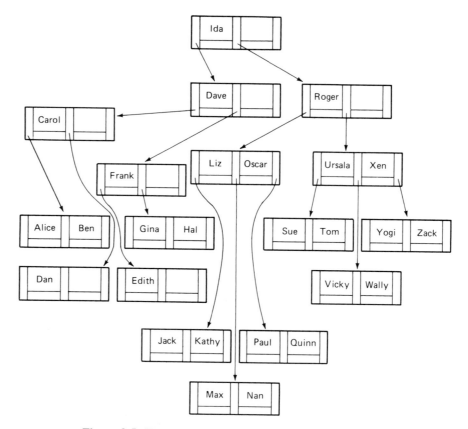

Figure 9.5 Homogeneous tree index after addition of "Dan".

It was inevitable that the tree grow to another level in this example, since it was already full. However, this algorithm can cause a tree that is far from full to grow as well. In the example above, it was only necessary for the three nodes involved to be full for the tree to grow another level. The remaining nodes could have been nearly empty and it would have made no difference.

These algorithms for adding and deleting entries (and ultimately nodes) have an advantage over many other algorithms in that the trees remain balanced in the face of additions. A **balanced tree** is defined as one in which the longest path from root to leaf differs from the shortest such path by no more than one level. Other things being equal, a balanced tree will have a shorter average search path than one that is not balanced. Balance is guaranteed, with these algorithms, because a new level can be created only at the root node. Other algorithms allow new levels to be created at leaf nodes and can lead to badly unbalanced trees with much longer search paths.

As a worst-case example of an algorithm that can result in an unbalanced tree, consider a binary homogeneous tree ($b = 2$). If entries are added in order by key (or reverse order by key), a very unbalanced tree results when the familiar algorithm for building a binary sort tree is used. This is *Algorithm 9.1*:

```
procedure ALGOR9.1(givenkey); (* adds a node with the given key
to the tree *)
        np := 0;  (* set the node pointer to the root node *)
        done := false;
        DO BEGIN  (* loop until new node has been added *)
                IF givenkey ≤ KEY(np) THEN   (* add node
                    to left subtree *)
                    IF LEFT(np) ≠ null THEN np := LEFT(np);
                        (* visit left son *)
                    ELSE BEGIN  (* insert new node as left
                        son of current node *)
                        LEFT(np) := GETNODE;  (* returns
                            pointer to empty node *)
                        np := LEFT(np);  (* set pointer
                            to new node *)
                        KEY(np) := givenkey;  (* insert
                            new key in new node *)
                        done := true;  (* signal
                            completion *)
            END
                ELSE   (* add node to right subtree *)
                    IF RIGHT(np) ≠ null THEN np := RIGHT(np);
                        (* visit right son *)
                    ELSE BEGIN  (* insert new node as right
                        son of current node *)
                        RIGHT(np) := GETNODE;   (* returns
                            pointer to empty node *)
                        np := RIGHT(np);  (* set pointer
                            to new node *)
                        KEY(np) := givenkey;  (* insert
                            new key in new node *)
                        done := true;  (* signal
                            completion *)
            END;
        END UNTIL done;
```

If keys are added in a random order, the tree will develop with some, but not gross, imbalance. However, if the keys are added in order, or nearly in order, the balance will be very poor. Figure 9.6 shows, on the right, such a tree where the keys were added in the order M, L, P, R, T, C, U, S, A, V, W, X, Y, Z. Because there is a high degree of order in the list, the tree is very poorly balanced. It requires 10 levels for the 14 nodes whereas these same values can be placed into a tree with only four levels. The difference for average search length is significant. The average search path for the balanced tree is 3.21 nodes, while the average search length for the unbalanced tree is 6.93 nodes, more than twice as many. Similar problems can be expected in trees with higher fan-out factors if the tree expands by adding nodes at the leaves rather than at the root.

In the next section we study one type of homogeneous tree that is maintained according to rules which guarantee that the tree will remain balanced in the face of unlimited additions and deletions. It will also have a mechanism to delete nodes when they are no longer necessary, and to maintain a high fan-out factor under all conditions. While many other kinds of trees can be, and are, used for indexes, the B-tree combines the best features of tree indexes while it avoids most problems.

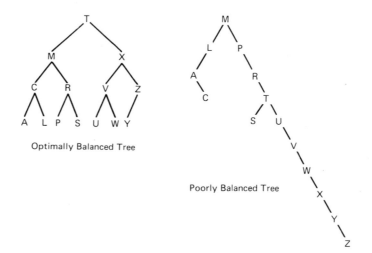

Figure 9.6 Two binary trees with same data.

9.4 B-TREE INDEXES

The origin of the term "B-tree" seems to be lost to history. It has been suggested that the "B" stands for balanced or bushy, both of which are descriptive, or that it stands for Boeing since much of the early work in developing B-trees was done there, or that it stands for Bayer who did much of the early work and publication on B-trees. Whatever the origin, the "B" definitely does not stand for binary. B-trees and binary trees are separate and disjoint ideas.

A **B-tree of order d** is defined as a homogeneous index tree with the following characteristics:

1. Each node can hold a maximum of $2d$ keys, with their data pointers, and $2d + 1$ tree pointers.
2. No node, except the root, may have fewer than d keys.
3. All leaf nodes are on the same level.

Because of these constraints, the fan-out factor for a B-tree will always range between $d + 1$ and $2d + 1$. The trees of Figures 9.4 and 9.5 are B-trees of order $d = 1$.

A B-tree grows as entries are added by the method described in the preceding section. When an entry is added to a node that is full, the node is split three ways. The middle entry is promoted to the father node, all entries to the left of the middle entry remain in the node, while all of those to the right are placed in a new node. Deletions likewise proceed as described in the preceding section, except that additional steps need to be taken to ensure that a node never has less than d keys. This is done by first rotating keys between nodes and then, as a last resort, combining nodes.

Throughout these operations of adding and deleting, the B-tree will remain balanced because of the algorithms it uses, and it will also remain "bushy" or low in height because of the lower limit allowed for the fan-out factor.

9.4.1 Algorithms for B-Trees

Of the six standard file functions that were defined in Section 3.3, four are applicable to the B-tree index: read a record with a specific key value, read all records in key order, add an entry, and delete an entry. It is these four functions for which we will consider B-tree algorithms. It must be remembered that, when a B-tree search has concluded, it is still necessary to access the data file. However, this is a separate operation and will not be considered here.

When making additions and deletions to a B-tree it will be convenient to use a node buffer that is slightly larger than the node. Specifically, the buffer should have room for $2d + 1$ keys (with their data pointers) and $2d + 2$ tree pointers. It will also save redundant reads from secondary storage if there is some way to preserve the nodes in primary memory that lie between the root node and the leaf node. It may be convenient to use a stack of node buffers for this purpose. Then, when it is necessary to move back up the tree, the needed node will always be on the top of the stack. Only nodes that are modified during an add or delete need to be written back to the index file.

Add (Algorithm 9.2).   Entries are always added at a leaf node. The basic process is to locate the appropriate leaf node and insert the new entry (key and data pointer) into it. Since there is always the possibility that the node was already full, it is necessary to check for an overflow of the node. If the node has overflowed, the first remedy is to redistribute the entries among the node, its father, and a brother node. If this cannot be done, the node is split into two nodes, with the middle entry being promoted into the father node.

These operations are illustrated in Figures 9.7 through 9.14. The first figure shows a B-tree of two levels. It is necessary to add entries with key values "Bob" and "Bill." The first addition (see Figure 9.8) fits into node 1 and no further processing is required. This kind of addition will be the rule rather than the exception when processing B-trees. The second addition causes

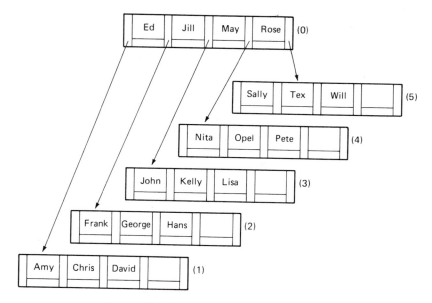

Figure 9.7 Two level B-tree of order $d = 2$.

the node to overflow. The dotted lines in Figure 9.9 indicate space that is available in the node buffer, but not in the index file. The overflow must be corrected before the node can be written back out.

Figure 9.8 Node 1 after adding entry "Bob".

Figure 9.9 Node 1 overflowing after adding entry "Bill".

The overflow in Figure 9.9 is corrected by redistribution. **Redistribution** means that the surplus entries are shared with an adjacent brother node that is not full. In this case node 2 has extra space and is selected for redistribution. The number of entries is divided equally between the two brother nodes. In this case there will be $(5 + 3) \div 2 = 4$ entries per node after the operation is complete. However, the entry for "David" cannot simply be shifted over to node 2, since the entry "Ed" in node 0 that separates nodes 1 and 2 would be incorrect. Instead, the redistribution must include this entry in the father.

The redistribution is done by including all the entries in nodes 1 and 2, plus the entry in node 0 which separates them. This will be all the entries in the sequence from "Amy" through "Hans." The middle entry of this sequence replaces "Ed" in node 0. Those entries before the middle go into node 1, while those that follow the middle go into node 2. These nodes can now be rewritten as shown in Figure 9.10.

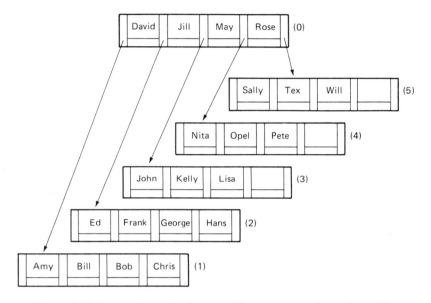

Figure 9.10 B-tree after redistribution of keys among nodes 1, 0, and 2.

The next entry to be added has the key value "Cal," which belongs in node 1. Again, this addition causes the node to overflow as shown in Figure 9.11. Now, however, there is no adjacent brother node with surplus space, so redistribution cannot be used. Instead, it is necessary to split the node. As was described in section 9.3, the node is split three ways. The middle entry is promoted to the father node. The entries to the left of the middle are left in the original node, while those to the right are placed into a new node. The split is shown in Figure 9.12.

Figure 9.11 Node 1 Overflowing after adding entry "Cal".

It is now necessary to insert the entry "Bob" into node 0, but again an overflow results, as shown in Figure 9.13, and there is no brother node for redistribution. Consequently, it is again necessary to split the node. Since node 0 was the root node, there is no father node into which the middle entry can be promoted. Therefore, it is necessary to create a new root node. This is the only time that a tree grows another level. The new root node is node 8, as shown in Figure 9.14.

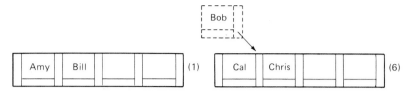

Figure 9.12 Node 1 after being split.

Figure 9.13 Node 0 Overflowing after adding entry ''Bob''.

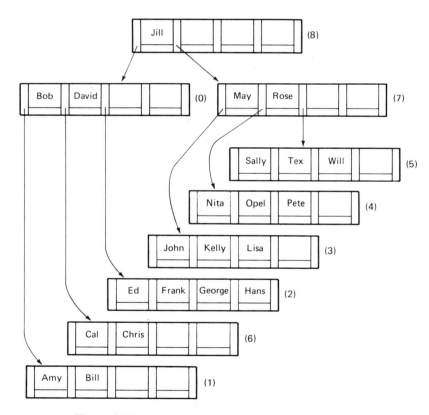

Figure 9.14 B-tree after splitting nodes 0 and 1.

Add (Algorithm 9.2). Algorithm 9.2 is not complicated in outline, but the details of reading, writing, and buffering nodes, and moving entries within and between nodes can become very involved. A detailed procedure for adding entries to a B-tree will require half-a-dozen to a dozen supporting procedures, if written in a proper written in a proper style. To avoid becoming bogged down in these details, the algorithm presented here will use a pseudocode, where functions such as insert, find, split, and redistribute are understood to be as described above. The algorithm is as follows:

```
procedure ADD(tree,entry);
        FIND LEAF node FOR KEY OF entry;
        INSERT entry INTO node;
        CHECK-FOR-OVERFLOW(tree,node);

procedure CHECK-FOR-OVERFLOW(tree,node);
        IF number-of-entries >  2*d THEN
                IF left-brother-node-entries < 2*d or
                        right-brother-node-entries < 2*d THEN
                                REDISTRIBUTE
        ELSE BEGIN
                SPLIT-NODE;
                IF root-node-was-split THEN BEGIN
                        GET-NEW-NODE;
                        INSERT middle-entry INTO
                                new-root-node;
                END ELSE BEGIN
                        INSERT middle-entry INTO
                                father-node;
                        CHECK-FOR-OVERFLOW(tree,
                                father-node);
                END;
        END;
```

The basic procedure ADD is simple and straightforward, except for the possibility of overflow. The complexities that can result from a node overflow are handled by the CHECK-FOR-OVERFLOW procedure. This procedure first determines whether or not an overflow has occurred. If there is an overflow, it first attempts a redistribution. Failing that, it will split the node. When a node is split and the middle entry is promoted, there is again the possibility of causing an overflow in the father. Thus, CHECK-FOR-OVERFLOW calls itself recursively as the overflow ripples up the B-tree. It must be remembered that the probability of an overflow occurring, even at the leaf level, is about $1 \div d$. The complications of the CHECK-FOR-OVERFLOW procedure are not often needed.

Delete (Algorithm 9.3).   This algorithm is nearly the inverse function of the add algorithm. The only difference occurs when the entry being deleted is not in a leaf node. For deletions that occur in leaf nodes, as most will, the entry is removed from the node. A check must then be made for node underflow. This happens when any node, except the root, has fewer than d entries.

The first recourse, in the case of underflow, is again a redistribution. If an adjacent brother node has more than d entries, the entries are redivided between the two nodes, just as they were when adding. The same procedure could be used for redistribution whether it is done as the result of adding or deleting. As before, the entry in the father node is also changed. If there is no adjacent brother node with more than d entries, redistribution fails, and the node must be combined with a brother node. This is the reverse of splitting nodes.

For example, if the entry "Cal" is removed from the tree of Figure 9.14, node 6 underflows. Node 2 is an adjacent brother with more than d entries, so redistribution is used to balance nodes 6 and 2. "David" moves into node 6 and "Ed" is rotated into node 0 as shown in Figure 9.15.

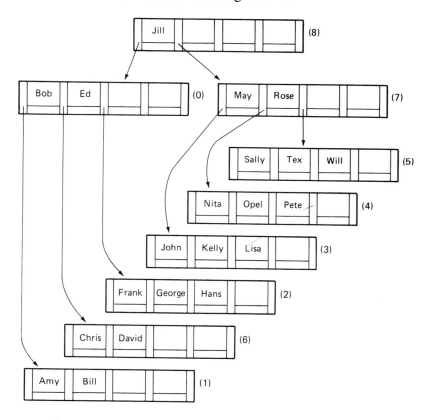

Figure 9.15 B-tree after deletion of "Cal" and redistribution.

Deletion of "Bill" again causes node 1 to underflow. This time there is no adjacent brother with more than d entries, so nodes must be combined. If nodes 1 and 6 are combined, the father entry that separates them, "Bob," is also included in the combined node. However, removing "Bob" from node 0 also causes it to underflow. Here, too, there is no adjacent brother node with more than d entries, so that it is necessary to again combine nodes. Nodes 0 and 7 are combined, and the combined node includes the entry "Jill," which is brought down from the father node. This leaves the root node empty, so that it may be deleted with node 0 again becoming the root node. The final tree is seen in Figure 9.16.

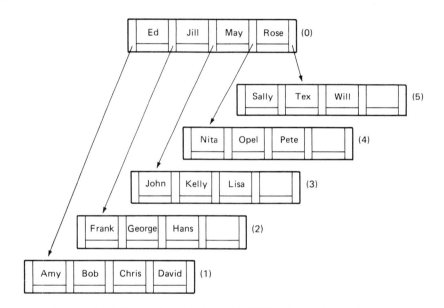

Figure 9.16 B-tree after deletion of "Bill" and combining of nodes.

The problem of deleting an entry in a nonleaf node is solved by replacing it with an entry from a leaf node. This transforms the problem into one of deleting an entry from a leaf node. As noted in Section 9.3, the leaf entry may be either the rightmost entry from the left subtree, or the leftmost entry from the right subtree. For the tree of Figure 9.16, the "Jill" entry could be deleted by moving either "Hans" or "John" up to replace it. This may cause an underflow in the leaf node which is handled as before.

As with Algorithm 9.2, pseudocode is used to describe Algorithm 9.3. The procedure CHECK-FOR-UNDERFLOW is analogous to the procedure CHECK-FOR-OVERFLOW found in algorithm 9.2. Algorithm 9.3 is as follows:

```
procedure DELETE(tree,key);
        FIND node WITH entry THAT MATCHES key;
        IF node-is-leaf THEN BEGIN
                DELETE entry FROM node;
                CHECK-FOR-UNDERFLOW(tree,node);
        END ELSE BEGIN
                FIND RIGHTMOST leaf-node OF left-subtree;
                REPLACE entry THAT MATCHES key WITH RIGHTMOST
                        entry OF leaf-node;
                CHECK-FOR-UNDERFLOW(tree,leaf-node)
        END;


procedure CHECK-FOR-UNDERFLOW(tree,node);
        IF number-of-entries < d THEN
                IF left-brother-node-entries > d or
                        right-brother-node-entries > d THEN
                                REDISTRIBUTE
        ELSE BEGIN
                COMBINE-NODES;
                DELETE entry FROM father-node;
                IF father-node-is-root and
                        root-node-is-empty THEN
                                RETURN-OLD-NODE(root-node);
                ELSE
                        IF father-node-is-not-root THEN
                                CHECK-FOR-UNDERFLOW(tree,
                                        father-node);
        END;
```

Again, the basic procedure is simple except for the possibility of under-flow. The recursive procedure CHECK-FOR-UNDERFLOW is used to process the occasional underflowing node and any ancestor nodes that might subsequently underflow.

Read a record with a specific key value (Algorithm 9.4). This algorithm is straightforward and less complex than the add and delete algorithms. The root node is first examined to locate either: (1) a key value that matches the given key, or (2) the place in the sequence of key values where the given key would be placed. If a match is found, the corresponding data pointer is returned. If a match is not found, the corresponding tree pointer is used to find the appropriate node at the next level of the tree. If there is no next level, the search fails and a null value is returned.

The algorithm is recursive, calling itself each time it descends another level in the tree. The functions KEY, LEFT, RIGHT, and POINTER are used to extract the key value, left tree pointer, right tree pointer, and the data pointer, respectively, that are associated with a given key. The keys are numbered left to right, beginning with 1. COUNT is a function that returns the number of active keys in the node. It is assumed that each node is stored as one physical record in the file. Algorithm 9.4 is as follows:

```
integer function FIND(tree,node,givenkey);
        (* returns data pointer if match found, null value if
            not found *)
        (* node is the root node for the initial call *)
        i := 1;  (* start search of node with first key
            in node *)
        WHILE KEY(node,i) < givenkey and i < COUNT(node)
            DO i := i + 1;
                (* sequential search of current node *)
        IF KEY(node,i) = givenkey THEN FIND := POINTER(i);
            (* match found *)
        ELSE BEGIN
                IF KEY(node,i) > givenkey THEN p := LEFT(node,i);
                    (* search left subtree *)
                ELSE p := RIGHT(node,i);  (* search right
                    subtree *)
                IF p ≠ null THEN BEGIN  (* search
                    next level of the tree *)
                    READ-DIRECT(tree,nextnode,p);  (* read
                        node at next level *)
                    FIND := FIND(tree,nextnode,givenkey);
                            (* recursive call for subtree *)
                END ELSE FIND := null;  (* no next level, search
                    has failed *)
        END;
```

Read all records in key order.   The standard function to read all records in key order can be implemented by an inorder traversal of the B-tree. Each entry will be visited in the proper order to retrieve the data in key order. The traversal begins with the leftmost entry of the leftmost leaf node and continues until the rightmost entry of the rightmost leaf node is reached. The traversal path goes up and down the tree as necessary to visit all entries in order. Again, it will save many redundant reads of the tree file if a stack is used to store all nodes from the root to the current node.

Algorithm 9.5 is a generalization of the inorder tree traversal. Instead of always beginning with the first entry and searching the entire tree, it allows the search to begin with any value and end with any higher value. Thus it is possible to read all keys in a given range of key values, including the range of all values. The functions KEY, LEFT, RIGHT, POINTER, and COUNT are used as they were in Algorithm 9.4.

The procedure TRAVERSE is called to perform the traversal of the B-tree. The tree and root node are passed as the first two parameters. The last two parameters are the lowest key value (lokey) and the highest key value (hikey) for the traversal. TRAVERSE calls FIND-START to locate the first qualified

entry and build the initial stack. The procedures GET-NEXT-KEY and
PROCESS are then called iteratively. GET-NEXT-KEY locates the data pointer
corresponding to the next key in the traversal and returns it for processing by
PROCESS. GET-NEXT-KEY returns a value of false when there are no more
qualified entries in the tree, and TRAVERSE terminates.

When traversing a tree, it is necessary to keep careful track of where one
is, has been, and is going. A stack is a useful structure for keeping one's place
in a tree. For this algorithm, we will use a stack local to TRAVERSE named
"nodestack" to keep places. Each element in this stack is a pair consisting of a
node of the B-tree, and an integer i that points to a particular entry in that node.
An entry will be stored in the stack if and only if it meets three conditions:

1. KEY(node, i) $\geq$ lokey
2. $1 \leq i \leq$ COUNT(node)
3. For all j such that $1 \leq j < i$, KEY(node,j) $<$ lokey, or has been
   processed

The procedure PUSH(nodestack,(node,i)) pushes a pair onto the stack.
The function POP(nodestack,(node,i)) takes the top pair off nodestack and
returns it if nodestack is not empty. POP returns true unless the stack is empty,
in which case it returns false.

```
procedure TRAVERSE(tree,node,lokey,hikey);  (* calls FIND-FIRST
        to locate starting point in tree, calls GET-NEXT-KEY to
        fetch the data pointer for each qualified key, and calls
        PROCESS to process each data record. *)
BEGIN
        local nodestack := null;  (* start with the node
            stack empty *)
        FIND-FIRST(tree,lokey,node,nodestack);
        WHILE GET-NEXT-KEY(tree,hikey,nodestack,ptr) DO
            PROCESS(ptr);
END;  (* of procedure transverse *)

procedure FIND-FIRST(tree,lokey,node,nodestack);
        (* builds nodestack such that top entry is the first
            key >= lokey *)
BEGIN
        i := 1;
        WHILE i <= COUNT(node) and KEY(node,i) <
            lokey DO i := i + 1;
        IF i <= COUNT(node) THEN BEGIN
                (* KEY(node,i) >= lokey and 1 <= j < i implies
                    that KEY(node,j) < lokey *)
        PUSH(ncdestack, (node,i));  (* save this node for
            future traversal *)
                np := LEFT(node,i);  (* starting entry may be in
```

```
                                        left subtree *)
                    END ELSE (* any possible beginning point must be in
                            rightmost subtree *)
                        np := RIGHT(node, COUNT(node));
                                (* observe that no (node,i) pair is
                                    pushed onto nodestack because no
                                    key in this node is included in
                                    the traversal *)
                    IF np ≠ null THEN BEGIN (* not a leaf, so check
                        out the subtree *)
                            READ-DIRECT(tree,node,np);  (* get next node
                                of subtree *)
                            FIND-FIRST(tree,lokey,node,nodestack);(*recursive
                                call for subtree*)
                END;
        END;  (* procedure FIND-FIRST *)


logical procedure GET-NEXT-KEY(tree,hikey,nodestack,ptr);
                (* If there is another key entry in the stack within the
                        specified range, this procedure returns a value of
                        true and ptr contains a pointer to the
                        corresponding data record: otherwise, a value of
                        false is returned. *)
        BEGIN
                ok := POP(nodestack,(node,i)); (* get the top entry
                    from the node stack *)
                IF ok (* nodestack not empty *) THEN BEGIN
                        IF KEY(node,i) > hikey THEN (* end of the
                            range *) ok := false;
                        ELSE BEGIN (* key is valid *)
                                ptr := POINTER(node,i);
                                np := RIGHT(node,i);
                                IF i < COUNT(node,i) THEN BEGIN
                                        i := i + 1; (* move to next
                                            entry *)
                                        PUSH(nodestack, (node,i));
                                            (* replace node on stack *)
                                END;
                                WHILE np ≠ null DO BEGIN  (* find
                                    leftmost leaf of subtree, if any *)
                                        READ-DIRECT(tree,node,np);
                                        PUSH(nodestack,(node,1));
                                        np := LEFT(node,1);
                                END;
                        END;  (* if key is valid *)
                END;  (* if ok *)
                GET-NEXT-KEY := ok;
        END;  (* procedure GET-NEXT-KEY *)
```

These four algorithms for B-trees are more difficult than presented here in that there will be numerous small details to be concerned with. However, if the procedures are implemented in a top-down manner, the details can be deferred to lower levels.

Sometimes these algorithms are implemented with variations from those shown here. There are several points at which the distinction between right and left is arbitrary and the implementation can go either way. Some implementations do not use redistribution in the add function. This can be done but will result in the tree having more nodes and consequently a lower effective fan-out factor.

An improvement can be made in both the add and delete functions by allowing the redistribution to span more than two brother nodes. This will permit the tree to maintain better balance and use fewer nodes.

9.4.2 B-Tree Statistics

The B-tree obeys the same rules for height as other homogeneous trees. Consequently, the statistics for tree height developed in Section 9.3 are valid. The problem is that the fan-out factor, b, is not a constant within a given tree. It can be no greater than $2d + 1$, or less than $d + 1$, but ranges widely within these limits. This creates considerable uncertainty about the height of the tree and therefore the number of accesses needed for a function.

Exact calculations can be performed for both the best-case tree ($b = 2d + 1$) and the worst-case tree ($b = d + 1$). Making these substitutions into formulas (9.1) and (9.2) yields

$$M = (d + 1)^k - 1 \qquad \text{(worst case)} \qquad (9.3)$$

$$k \geq \log_{(d + 1)}(M + 1) \qquad \text{(worst case)} \qquad (9.4)$$

$$M = (2d + 1)^k - 1 \qquad \text{(best case)} \qquad (9.5)$$

$$k \geq \log_{(2d + 1)}(M + 1) \qquad \text{(best case)} \qquad (9.6)$$

These formulas can serve as absolute upper and lower bounds on tree height and capacity but are not effective for calculating the average case.

The average value for occupancy of nodes, in the face of many random inserts and deletes, will range between 69 and 75%, depending on the exact algorithms used. For simplicity, the following analysis will use the 75% figure in developing statistics. The actual figure for any given tree will depend both on the exact insertion and deletion algorithms used and the degree to which inserts and deletes are ordered.

With these assumptions, formulas (9.1) and (9.2) may be revised for the average case as follows:

$$M = (1.5d + 1)^k - 1 \qquad \text{(average case)} \qquad (9.7)$$

$$k \geq \log_{(1.5d + 1)}(M + 1) \qquad \text{(average case)} \qquad (9.8)$$

When making a successful search for a unique key value, the search will sometimes terminate before a leaf node is reached, owing to the presence of keys in the higher-level nodes. Consequently, the average search is somewhat shorter than k. Consider, for example, a B-tree of three levels ($k = 3$), and order ($d = 20$). The average number of keys in this tree, by formula (9.7), is $31^3 - 1$ = 29,790. The number of keys at the root level is $1.5d = 30$. The number of keys at the second level is $31 \times 30 = 930$. The number of keys at the leaf level is $31^2 \times 30 = 28,830$. The average search is found by summing the product of the level depth and the probability of the search terminating at that level for all levels: $1 \cdot (30 \div 29{,}790) + 2 \cdot (930 \div 29{,}790) + 3 \cdot (28{,}830 \div 29{,}790) =$ 2.967. Thus the average search requires slightly less than three levels, which is what would be expected since the vast majority of the keys are at the leaf level. This calculation can be generalized for any order and level of tree as

$$L = (1.5d \div M) \cdot [k \cdot (1.5d + 1)^{(k + 1)} - (k + 1) \cdot (1.5d + 1)^k + 1)] \div (1.5d)^2 \ (9.9)$$

where L is the average number of levels that must be searched. If M is assumed to be the value given by formula (9.7), the average number of levels required by the average successful search for various values of d and k is shown in Figure 9.17. As can be seen, this value is only slightly less than k, except where d is small. This number will be referred to henceforth as k^-.

k	5	10	d 20	50	100
2	1.894	1.941	1.969	1.987	1.993
3	2.872	2.934	2.967	2.987	2.993
4	3.867	3.933	3.967	3.987	3.993
10	9.867	9.933	9.967	9.987	9.993

Figure 9.17   Average number of levels searched (k^-) for average B-tree.

The add and delete functions will require slightly more than the number of physical reads required by the retrieval function. This is because of the need to access brother nodes occasionally. Since the retrieval function requires slightly less than k reads, the value of k is a close approximation to the number of nodes read. In addition, the add and delete functions must write back all modified nodes. This will be slightly more than one node. The leaf node must always be written back, as well as any other nodes modified. Since adds and deletes are much less frequent, in most systems, than retrievals, the value of $k + 1$ physical accesses will be a sufficiently close approximation for adds and deletes.

9.4.3 B-Tree Summary

The B-tree is such an effective structure for an index that other structures are seldom used in modern file systems. It has all the good properties that can be expected of an index: order $\log(N)$ access requirements; self-balancing; low tree height; and efficient update statistics.

As a result, the B-tree index is found in many database systems, as well as some file access methods: IBM's Virtual Sequential Access Method (VSAM) and Hewlett-Packard's Keyed Sequential Access Method (KSAM), to name two. B-trees would usually be implemented through a similar "method" or by means of a library of procedures which are general in their application.

9.5 B-TREE VARIANTS

There are several variations of B-trees commonly used which have an advantage in some situations. They are not of sufficient general value to have been adopted as universally as the B-tree, but are encountered frequently enough that their special features should be known.

The **B*-tree** is identical to the B-tree except that the second rule (Section 9.4) is changed to say that each node may have a minimum of $(4/3)d$ keys instead of d keys. The insertion algorithm (Algorithm 9.2) is modified so that a split requires that the entries in two full, adjacent, brother nodes are divided among three nodes, one of which is new. Similarly, when deleting causes an underflow, three nodes are combined into two nodes.

The B*-tree has an advantage in that the average occupancy rate, and hence the effective fan-out factor, is higher than would be the case for the corresponding B-tree. Consequently, file space is saved and the tree height might be reduced by one level in some cases. The disadvantage is that overflows and underflows will occur more often with the attendant increase in I/O operations.

The **B⁺-tree** differs from the B-tree in three respects. First, it is a heterogeneous tree rather than a homogeneous tree. All the keys appear in the leaf nodes. Data record pointers occur only in the leaf nodes and son pointers only in the nonleaf nodes.

Second, keys are duplicated in the tree. Since all keys appear in leaf nodes, some of them must be duplicated to provide entries for the higher levels of the tree. The usual rule is to use the rightmost leaf key of the left subtree to find a key value for use higher in the tree.

Third, in addition to the data record pointers, each leaf node has one brother pointer which points to the next leaf node in sequence. Thus it is possible to traverse the index by following the brother pointers from leaf node to leaf node instead of using a tree traversal. This allows a very simple traversal instead of the complexity of Algorithm 9.5. Doubly linked lists are sometimes used to simplify the addition and deletion of leaf nodes.

With these exceptions, B⁺-trees are managed similarly to B-trees. The basic B-tree algorithms can be modified to accommodate the B⁺-trees.

Slightly more accesses are required to find a record with a given key value since the search must always continue to a leaf. Thus the depth of the search always equals the height of the tree. On the other hand, traversals require fewer accesses since it is only necessary to locate the start of the traversal in a leaf and follow the linked list.

Figure 9.18 shows a B⁺-tree. The light arrows represent the son pointers while the heavy arrows show the brother pointers. Leaf nodes have square corners and nonleaf nodes have round corners.

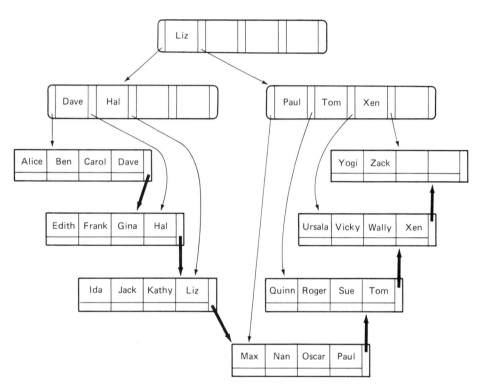

Figure 9.18 B⁺-Tree.

Another variation of the B-tree is to include more data in each entry than that required for the key. If the amount of data is small compared with the entire data record, and that data is accessed much more often than the rest of the data in the record, the operation of accessing the data record may be avoided in many cases, thus reducing the time required. The disadvantage is that the added data requires space. Thus the order, d, of the index is reduced. All other things being equal, this may increase the number of levels of the tree. This variant does not yet have a generic name.

9.6 SUMMARY

An index is a data structure containing a function that maps key values into record numbers of the corresponding records. Indexes may take the form of *linear list indexes*, which are simple but difficult to update, or of *tree indexes*, which are more complex but more flexible in updating and which generally provide faster access than linear lists.

Tree indexes are either *heterogeneous trees*, where only the leaf nodes contain pointers to the data file, or *homogeneous trees*, where all nodes have the same form and include pointers to the data file. The height, or number of levels, of a tree depends on the number of entries in the index, the fan-out factor of each node, and the balance of the tree. The *fan-out factor* is the number of son nodes that each nonleaf node owns. A *balanced tree* is one where the longest path from root to leaf differs in length from the shortest such path by no more than one level.

A *B-tree of order d* is a homogeneous index tree with three constraints. First, each node has a capacity of $2d$ keys with data file pointers and $2d + 1$ tree pointers. Second, no node except the root may have fewer than d keys. Third, all leaf nodes are on the same level. Algorithms 9.2 through 9.5 show how to add, delete, and find entries in a B-tree index. An important factor in the add and delete algorithms is the *redistribution* of entries between nodes to keep the tree balanced and minimize the adding and deletion of nodes. Tree height and average search lengths can be calculated for the best-case and worst-case B-trees and approximated for the average case.

There are several common variations on the basic B-tree. These include storing some or all of the data of the file in the tree instead of just the key. This increases the tree height but may prove effective if the data record is short. *B*-trees* are like B-trees except that the minimum node population allowed is $(4/3)d$ keys. This results in denser nodes and lower tree heights but creates additional complexity in the add and delete algorithms. *B+-trees* are heterogeneous forms of B-trees where only the leaf nodes contain pointers to the data file and the leaf nodes are also linked to form a linear list. This variation has some of the advantages of both the linear list and the B-tree.

9.7 PROBLEMS

9.1. Some files, such as the ordered relative file and the indexed sequential file, are said to be "self-indexing." Why, then, is there an advantage to having a separate index for such a file?

9.2. Why does a tree search usually require fewer accesses than when the binary search (Algorithm 5.2) is applied to the same-sized index organized as a linear index?

9.3. In Section 9.3.2, the assertion was made that

$$(b^0 + b^1 + b^2 + \ldots + b^{(k-1)}) \times (b - 1) = b^k - 1$$

Prove that this is true.

9.4. Show that a balanced tree will always remain balanced if levels are added or deleted only at the root.

9.5. Redraw the tree index of Figure 9.10 after the keys "Edward," "Edwin," and "Ethel" have been added in order.

9.6. It was seen in Figure 9.6 that adding keys to an index in order creates a worst-case situation. For the B-tree shown in Figure 9.19, create a worst case by adding the 15 keys in the range 6 through 20, in order. Use Algorithm 9.2. Draw a diagram of the final tree.

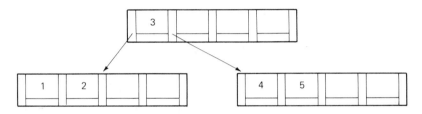

Figure 9.19

9.7. Repeat Problem 9.6 using Algorithm 9.2 *without* redistribution. When a node overflows, it is always split. Compare the results.

9.8. Verify Algorithm 9.5 by walking through it with the tree of Figure 9.14. Use values of "C" and "Q" for lokey and hikey.

9.9. Write a set of procedures to implement Algorithms 9.2 through 9.5 in a general way. This can be a team project. The generality should allow for trees of differing order (d), number of levels (k), and key lengths. Begin by designing the node structure and tree file structure. Next, define and develop the lower-level procedures needed. Then write procedures for each of the four algorithms. Finally, write a test program that will exercise the four functions. This program will allow entries to be added, deleted, displayed, and a range of entries to be displayed.

9.10. For an average B-tree, is the capacity, as given by formula (9.7), closer to the best case or the worst case? Why?

9.11. According to the numbers in Figure 9.17, the difference between the number of levels searched (k^-) and the number of levels of the tree (k) decreases with increasing order (d). Explain why this is. Should this be an argument in favor of keeping d small?

10

Multi-indexed Files

10.1 DESCRIPTION AND ORGANIZATION

A *multi-indexed file* is a data file that is associated with one or more logically separate index files. Each index file contains keys and pointers that point to records in the data file, as shown in Figure 10.1. Any changes that affect key values, or data record locations, including adds and deletes, must be made on both the data file and the indexes at the same time to keep them consistent with one another. By allowing more than one index, it is possible to retrieve records by more than one key. This greatly reduces the problem of file design where multiple keys are necessary.

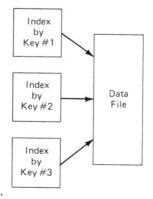

Figure 10.1 Data file with multiple indexes.

The data file may be organized by any of the methods studied in Chapters 3 through 8 or by any other convenient methods. The primary functions to be considered are adding and deleting records. Where it is frequently necessary to read the file in order by some key, the ordered relative file may result in fewer accesses because it allows full advantage to be gained from the blocking factor.

Similarly, the indexes may be of any type. However, the B-tree will be superior to other forms for most applications. Each index may be in a separate file; all of the indexes may share one file; or the indexes may occupy a separate part of the data file. All of these schemes have been used, and the difference is not important for most purposes. We will assume, in the following discussion and examples, that each index is contained within its own file.

The choice of pointers used to link each index entry to the data file is important. If the data file type is such that a record will never be relocated, the obvious choice for the pointer type is the record number. However, there are some file types, such as direct access files, where a record may be relocated because of the addition or deletion of another record. Where this situation can exist, there are two options. Either the procedures that may relocate a record must also change the pointers in all indexes whenever a record is moved, or a pointer type must be selected whose value is unaffected by relocation.

For example, both the ordered relative file and the direct access file using hashing with replacement will have records moved by additions and deletions. The ordered relative file must be reorganized to affect adds and deletes, while hashing with replacement causes records to move about in several different situations. Both file types, however, have a primary key that may be used to identify each record uniquely. These primary keys may always be used to locate the record, regardless of its physical location. In this situation, the index becomes a means of transforming one key value (a secondary key) into another key value (the primary key) with which the record can be located.

Whether the index pointers are updated when a move is made, or a primary key is used for a pointer, is a design choice. The procedures that perform adds and deletes are complicated by the former method, especially if they are designed to modify an arbitrary number of indexes. The number of accesses is increased by the need to update each index. The latter method may require additional accesses to find the data record, as when a binary search is used to locate a record in an ordered relative file.

10.1.1 Inverted Files

A distinction is sometimes made, in a multi-indexed file, between primary and secondary keys. Where this distinction is made, the data file is usually organized as a direct access file, ordered relative file, or a similar structure where the *primary key* determines the physical location of the record in the file.

When the file is structured as a sequential-chronological file, or other structures where a key does not determine the location of the record, all keyed access must employ an index. Keys that are used for indexed access are sometimes call **secondary keys**.

In an unindexed file, a value of the primary key is used to find the corresponding values of the other fields. This can be likened to a function where the primary key is the argument and the remaining fields are the values of the function. Where indexes are available on secondary keys that return the corresponding value of the primary key, they correspond to inverting the function (i. e., given the value of the function, the corresponding argument is returned). Because of this, files on which all fields are indexed are sometimes called **inverted files** or **fully inverted files**. Those where some, but not all, fields are indexed are called **partially inverted files**.

The choice of keys by which the file is indexed is completely arbitrary and will be dictated by the functions that must be exercised against the file. It may be tempting to index any and all keys that might ever be even slightly helpful. This should be resisted however, since each index will carry a penalty of overhead. Too many indexes will cause performance to suffer, especially when making additions and deletions. It may be true that fewer resources are needed to dynamically create and destroy indexes for temporary use than to maintain seldom used indexes.

10.1.2 Multilist Files

Usually when an index is constructed on a secondary key, the key value for each record is represented in the index. If there are N records in the file there are N entries in each index. Where the same key values occur in different records, it is possible to reduce the size of the index by indexing each key value only once. The index entry then points to one of several records having that value. All records sharing the same value of the key are joined together by a doubly linked list. The list is doubly linked to ease the problems of adding and deleting records to the chain. It may be linear or circular.

Several different keys may be indexed by this method in the same file. Figure 10.2 shows a small portion of an enrollment file from the student records problem. All enrollments for one student are linked together because they share a common value for the SSN field. Similarly, all enrollments for the same course are linked together.

A file in which records that share values of fields are linked together is called a **multilist file**. This file type can have several advantages over conventionally indexed files.

First, the indexes can be considerably smaller, perhaps enough so to remain entirely resident in primary memory. For example, in the student records problem with 2000 students there are 12,000 enrollments. A multilist enrollment file would require only $12,000 \div 30 = 400$ entries for a course index.

SSN Index	
123-45-6789	1
246-80-9753	2
753-19-4567	4
.	.
.	.
.	.

Course Index	
CS 150	1
EN 225	4
MA 331	2
PH 201	6
.	.
.	.
.	.

Record Number	SSN	Forward Student Pointer	Backward Student Pointer	Course	Forward Course Pointer	Backward Course Pointer	Other Data
1	123-45-6789	3	Null	CS 150	5	Null	...
2	246-80-9753	5	Null	MA 331	3	Null	...
3	123-45-6789	6	1	MA 331	8	2	...
4	753-19-4567	8	Null	EN 225	7	Null	...
5	246-80-9753	7	2	CS 150	10	1	...
6	123-45-6789	Null	3	PH 201	9	Null	...
7	246-80-9753	9	5	EN 225	Null	4	...
8	753-19-4567	10	4	MA 331	Null	3	...
9	246-80-9753	Null	7	PH 201	Null	6	...
10	753-19-4567	Null	8	CS 150	Null	5	...
.	.	.	.	.	.	.	.
.	.	.	.	.	.	.	.
.	.	.	.	.	.	.	.

Figure 10.2 A multilist enrollment file.

A second advantage is the ability to **navigate** through the file by jumping from one linked list to another at appropriate records. For example, suppose that we wish to determine the names of all students who are enrolled in both MA 331 and PH 201. One way to solve the problem is to locate one of the courses, say MA 331, in the course index of the enrollment file. The course linked list is then followed to each of the enrollments for that course. At each enrollment, we jump over to the student linked list and examine each enrollment for that student. If an enrollment record is found to contain the other course (PH 201) the student's name is added to the list. A program to perform this function could be structured as follows:

```
search index for pointer to enrollment for course 1;
WHILE more entries on linked list for course 1 DO BEGIN
        READ record of next enrollment for course 1;
        get pointer for student linked list for this enrollment;
        WHILE more entries on linked list for student DO BEGIN
                READ record of next enrollment for student;
                READ record of next enrollment for student;
                IF course of enrollment = course 2 THEN
                        add student's name to list;
        END;
END;
```

There are also several disadvantages to multilist files. An obvious one is the space required to maintain a linked list for each indexed field. Where most or all fields are linked, the space for pointers can exceed the space for the data. In some applications the cost of this storage will exceed the benefits of a multilist file.

A second disadvantage is the complexity demanded by the need to maintain the linked lists when adding, deleting, and updating records. A new record must be linked into a list for each field indexed. Similarly, a deleted record must be unlinked from each list. An updated record must be unlinked and relinked to a list for each indexed field that is changed. Moreover, some comparison must be made between the old and new values to determine which fields must be relinked.

10.2 ALGORITHMS

The algorithms for using a multi-indexed file are, for the most part, combinations of the algorithms used for the underlying indexes and data files. They should be thought of as another layer of library procedures (see Figure 10.3) that are supported by those algorithms studied earlier in this text. The choice of exactly which lower-level algorithms are used will depend on the type of data file and index used.

For example, if the data file is an ordered relative file, and the index is a B-tree, the algorithm for finding a record by a nonprimary key value might consist of a call to Algorithm 9.4 to locate the entry in the index, followed by a call to Algorithm 5.2 to perform a binary search on the data file to locate the specific record.

10.2.1 Access Method Libraries

Because the number of combinations of index types, data file types, and pointer types is so extensive, no attempt will be made to list all the possible algorithms for accessing multi-indexed files. However, these algorithms are simple to build on top of the previously studied algorithms. For the most part the lower level algorithms are combined in an obvious and straightforward manner. Complica-

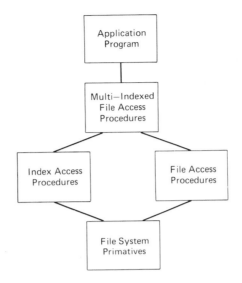

Figure 10.3 Relationship of multi-indexed file procedures to others in system.

tions will arise where the data file type is such that records may move, and record numbers are used for pointers. Care must also be exercised when updating fields that are included in one or more keys. In this situation it is necessary to delete and add back the corresponding index entries.

A library of "access method" procedures is commonly found on computer systems. The library consists of the multi-indexed file access procedures and those procedures needed to support them at the lower levels. A set of utility programs to aid in the creation and maintenance of the files and indexes is typically included as well. Such a package greatly reduces the effort needed to use multi-indexed files.

10.2.2 Conjunctive Queries

Multi-indexed files are useful not only for retrieving records by different keys, but also for searches that are specified by the values of multiple keys. Such searches are sometimes called *conjunctive queries*.

For example, suppose that a scholarship is available only for sophomores from Ohio with a grade-point average of 3.0 or more. A crude method of generating a list of eligible students would be to examine the records of all students during a sequential read of the entire file. The names of those qualified would be printed.

This might require many times more accesses than a more sophisticated search. If 10% of the students are from Ohio, 25% are sophomores, and 20% have grade point averages of 3.0 or higher, we might expect only 1 student in 200 to qualify for the scholarship. The reads of the remaining 99.5% of the records are unnecessary.

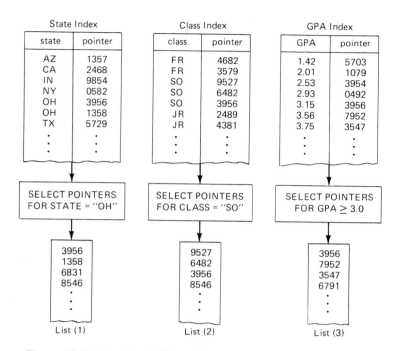

Figure 10.4 Lists of partially qualified pointers for conjunctive query.

If the fields used for the query are indexed, it is possible to determine which records qualify without having to read them. For the scholarship example, each of the three indexes (state, class, GPA) can be searched for the pointers to records that qualify by the value of one attribute. The result is three lists of record pointers as shown in Figure 10.4.

Since all three qualifications must be met, we need to find the intersection of the three sets of record pointers (i. e., those pointers common to all three lists). One method of finding the intersection is to order the lists by pointer value and merge them. Since the lists will frequently be short, an internal sort will usually be sufficient for this purpose.

After the lists are sorted, they can be processed by a merge algorithm to generate a fourth list, containing pointers to the fully qualified records. This algorithm has an added benefit when record numbers are used for pointers. The access will be ordered by record number so that any possible benefit of blocking to reduce physical accesses will also be realized.

An algorithm for finding the intersection of an indefinite number of pointer lists is shown below. *Algorithm 10.1* accepts j lists, each of indefinite length and returns a list of pointers that represents the intersection of the pointers in the j lists. The functions READ-NEXT, WRITE-NEXT, and AP-PEND are used to read and write values to the lists. The function SORT arranges all the pointers in one list into ascending order. The functions MAX and MIN return the largest and smallest pointer values respectively from the array p.

```
procedure intersect(list, j);   (* list is an array of
    (j + 1) lists, each of indefinite length.  The first
    j lists contain pointers.  The intersection of the lists
    is returned in list(j + 1).  *)
local p(1..j);  (* array to hold one value at a time from
    each list *)
FOR i := 1 TO j DO APPEND(list(i), top);   (* top is
    a named constant of pointer type whose value is greater than
    that of any pointer.  It serves as an end-of-list
    sentinel.  *)
FOR i := 1 TO j DO SORT(list(i));
        (* order the pointers in all lists *)
FOR i := 1 TO j DO READ-NEXT(list(i),p(i));
        (* read first pointer from each list *)
WHILE MAX(p) < top DO BEGIN (* loop until all matches
    have been found *)
        IF MAX(p) = MIN(p) THEN BEGIN   (* match has been
            found *)
                WRITE-NEXT(list(j+1),p(1));   (* add match to
                    output   *)
                FOR i := 1 TO j DO READ-NEXT(list(i),p(i));
                        (* refill the pointer array *)
        END ELSE (* replace entries less than MAX with next
                entries *)
                FOR i := 1 TO j DO
                        IF p(i) < MAX(p) THEN
                                READ-NEXT(list(i),p(i));
END;
```

Often queries are joined by operators other than *and*. It would be necessary to write a specific variation of Algorithm 10.1 to accommodate each query if operators other than *and* are allowed. This can be avoided by building the lists more selectively.

For example, suppose that the donor of the scholarship in the earlier example wishes to eliminate the requirement of a 3.0 grade-point average for students from Akron. The qualifying predicate becomes (state = "OH" *and* class = "SO" *and* (GPA $\geq$ 3.0 *or* city = "Akron")). This can be processed by Algorithm 10.1 without modification by adding one additional step before the merge.

The three lists are built, as before, from the state, name, and GPA indexes. A fourth list is built using entries from the city index having the value "Akron." The fourth list is then appended to the third list. Thus a sophomore from Ohio can qualify by appearing in the third list either because his GPA is high enough or because he is from Akron. A student who qualifies both by GPA and being from Akron will only appear once on the output list generated by Algorithm 10.1.

Thus, while the conjunctive query algorithm operates only with *and* logic, it may readily be adopted to any general boolean expression by placing pointers in the appropriate lists before the merge. Because indexes are generally much smaller than the underlying data files, and because either specific values or ranges of values are used to qualify the selected records, it is possible to satisfy most conjunctive queries with far fewer physical accesses by using the merge algorithm.

Where indexes are not available for all the attributes in the query predicate, conjunctive queries can still be made more efficient by use of the merge algorithm. For example, consider the case where a GPA index is not available in the scholarship problem. The GPA may not be indexed, or it may not even exist as a separate field. It may be necessary to calculate GPA by dividing credit points by credit hours each time it is needed.

In this situation, the best strategy is to use the available indexes and the merge algorithm to produce a list of pointers to partially qualified records. Each of the partially qualified records is then read and the fully qualified ones are processed.

For the scholarship example, the lists by state and class can be generated and merged. The pointers in the merged list are then used to access the records of all sophomores from Ohio. The GPA is calculated for each record and the names of those who are fully qualified are produced. By first partially qualifying the records, it is necessary to read only about 2.5% of the records in this example.

10.3 SUMMARY

Multi-indexed files are data files associated with one or more logically separate index files. Indexes contain pointers either in the form of record numbers or *primary keys*. Indexed keys are sometimes called *secondary keys*. Files with indexed attributes are sometimes referred to as *inverted files*. Those with all attributes indexed are *fully inverted* while those with some, but not all, attributes indexed are *partially inverted*.

Multilist files index each attribute value only once. Records that share an attribute value are joined together by a linked list. By jumping from one linked list to another, it is possible to *navigate* through a multilist file to locate the desired data.

Access methods are libraries of procedures and utilities that combine data file and index accessing procedures in a convenient package.

Conjunctive queries are those that specify the characteristics of the desired records by values of multiple keys. Such queries can be processed efficiently by using the key indexes to compile lists of *partially qualified records*. These lists can then be *merged* to yield a list of *fully qualified records*.

By using an efficient type of index structure, and building indexes for several different keys, it will be possible in most cases to reduce the statistics for an application to order $N\log(N)$. For applications that require any kind of ordering, this is the best order of statistics that can be attained.

This dramatic improvement does not mean that it is no longer necessary to give attention to the more mundane design factors such as blocking factor and data file structure. These elements will affect the constants of the system statistics just as they always have. Carefully made choices will still have a major benefit on the final performance of the system.

The use of the best design possible will always be important. The improvements in file design over the years have allowed applications to move from batch only environments to on-line environments that are now accepted as the norm. Further improvements will decrease response time, allow larger applications to be implemented, and require less hardware to support them. As a case in point, applications are routinely implemented today on microcomputers that would have required a medium sized batch system two decades ago. While a significant part of the change is due to improvements in the hardware, the improvements in the file structures and algorithms have been equally important in facilitating this change. The multi-indexed file represents the pinnacle of development for single data file applications. Further improvement is possible only by introduction of the concepts of databases. These are explored in Chapter 11.

10.4 THE STUDENT RECORDS PROBLEM

The decision tree for this problem has now become a very thick and tall bush. The number of options has increased at each decision point, and decisions must be made about both the data file and the indexes. Exhaustive analysis is not feasible, and intuitive judgments must be applied.

As a starting point, we might consider all the previously derived solutions for this problem. The most attractive solution so far is that seen in Section 6.6.1, which used a student record file organized as a direct access file using hashing with replacement. Besides having the best statistics of all the solutions, this file allows access directly by one key, and it is self organizing; we do not have to reorganize it periodically or otherwise manage the placement of records within the file.

The course record counterpart is found in Section 6.6.3. The same file organization is used, but the record and key are different. Both of these solutions worked well except for one or two functions which required accesses of order M^2. With the use of indexes, it should be possible to eliminate the M^2 statistics in favor of more reasonable ones. The penalty will be in the form of additional accesses required for the indexes and some additional file space for the indexes.

10.4.1 The Student Record File

The data file used here will be exactly as described in Section 6.6.1. The key will be the SSN and the blocking factor is nine. The file will be filled to about 90% of capacity, which from Figure 6.10, will result in an average of 1.12 physical accesses per retrieval.

There are two indexes needed to allow all functions to be performed in the most effective manner. The problems with the solution of Section 6.6.1 occurred in the roster and grade input functions, where access by course was required. Obviously, an index by course will be most helpful in those functions. The requirement to produce the rosters in alphabetic order can be met if the course index uses a key consisting of the course followed by the name. A traversal of the portion of this index that contains entries for one course will result in all students in that course being accessed in alphabetic order by name. In addition, the requirement to have the grade reports produced in order by name can be met with the aid of an index by name. This same index could also serve as a secondary method of accessing a student's record if the SSN should not be available.

The indexes will be of order $d = 50$. This is an arbitrary decision but results in reasonable parameters. The size of the course-name index nodes will be as follows:

$$100 \times (7 + 30) + 100 \times 9 + 101 \times 2 = 4802 \text{ bytes}$$

where the key consists of two fields: course, 7 bytes, and name, 30 bytes; and the data pointer is the SSN of 9 bytes. The tree pointers are 2 bytes each.

The number of levels, as determined by formula (9.8) for the average case, will be 2.17 for $M = 6 \times 2000$, and 2.54 for $M = 6 \times 10,000$. Rounded up, these give expected values for k of 3 for the index. The usual practice of keeping the root node in primary memory at all times will be assumed in calculating the statistics.

The name index will also be of order $d = 50$. The key is shorter since only the name field is included. The index node size is also shorter:

$$100 \times 30 + 100 \times 9 + 101 \times 2 = 4102 \text{ bytes}$$

The number of levels, as determined by formula (9.8) for the average case, will be 1.76 for $M = 2000$ and 2.13 for $M = 10,000$. Rounded up, these give expected values for k of 2 and 3, respectively, for the index.

An assumption similar to that of Section 6.6 is made: that the student record file and the associated name index have already been created before registration begins. Since no students are added or deleted by any of the functions, there is no maintenance needed on these objects.

Registration is performed by directly accessing each student's record and adding the enrollments required. The record is then written back out. Following this, the course index must be updated once for each of the six courses for which the average student enrolls. To find the node in which the new entry is added requires $k - 1$ physical accesses, since the root is already in primary memory. After the node is updated, it must be rewritten, requiring one more access for a total of k physical accesses.

Changes of schedule are performed in a very similar manner; the difference being that an average of three courses are dropped and two courses are added. Each of these requires the appropriate updating of the course index.

Rosters are produced by using the FIND-RANGE procedure of Algorithm 9.5 to search for all students enrolled in a given course. As the tree is traversed, the pointer to each enrolled student will be retrieved so that the students are found in alphabetic order by name. Most of the time, all students for one course will be found in one leaf node of the B-tree index. However, about $30 \div 1.5d$, or 40% of the time, a course will overlap between two nodes. In these cases it is necessary to read an additional node. Thus the average traversal for this function will require $k - 1 + 0.4 = k - 0.6$ accesses.

Grades are entered by nearly the same processes as producing rosters. The only difference is that the data record is updated after the grade is entered.

The grade reports are produced by traversing the entire name index and retrieving each student's data record in order. The index will contain an average of $M/1.5d$ nodes, each of which must be read exactly once.

The total statistics for this solution are shown in Figure 10.5. The total is of order $M \cdot k$. However, since k is a logarithmic function of M, this is equivalent to the total being of order $M \cdot \log(M)$. This represents a considerable improvement over the order M^2 statistics seen in Section 6.6.1. In addition, the numbers are much improved, especially for the larger values of M, as might be expected.

10.4.2 The Course Record File

The data file for the course record file will be that described in Section 6.6.3. The key for this file is the course, and the blocking factor is 1, owing to the very large record size. The file will be about 90% filled, which will result in an average of 1.45 physical accesses per retrieval.

It was possible to perform all functions efficiently with the file of Section 6.6.3 except production of grade reports. The addition of an index by name would greatly simplify this function. The data pointer would be the course field.

Again a B-tree of order $d = 50$ will be used. The number of levels will be 3 for both M = 2000 and M = 10,000 since there are six courses indexed for each student. There will be a small difference in the space required for each node, since the course field (7 bytes) is used for the data file pointer instead of the SSN (9 bytes). The node size is

$$100 \times 30 + 100 \times 7 + 101 \times 2 = 3902 \text{ bytes}$$

Function	File	Algorithm	Physical Accesses per Record	Number of Records	Mult.	Total
Registration	Data	6.11	1.12	1	M	$1.12M$
	Data	Update	1	1	M	$1.00M$
	Course index	8.2	k	6	M	$6Mk$
Change	Data	6.11	1.12	1	M	$1.12M$
	Data	Update	1	1	M	$1.00M$
	Course index,	8.3	k	3	M	$3Mk$
	Course index	8.2	k	2	M	$2Mk$
Rosters	Course index	8.5	$k - 0.6$	1	$2M/5$	$0.4Mk - 0.24M$
	Data	6.11	1.12	30	$2M/5$	$13.44M$
Grades in	Course index	8.5	$k - 0.6$	1	$M/5$	$0.2Mk - 0.12M$
	Data	6.11	1.12	30	$M/5$	$6.72M$
	Data	Update	1	30	$M/5$	$6.00M$
Grades out	Name index	8.5	1	$M/1.5d$	1	$0.013M$
	Data	6.11	1.12	M	1	$1.12M$
Total accesses						$11.6Mk + 31.17M$

Note: For $M = 2000$, $B = 9$ $d = 50$, $k = 3$, accesses = 131,940; for $M = 10,000$, $B = 9$ $d = 50$, $k = 3$, accesses = 659,700 (M, number of students; B, blocking factor; d, order of tree; k, number of levels).

Figure 10.5 Function analysis for student record file.

Initially, all records will be present in the course file, one per course. There are no enrollments in the course file, and the name index is empty, since there are no students enrolled.

Registration is done by accessing each course record as each student enrolls. As each enrollment is entered, an entry must be added to the name index linking the student's name with the course.

Changes are made by accessing and updating the record of each affected course. The corresponding changes must also be made in the name index.

As before, rosters are produced very simply by accessing the record for the course desired. Only a single record is retrieved for each roster produced.

The grade input function is very similar to the roster function, except that the course record is updated after the grades for the course are entered.

The name index, which has been only a burden so far, is used to produce the grade reports. The entire index is traversed, resulting in the course records for each student being accessed. Each course record will be accessed once for each student enrolled in the course, for an average of 30 accesses per course record.

The total statistics are summarized in Figure 10.6. Again the total is of order $M \cdot \log(M)$ since k is a logarithmic function of M.

Function	File	Algorithm	Physical Accesses per Record	Number of Records	Mult.	Total
Registration	Data	6.11	1.45	6	M	8.70M
	Data	Update	1	6	M	6.00M
	Name index	8.2	k	6	M	6Mk
Change	Data	6.11	1.45	5	M	7.25M
	Data	Update	1	5	M	5.00M
	Name index	8.3	k	3	M	3/Mk
	Name index	8.2	k	2	M	2Mk
Rosters	Data	6.11	1.45	1	2M/5	0.58M
Grades in	Data	6.11	1.45	1	M/5	0.29M
	Data	Update	1	1	M/5	0.20M
Grades out	Name index	8.5	1	6M/1.5d	1	0.08M
	Data	6.11	1.45	M/5	30	8.70M
Total accesses						11Mk + 36.80M

Note: For $M = 2000$, $B = 1$ $d = 50$, $k = 3$, accesses = 139,600; for $M = 10,000$, $B = 1$ $d = 50$, $k = 3$, accesses = 698,000 (M, number of students; B, blocking factor; d, order of tree; k, number of levels).

Figure 10.6 Function analysis for course record file.

10.4.3 The Enrollment Record File

There is no obvious structure for the enrollment record data file. There is no single field that can serve as a primary key. Consequently, the direct access file cannot be used unless a key is created by combining two or more fields. As a result of these considerations, a relative file will be used for the enrollment data.

A bit map, as described in Chapter 3, will be used to determine which slots are occupied and which are vacant. Since the entire bit map for a file of 60,000 records requires only 7500 bytes, it may remain in primary memory while the file is open. Consequently, no accesses will be tallied for the bit map.

Blocking in the data file will have a negligible effect on the number of physical accesses. This is because the data records will always be accessed by record number and sequential reads are never performed. This characteristic is unique to this particular problem and should not be assumed for other problems. The considerations of storage efficiency are still valid and care must still be exercised in choosing the blocking factor.

Three indexes are required to allow the appropriate access for all of the functions. An index by SSN is needed to access enrollments by student for the change of schedule. A course index is needed for the roster and grade input functions. As before, we will use a key consisting of the course and name so that these functions will be done in alphabetic order. Finally, an index by name is needed to produce the grade reports in alphabetic order. All three indexes will index each of the $6M$ enrollments. The data pointer will simply be the record number, which is assumed to be 2 bytes long. The SSN index will be of order $d = 100$ while the other two will be of order $d = 50$. The difference is due to the shorter key for the SSN, which allows more entries to be fit into a reasonable-sized node. The node size for the SSN index is

$$200 \times 9 + 200 \times 2 + 201 \times 2 = 2602 \text{ bytes}$$

The course index nodes are

$$100(7 + 30) + 100 \times 2 + 101 \times 2 = 4102 \text{ bytes}$$

While the nodes for the name index are

$$100 \times 30 + 100 \times 2 + 101 \times 2 = 3402 \text{ bytes}$$

The course and name indexes will require three levels for both the 2000 and 10,000 student populations, as has been calculated in earlier examples. The SSN index will require only two levels for 2000 students and three levels for 10,000 students owing to its greater order. Formula (9.8) yields values for k of 1.87 and 2.19, respectively, for the two populations in the SSN index.

Both the data file and the indexes will be empty initially. They are filled as enrollments are added.

The registration function is performed by adding each enrollment to the data file, using the bit map to determine where empty slots are available. As each enrollment is added, it is necessary to insert the corresponding entry into each of the three indexes, using Algorithm 9.2.

The changes are performed by using the SSN index to locate all the enrollments for the student. Since the average student is enrolled in six courses and the average leaf node for this index will have 150 entries, the odds of having to look in more than one leaf node for all of the enrollments for one student is very small. Similarly, the odds are very high that this index can be updated by just writing back the one leaf node. Deletions in the data file are done by flagging the slot empty in the bit map. Additions are made as they were for registration. The adds and deletions must be reflected by updating the course and name indexes as well as the SSN index.

Rosters are produced by traversing the course index and accessing each enrollment for the required course. Since the key includes the name, the enrollments will be accessed in alphabetic order by name.

Grades are entered by the same process that the rosters were produced, except that the data record is updated after each grade is entered.

The grade reports are produced in alphabetic order by traversing the name index. The entire name index tree must be read once. As each enrollment pointer is encountered in the index, the corresponding record is read and processed.

Function	File	Algorithm	Physical Accesses per Record	Number of Records	Mult.	Total
Registration	Data	4.1	1	6	M	$6M$
	SSN index	8.2	$k1$	6	M	$6Mk1$
	Course index	8.2	$k2$	6	M	$6Mk2$
	Name index	8.2	$k2$	6	M	$6Mk2$
Change	SSN index	8.5	$k1 - 1$	1	M	$Mk1 - M$
	SSN index	Update	1	1	M	M
	Data	3.2	1	3	M	$3M$
	Data	4.1	1	2	M	$2M$
	Course index	8.3	$k2$	3	M	$3Mk2$
	Course index	8.2	$k2$	2	M	$2Mk2$
	Name index	8.3	$k2$	3	M	$3Mk2$
	Name index	8.2	$k2$	2	M	$2Mk2$
Rosters	Course index	8.5	$k2 - 0.6$	1	$2M/5$	$0.4Mk2 - 0.24M$
	Data	4.1	1	30	$2M/5$	$12M$
Grades in	Course index	8.5	$k2 - 0.6$	1	$M/5$	$0.2Mk2 - 0.12M$
	Data	4.1	1	30	$M/5$	$6M$
	Data	Update	1	30	$M/5$	$6M$
Grades out	Name index	8.5	1	$M/1.5d$	1	$0.08M$
	Data	4.1	1	$6M$	1	$6M$
Total accesses						$7Mk1 + 22.6Mk2 + 40.72M$

Note: For $M = 2000$, $k1 = 2$ $k2 = 3$, accesses $= 245,040$; for $M = 10,000$, $k1 = 3$, $k2 = 3$, accesses $= 1,295,200$ (M, number of students; k, number of levels).

Figure 10.7 Function analysis for enrollment record file.

The statistics for the enrollment record file are shown in Figure 10.7. As before, the total is of order $M \cdot \log(M)$. The numbers are higher than the previous two examples because there are many more records in this file than in the others. This not only creates more accesses to the data file, but also requires more entries in the indexes with their corresponding accesses.

10.4.4 Critique

With the introduction of the multi-indexed file, we have found solutions for the first time that are not of order N^2. This has allowed a very dramatic reduction in the number of accesses required for the system. The numeric solutions are more than 10 times better for the case with 10,000 students than any of the previous ones. The improvement in the course record file was even more dramatic with the reduction in accesses exceeding the best previous solution by a factor of more than 30, to make this file competitive for the first time.

That these improvements are possible is no surprise when the difference is in functions of order $N \cdot \log(N)$ compared with function of order N^2. Even though there may be as many as four files to access (including the indexes), the improvement in the order of the statistics is paramount.

Of the three solutions developed, the student record file is still probably the best. It will require less space than the course record file and its statistics will be better until the number of students increases to a very large number. The enrollment record file simply has too many records which are accessed individually to be competitive.

It must be noted that because the student and course record files can be accessed directly by key, that one index has been eliminated for each of them. This was not true for the enrollment record file, which is the reason it has more indexes than the others. Most "access method" packages do not allow the freedom to select the data file type. Consequently, when using these packages, it will usually be necessary to develop a solution similar to that done here for the enrollment record file, indexing all of the keys.

10.5 PROBLEMS

10.1. List all of the file types for which it is true that data records, once added to the file,
  (a)   never move until deleted.
  (b)   may be moved as part of normal file maintenance.

10.2. Write an algorithm to add a record to a file when the indexes are B-trees and the data file is
  (a)   sequential-chronological (record number pointer).
  (b)   ordered relative (primary key pointer).
  (c)   direct access using hashing with replacement (primary key pointer).

  Use calls to any procedures that contain algorithms previously studied as you build this higher-level function.

10.3. The navigation example in Section 10.1.2 arbitrarily selected one of the two courses to begin the search. This does not always result in the most efficient search. Assume that MA 331 has 50 enrollments, PH 201 has 20 enrollments, and students average 5 enrollments each. Compare the total number of enroll-ment records read when the search begins with MA 331 with the number read when it begins with PH 201. What general rule can be concluded from this ex-ample?

10.4. Devise an algorithm with the same parameters as Algorithm 10.1 which finds the union of the lists instead of the intersection. Note that the union operation requires each pointer value to appear in the output list exactly once regardless of the number of input lists in which it appears. This algorithm could be used for queries where the parts of the predicate are joined by the "*or*" operator. Why is union not as useful as intersection in this application?

10.5. Calculate the expected fraction of records accessed by a conjunctive query where the predicate has four qualification joined by the "***and***" operator and the fraction of records that satisfy each partial qualification are 0.3, 0.1, 0.5, and 0.25. Assume that the qualifying attribute values are independent of one another.

10.6. What proportion of the file accesses is caused by accesses to indexes rather than to the data file for
  (a)   the solution of Section 10.4.1?
  (b)   the solution of Section 10.4.2?
  (c)   the solution of Section 10.4.3?

10.7. The indexes for both the student record file and the course record file were of three levels.
  (a)   By how much would the number of physical accesses be reduced for these two solutions if the indexes were of two levels?
  (b)   The B-tree indexes would need to be of what order (*d*) for the level of the trees to be reduced to two for 2000 students?

10.8. Develop two solutions to the student records problem that are substantially dif-ferent from those in Section 10.4. Compare your solutions to those of Section 10.4 by means of a graph similar to Figure 5.7. Be sure to include the space required for the indexes in your comparison.

10.9. Develop a solution for the computer equipment problem described in Section B.2. Be prepared to defend the choices made in the design.

10.10. Develop a solution for the parts supply problem described in Section B.3. Be prepared to defend the choices made in the design.

11

Database Systems

11.1 DATABASE CONCEPTS

The solutions found for the student record problem in Chapter 10 are about as good as can be found when using a single data file. There are some obvious problems still remaining with the system and some equally obvious improvements that can be made if the data is divided between several files. Such multiple file solutions have been used nearly as long as files have been used.

Over the years many helpful concepts have been developed for such multiple file systems. These concepts, together with tools to apply them, have evolved into the database systems that are commonly used today. There is no rule that one must have a database system to use database concepts. It is feasible to implement a database using tools no more sophisticated than those already presented in this book. The database system only makes the implementation easier.

However, there are many problems that can occur in a system with multiple files. Systematic methods and concepts have been developed to avoid most of these problems so that the result is a flexible and efficient database. These concepts are fundamental not only to the understanding of database systems, but also to the effective use of file systems. Thus the first section of this chapter is devoted to an exposition of these concepts.

11.1.1 Eliminating Redundancy

All of the solutions for the student record problem have suffered from *redundancy*. For example, the student record must contain all of the data for each course for which the student is enrolled. This course data is repeated an average of 30 times. All but one of the 30 occurrences is redundant data. The other designs also required redundant data. For example, both student and course data are repeated in the enrollment record file.

There are four major problems with the redundancy of data. First, and most obvious, is the waste of space. Every time data is repeated, it requires wasted space to store the repetition. This can add up to a considerable amount, even the majority of the space required for an application.

Second, redundant data requires that multiple updates are required to change a simple data item. For example, in the student records problem with the student record file, a change in the room for a course will require that the records of all students enrolled in the course be located and updated. This will require an average of 30 times as many disk accesses as would be needed if the course data was stored in only one place.

The realization that multiple updates are necessary leads to the third problem with redundancy of data: inconsistency. When there are many supposedly identical copies of the same data, there is always the possibility that they are not identical. There are many ways that this can happen, ranging from human error to program bugs to machine failures. To quote the often-cited law of Murphy: "If something can go wrong, it will go wrong, at the worst possible time." This is probably the worst aspect of redundancy and the one that is most important to eliminate.

Fourth, redundancy usually also leads to *insertion and deletion anomalies*. These occur when the first entry of a set of (potentially) redundant data is added, or the last copy is deleted. Suppose, for example, that the last student enrolled in a course drops the course. With the student record file, deleting the last enrollment also deletes *all* the information about that course that is in the file. The reverse problem occurs when enrolling the first student for the course. The data needed to describe the course does not exist anywhere within the system. Such anomalies are usually the result of not formally recognizing an entity in the structure of the data.

The problems of redundancy and anomalous behavior can be eliminated through the process of normalizing the data. This will be examined in the next subsection.

11.1.2 Normalization

When there is more than one file in a data system, the problem of organizing the data becomes much more complex. It is helpful to have a *data model* of how the data is organized into files and how these files are related to each other. The model includes a list of the fields in each record type, the keys used to access the records, and how the records in one file are related to records in other files. The data model not only serves as documentation for the system, but it is essential to the system designer's being able to think clearly about the data organization and subsequent processing.

Normalization is the systematic, reversible transformation of a data model to remove logical structures which result in anomalous behavior. The result of normalization is a data model in which redundancy has been greatly reduced or eliminated, and in which the nonkey data items are functionally dependent on their keys. To state it another way, normalization is the process of discovering the entities in a system and the proper keys for each entity.

When a system is normalized, several important benefits are derived. First, as noted above, redundancy is greatly reduced or eliminated. Where it is not completely eliminated, it is usually for reasons of efficiency and is clearly obvious. Second, since entities are separated, the anomalous behavior is eliminated. Third, because there are no complex hidden relationships in the data, the system is much more flexible. It is usually possible to add new functions to the system without having to restructure the model, and hence the data, to accommodate them. It becomes relatively simple to use ad hoc queries that were not anticipated when the system was designed.

Normalization is done in a series of steps, each of which leaves the model in a specific "normal form." Each normal form includes all the constraints of the previous normal forms, so they must be applied in strict order. The normal forms usually applied include first normal form, second normal form, third normal form, Boyce/Codd normal form, fourth normal form, and fifth normal form. Typically, most transformations are achieved by third normal form and the remaining forms are increasingly subtle and relevant to fewer and fewer systems.

Normalization is properly the topic of a course in databases and will be described here only briefly. For purposes of this example, we will use the student records problem with some additional data. Let us assume that in addition to the data described in Appendix B, the course information includes the instructor's office and telephone numbers. In addition, let us separate the section number from the remainder of the course number and treat it as a separate attribute.

While we could begin with any complete model of the data and arrive at the same normalized model, for this example we begin with the student record as shown in Figure 11.1. The underlined attributes indicate keys, and the ellipsis indicates repeated attributes.

First normal form (1NF) requires that every attribute must be single valued. This means that repeating groups are not permitted in a model that is in first normal form. Where repeating groups exist, it is a sign that there is another entity "hiding" in the record. The hidden entity must be broken out into a separate file. For example, the student record has a repeating group that consists of course and enrollment information that is repeated for each enrollment. The student record, if it is in first normal form, may contain only student information. The other data is removed to separate files. The result is seen in Figure 11.2. The arrow indicates that each student record is related in some manner to any number of enrollments.

SSN, name, address, birthdate
Course, section, course title, instructor, office, telephone, time, room, credit, grade, absences
Course, section, course title, instructor, office, telephone, time, room, credit, grade, absences
Course, section, course title, instructor, office, telephone, time, room, credit, grade, absences
Course, section, course title, instructor, office, telephone, time, room, credit, grade, absences

.
.
.

Figure 11.1 Original student record.

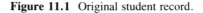

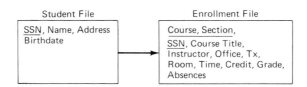

Figure 11.2 Student records problem in 1NF.

Second normal form (2NF) requires that the model be in 1NF, and that attributes that are not part of any key may not be "partially dependent" on any key. This means that if the same attribute value always occurs in combination with the same value for part of the key, the model is not in 2NF. For example, in Figure 11.2 it may be seen that description, time, instructor, room, office, and telephone will all have the same values whenever course and section have the same value. This means that these attributes are partially dependent on the course–section part of the key. The solution is to remove these attributes, with their key(s) to another file as shown in Figure 11.3.

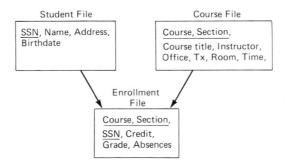

Figure 11.3 Student records problem after first change for 2NF.

This still does not leave the model in 2NF, however, because description will always have the same value whenever course has the same value. In other words, the description attribute is partially dependent on the key. Again, this attribute is removed, with its key, to another file as shown in Figure 11.4. This model is now in 2NF.

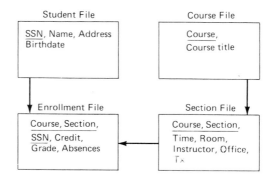

Figure 11.4 Student records problem in 2NF.

Putting the model in 2NF does two things. First, like 1NF, it forces us to recognize entities that were previously mixed in with other entities. Second, it helps to eliminate redundancy. There is no need for the time, room, instructor, office, and telephone attributes to be repeated for each student enrolled in the section. Nor is it of any help to have the course description repeated for each section. By bringing the model into 2NF, these redundancies have been eliminated, and two more entities have been identified.

Third normal form (3NF) requires that the model be in 2NF and that attributes that are not part of any key be independent from each other. The model of Figure 11.4 is not in 3NF because the same values of instructor, office, and telephone always go together. Instructor is the proper key for this entity, and office and telephone are nonkey attributes. Like 2NF, 3NF helps to eliminate redundancy and recognize entities. Figure 11.5 shows the resulting model in 3NF.

This model could have been arrived at regardless of the starting model. As long as the attributes are consistently defined, the outcome should always be the same.

It is worth asking when an attribute becomes an entity. As was discussed in Chapter 1, this is a matter upon which reasonable people can disagree. As a rough rule of thumb, it can be noted that entities seldom have a single attribute. For example, the entity of "instructor," which was discovered in putting the model into 3NF, would not exist if it were not for the attributes "office" and "telephone." There would be no redundancy due to the values of this triplet being repeated, and no need for the last transformation. Similarly, if "description" were different for each section, there would be no separation of course and section. They would remain one entity.

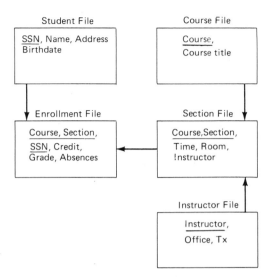

Figure 11.5 Student records problem in 3NF.

The normalization process has helped identify the entities and their relationships. While some people have, through long and costly experience, developed a good intuitive sense of normalization (often without any formal knowledge of normalization), there is no substitute for working through the formal process when designing the data model.

11.1.3 Entity Relationships

A problem is created by separating the entities into different files. It is not automatically clear how entities of different types are related to each other. For example, when the enrollments were kept in a student record, the association between student and enrollment was implicit in the placement of the enrollment. When the enrollments exist in another file, as in Figure 11.5, there needs to be some way to associate each enrollment with the corresponding student and section.

Entity relationships, or *associations* as they are sometimes called, can be classified as being of one of three types: 1:1, 1:N, and M:N. The 1:1 relationship means that exactly one of each of two types of entities are mutually associated (see Figure 11.6). For example, husbands and wives (legally) have a one-to-one relationship.

The one-to-many or 1:N relationship is the most common. This means that the first entity may have any number of the second entities associated with it, but each of the second entities must have exactly one of the first associated (see Figure 11.7). For example, a student may have many enrollments, or none, while an enrollment must be associated with exactly one student.

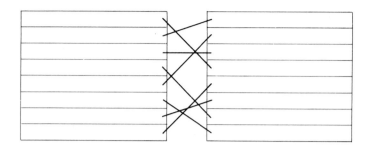

Figure 11.6 One-to-one entity relationships.

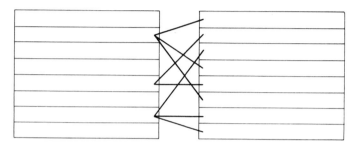

Figure 11.7 One-to-many entity relationships.

The many-to-many or *M:N* association is usually a symptom of a data model that is not fully normalized (see Figure 11.8). For example, there may appear to be such a relationship between students and courses. This would occur only if the intermediate entity, in this case the enrollment, has not been recognized. Sometimes it seems artificial to create such an intermediate entity. However, it nearly always happens that once such an entity has been discovered, it has other attributes. The enrollment, for example, has attributes of credits, grade, and absences.

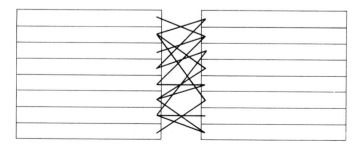

Figure 11.8 Many-to-many entity relationships.

There are three methods commonly used to implement the association of entities in database systems. The first is to use pointers in the record of each entity that point to related entities. This method has difficulty with the $1:N$ relationship since there is no way to know how much space must be reserved for the variable number of pointers required for the first entity. This can be mitigated by using a single pointer in the first entity to one record of the second entity, and maintaining linked lists within the file of the second entity to join all of the N records together. This makes the second file a multilist file as discussed in Chapter 10.

Databases that use pointers are referred to as ***network data model*** databases. Network models are commonly diagrammed with arrows shown to represent the entity relationships. The arrow points from the "1" entity to the "N" entity. For example, the arrow linking students to enrollments in Figure 11.5 points from student to enrollment because one student is linked to many enrollments.

For a variety of reasons, most network model database systems do not permit $M:N$ relationships. They are designed to implement $1:N$ relationships, with $1:1$ relationships being a special case of the $1:N$ type.

The network model databases are relatively efficient because access to related entities can be made directly, using the record number. Chains of pointers can also be followed with equal ease. The entity relations must be explicitly declared in network systems, and where pointers have not been declared, much less efficient access methods must be used. Figure 11.9 illustrates two of the files from Figure 11.5 joined by pointers and chains.

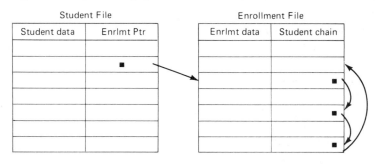

Figure 11.9   One student linked to four enrollments by pointers (network model).

A second method does not require that associations be anticipated, but allows entities to be associated together based on the value(s) of common attributes. For example, a student may be associated with an enrollment based on their both sharing a common value for the attribute SSN. This requires that both entities carry the same attribute, which is a form of redundancy. Here, however, the redundancy is necessary to connect the two entities. Logically, it replaces the pointer that was used in the network model. Databases that use this method are referred to as ***relational data model*** databases. Unlike the network model, it is not necessary to anticipate which entities may be associated. However, it is necessary to have enough information in the attributes of each entity type so that the associations can be made. It is frequently helpful to have an index on each attribute that is likely to be used for such associations, since the alternative is to exhaustively search the file when associations are made. An association between students and enrollments that is based on common values of SSN is illustrated in Figure 11.10.

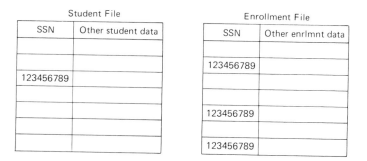

Figure 11.10 One student linked to enrollments by values of SSN (relational model).

The third method of associating entities is to store the records for the related entities together in a common file. Entities that are associated together are physically stored together, usually in the same block. Although this method can be very efficient in some applications, there are several difficulties with it. First, the associations must be anticipated when the database is built. It is not feasible to add associations afterward. Second, there is a limit to the manner in which relations can be established due to the way they are stored. Specifically, all entity relations must be connected in a tree structure. For this reason such systems are referred to as *hierarchical data model* systems. They tend to be very inflexible but enjoy excellent efficiency in limited applications. The student record and course record of Section 3.6 are essentially hierarchical.

Most modern systems are based on either the network or the relational model. The hierarchical model can be viewed logically as a subset of the network model, although they are usually implemented differently. Some systems combine features of the network and relational models so that the efficiency of the network model and the flexibility of the relational model may both be enjoyed.

11.1.4 Data Abstraction

Data abstraction means that details of the physical storage of the data are hidden from the user. This is true even when the user is a programmer. There are three motives for abstraction.

First, many of the details of storage such as file maintenance, index maintenance, and pointer maintenance are low level matters that are only distractions to a user working at a higher level. If the programmer or other user does not have to be concerned with these details, he is free to concentrate on the higher-level design issues. Thus a user of a database is seldom forced to think about record layouts, blocking factors, or pointer values. The database system will automatically calculate appropriate values and designs for these from a higher-level description of the data. Such a higher-level description is called a *schema*. These can be of many different forms and are usually implemented by means of a ***data definition language*** (DDL).

A second reason for data abstraction in database systems is ***data independence***. This means that changes in the description of the data at a lower level do not cause a change in the description of the data at a higher level. Consequently, programs that were compatible with the data before a change may still be compatible after the change. For example, suppose that the solution to the student records problem that was developed in Section 6.6.1 had been implemented. Subsequently, it was determined that the instructor's office and telephone numbers should be included in the course data. This would require that the repeating group of course and enrollment data must be expanded, resulting in a longer record size, different placement of the fields in the record, and probably a different blocking factor. All programs that access the file would have to be modified to accommodate the larger record. Had there been data independence, the only programs that would have needed modification would be those that needed to access the new fields. The other programs would continue to use the older, high-level descriptions of the data. The database system would mediate between this logical view and the physical storage.

The third reason for data abstraction is that it allows different users of the data to have different logical views of the data. Separate descriptions of the data may be provided to different users. Each user sees only that portion of the data that is relevant to his applications or functions. These separate descriptions are variously called ***subschemas*** or ***views***, depending on their scope. For example, an instructor may have a view of the data of the student records problem that appears to be a separate file of enrollments for each course the instructor teaches. Each such "logical file" contains the name, SSN, credits, grade, and absences for each student in the course. The other data in the database is hidden from the instructor. Moreover, the instructor is able only to change the grades and absences. The other fields are "read only" in this view. The fact that the data in each such view may reside in five different physical files, as shown in Figure 11.5, is totally hidden from the instructor's view. Such differing logical views not only allow data security to be enforced automatically but can also greatly simplify the appearance of the database for users.

It is not easy to implement data abstraction in an efficient manner. Frequently, the most difficult problems, both in the design of a database and in the design of database systems, arise from the conflict between data independence and efficiency.

11.2 DATABASE SYSTEMS

A *database system* is an aggregation of languages, programs, procedures, methods, and documentation that aid in the implementation of databases. It is supported by the operating system and file system. It in turn supports application programs and end users by performing functions on the physical data. There is considerable variety among database systems, both in the methods they use and the services they provide. The following descriptions cover the most common features of database systems. Not all systems will have all of these features, and many systems will have features not described here. However, these are probably the most important features needed to understand database systems.

11.2.1 Data Definition Language

The schema, or description of a database, must be stated in some regular form so that the database system can process it. A few systems have used extensions of some common programming language, such as COBOL or PL/1. Most, however, have elected to define a new language especially for the database system. These data definition languages (DDLs) are declarative in nature. They describe the data and how it is to be organized, but do not describe operations performed on the data.

There are about half-a-dozen aspects of a database that are usually described in the schema. The order of these is not important and varies considerably from system to system. Each will be described briefly here.

The most elementary part of a schema is used to describe each data item or field that appears in the database. The description includes the name and data type. Frequently, it will also allow more detailed descriptions such as external format, range of allowed values, and security provisions. Since any given data item may appear in several files, many systems allow it to be described once and referred to by name thereafter.

The data items are organized together into records. The records are, in turn, organized into files. A part of the schema contains the name of each file and a list of the data items that the records of that file contain. While we would prefer to think of these files as holding entities, there is nothing in most database systems to enforce normalization. The files may be declared to hold any combination of attributes, whether or not it is reasonable. In relational systems, files are sometimes referred to as tables and records as tuples or rows. The file descriptions include the capacity of each file.

The entity relationships are described in a variety of ways. In hierarchical systems, these associations are very tight and must be made with extreme care. They will result in the physical placement of differing types of records into the same file so that entities that are associated will be in close proximity. In network systems, the associations are reflected in the pointers that are declared to link the entities together. Since space must be allocated for the pointers, these associations become an integral part of the physical database. The entity relationships in relational systems are usually reflected in the indexes that are specified for the entities. Associations are not explicitly defined in relational systems as they are in the other models. However, the linkages will usually be very inefficient unless there are appropriate indexes available to help the system make the connections. For example, it would be appropriate to index the enrollment file by both course-section and SSN if the database of Figure 11.5 were implemented as a relational database.

Views and subschemas range from nonexistent in some systems to a major part of the schema in others. Where subschemas are used, they generally follow the syntax used for the main schema and are constrained to be a subset of the main schema. Views are frequently subsets of either a single file or several files that are joined by entity relationships. In either case a view usually appears as a single logical file. A subschema may include one or more views.

Schema *security* provisions may commonly be invoked at several different levels. Frequently, users are assigned to sets or classes of users. Each user class is allowed access to data items, files, views, and subschemas as is necessary. Access may be defined as read only, append only, read/write, update, delete, or combinations thereof. Users are usually required to enter passwords, which may be part of the schema, to verify their identity. At other times, user classes may be defined by the terminals used or by means outside the database system. It is essential for good security that the operating system also have some means of assuring that the database cannot be compromised by access to the underlying files by direct methods such as using the file primitives.

11.2.2 Data Manipulation Language

Where the DDL describes the data in a database, the ***data manipulation language*** (DML) is used to perform the operations on the database. While there are exceptions, most systems have two versions of DML.

One version is designed to be used from applications programs. It may take the form either of calls to procedures that perform specific functions on the database, or of extensions to the programming language. When the latter form is used, there is usually a preprocessor that changes the language extensions into procedure calls. The functions performed by the procedures are typically those of manipulating records, such as reading, writing, updating, or locating. Some functions allow operations on entire files and include indexing and copying subsets. Other functions retrieve information about the schema, file occupancy, and other database information.

The other version of the DML is usually in the form of a "fourth generation" or "query" language. This is a higher level language where operations are typically performed on entire files or views rather than on single records. Many of these languages are simple enough that nonprogrammers can formulate their own transactions. They are very powerful tools, and when used carelessly, can consume inordinate resources.

11.2.3 Utilities

There are many utility functions that are usually needed to manage a database. These include a schema processor, tools to build the databases, to restructure them, and to checkpoint and recover them.

A *schema processor* works something like a compiler for a programming language. The analogy is so strong that programmers frequently talk about "compiling" a schema (see Figure 11.11). A schema processor reads the "source schema," which is usually in a high-level form that is convenient for people to read and understand. The processor checks for syntax errors and inconsistencies, much as a compiler checks for similar errors. If no errors are detected, a report is generated showing the number and size of the various files that are required to implement the database and other statistical measures of the database. A file is also created into which a form of the schema is stored. This copy of the schema is designed for quick reference by other parts of the database system and is usually highly encoded for speed. It is this "object schema" to which all other components of the database system refer when information about the structure of the database is needed.

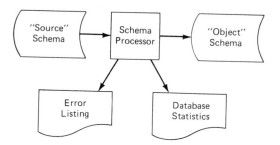

Figure 11.11 "Compiling" a schema.

The database files are usually created by a utility program that reads the "object schema" and builds the required files, initializing the records as required. The same or a similar program is used to restructure a database. This is done by comparing two object schemas and copying data from the original database to new files, and then purging the old files.

Databases can be *checkpointed* by storing copies of the object schema and data files to another medium, such as magnetic tape. In case the database is destroyed, for example by a disk head "crash" or a program error, the tape can be copied back to the disk and the database is restored to the state that existed at the checkpoint. Utilities for these purposes are usually part of a database system.

There may be other utility programs in addition to these. One class of utilities generates reports on the database usage, including the occupancy of files, the frequency of access to files, the usage by user classes, and so on.

11.2.4 Integrity and Recovery

A database is a more fragile object than a file since the loss of even a small part may render the remainder useless, and the cost of reconstructing all the data is so high. Consequently, great care is usually taken to ensure that the integrity of the database is not compromised and if it should be compromised, that there is some method to recover the lost data.

The checkpoint and recovery utilities, discussed above, are usually one part of the integrity and recovery system. Another component is the concurrency management system that will be discussed in the next subsection. A third element is frequently some form of **transaction logging**. As each transaction that modifies the database occurs, it is recorded on a separate medium from the database, frequently magnetic tape. In the event of a catastrophe to the database, it can be recovered by using the checkpoint tape and the logging tape. The database is first restored to the state of the last checkpoint, as described above. Then the logging tape is read by a utility program that processes each transaction against the database, in the order that they originally occurred. When all of the logged transactions have been processed, the database is recovered to the state it was in immediately preceding the catastrophe. This is known as a *"roll forward" recovery*.

It is also possible to recover from some types of catastrophes, such as program errors, by what is called a *"roll backward" recovery*. In this situation the logging tape is processed from back to front and each transaction is backed out in the reverse order that they occurred. When all of the "bad" transactions have been backed out, the database is recovered to the state it had before the program ran. A checkpoint tape is not needed for this kind of recovery.

11.2.5 Concurrency

Concurrency management may be defined as controlling the access of multiple users, whose functions are being performed at the same time, so that each user sees a consistent set of data. If all users are in a read-only mode, there is never a problem. If, however, one or more users can make changes in the data, there must be some global control to assure consistency. Consider, for example, a file that is being updated by both user A and user B. If both users attempt to update the same record, there may be a loss of data. First, user A loads his buffer with a copy of the record. User B follows by loading his buffer with an identical copy of the record. Each user modifies his copy of the record, changing different fields. User A then updates the record by writing out his modified copy to the file. Finally, user B writes his modified copy to the file. This sequence will result in the loss of A's update since it was never reflected in B's copy which was written over A's update.

The problem can be solved, in this case, by forcing B to wait to read the record until A has completed his transaction. Then the copy read by B will contain A's update which will be preserved.

When a database is used, however, the concurrency problems are multiplied; not just because there are multiple files, but because the data in these files are closely related. For example, in the database of Figure 11.5, if an enrollment is deleted, it is not only necessary to delete the record, but also to change the pointers that connect the associated course and student to that enrollment. If user A were to read a student record and pick up the pointer to that student's enrollments while user B was deleting those same enrollments, user A would find "garbage," or receive an error condition. Consequently, it is necessary for the system to either prevent A from beginning his transaction, or to restart the transaction when it is discovered to have collided with B.

As can be seen from this example, concurrency control in a database is a complex problem. It is usually solved by locking some subset of the database for the duration of one transaction so that only one user has access to the subset. Defining the appropriate subset and screening all other requests while the lock is in effect is a major task. If it is not done skillfully, serious performance problems can result. If it is not done correctly, data losses and inconsistent databases will result.

11.3 SUMMARY

An efficient solution to a problem with multiple entities will usually require multiple files. The design of a multiple file system is much more complicated than the design of a system with a single file. Methods for coping with these complexities are called *database concepts*.

One such concept is that of a *data model* that shows how the data in each of the files is organized and how it relates to data in other files.

Problems encountered in multiple file systems include *redundancy* and *insertion and deletion anomalies*. These can be minimized by *normalizing* the data model through a series of reversible transformations.

Entities of different types are joined by *entity relationships* or *associations*. These are either *1:1, 1:N,* or *M:N* relationships. The method used to implement the associations determines the type of model and database system used. *Network model* databases use pointers or linked lists to join the entities. *Relational model* systems join entities on the basis of common attribute values. *Hierarchical model* systems group or cluster together records of different entity types in a common file.

Data abstraction hides the details of the physical storage from the programmer or user. This not only simplifies the use of the database, but allows *data independence* between programs and the database. This means that changes in the programs and database can be reasonably independent of each other. It also allows the database to present different appearances or *views* to different users.

A database is described by a *schema* written in a ***data definition language*** (DDL). The manipulation of the data is expressed in a ***data manipulation language*** (DML).

A database system usually includes several utilities such as a ***schema processor***, and ***checkpointing, logging***, and ***recovery*** utilities. Recoveries may be either ***roll forward*** or ***roll backward***, depending on the cause. A ***database system*** is an aggregation of languages, utilities, procedures, methods, and documentation that aid in implementing databases. Although a database system is not essential for implementing a database, it is very helpful.

Controlling multiple users accessing one or more files simultaneously is called ***concurrency management***. It is usually implemented by giving one user at a time exclusive access to some subset of the database.

11.4 THE STUDENT RECORDS PROBLEM

In this section two databases are analyzed for the student records problem. To make the comparisons more meaningful, both will be based on the attributes and entities as described in Appendix A, not on the augmented data that was the basis of the normalization example in Section 11.1.2.

The network and relational models will be used for the two solutions. The hierarchical model will not be used for several reasons. First, it does not fit this problem very well and would not produce a solution that would be competitive. Second, several of the solutions found earlier in this book were essentially hierarchical solutions. The repeating groups that were present in the files are very similar to the physical organization of the data that a hierarchical database system would use. Thus there would be little new to learn from this model.

It should be noted that the solutions presented in this section do not assume that a database system is being used. The techniques used have all been presented earlier in this text. The difference is that database concepts are being used. Entities have been separated into different files, and mechanisms are provided to aid in establishing the entity relationships. Although these solutions would be much easier to implement with the help of a database system, there would be no fundamental differences if they were implemented as ordinary files.

11.4.1 The Student Records Problem Using the Network Model

The normalization process will produce three entities: student, course, and enrollment. Each of these will occupy a separate file. In addition, it will be helpful in producing the grade reports in alphabetic order if there is an index by name for the student file. The model is illustrated in Figure 11.12.

These files may each have different designs. Some database systems force all files to be organized in the same manner or allow only a very limited number of file types. Other systems may be flexible in the file types that are al-

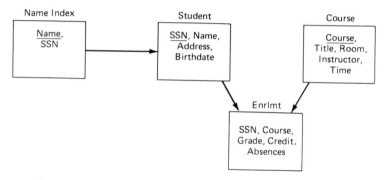

Figure 11.12 Data structure diagram for network model database.

lowed. We will assume, for purposes of this example, that we are free to choose the most appropriate file types.

The Student file will be organized as a direct access file using hashing with replacement. The key will be the SSN. The file will be targeted for a maximum load factor of 90%. In addition to the attributes of the student entity, it will need to have two pointers of two bytes each for the doubly linked synonym chain, and another pair of pointers to link each student with his enrollments. One pointer will point to the first enrollment in the student's enrollment chain, the other to the last enrollment. Thus the chain will be both doubly linked and circular, linking together one student record with any number of enrollment records.

The fields required by the student record are as follows:

Field	Length (bytes)
Name	30
SSN	9
Address	40
Birthdate	6
Synonym chain pointers	4
Enrollment chain pointers	4
Total record length	93

The blocking factor will be 50, although there is no advantage, other than storage efficiency, to having a large blocking factor. The number of slots in the file will be a prime number such that the load factor will never exceed 90%. For $M = 2000$, this will require 2237 slots. For $M = 10,000$, 11,113 slots are needed.

The course file will be organized in the same manner, as a direct access file using hashing with replacement and 90% load factor. The key is the course.

This file will also need pointers, one pair for the synonyms and one pair for the enrollment pointer chain. This chain will link each course with all the enrollments in the enrollment file for that course.

The fields in the course record are as follows:

Field	Length (bytes)
Course	7
Title	20
Instructor	20
Room	6
Time	7
Synonym chain pointers	4
Enrollment chain pointers	4
Total record length	68

The blocking factor will also be 50 here, and again, there is no performance gain derived from the blocking factor. As with the student record, the file capacity is chosen to be a prime number allowing for a maximum of 90% load factor. Since there are $M/5$ records, the capacities will be 449 and 2237 for M of 2000 and 10,000, respectively.

The enrollment file will be organized as a relative file. Record numbers will be assigned by using a bit map to locate free slots. There are no internal keys since all access will be via pointers in the student and course files. This file will also have two pairs of pointers. One pair will form a doubly linked list that links together all the enrollments for each student. The other pair will form a doubly linked list to join all the enrollments for each course. The first and last enrollments in each chain will be pointed to by the pointers in the student and course records, as shown in Figure 11.9.

The fields for the enrollment file are as follows:

Field	Length (bytes)
SSN	9
Course	7
Grade	1
Credit	2
Absences	2
Student chain pointers	4
Course chain pointers	4
Total record length	29

The blocking factor will be 100, since the record is so short. Here there is an advantage to be gained from the large blocking factor as we will assume that it is always possible to place all of the enrollments for one student in the same block. This will be reflected in the statistics. The total number of slots needs only to be sufficient to hold all of the enrollments. For $M = 2000$, there will be 12,000 enrollments and 60,000 enrollments are required when $M = 10,000$.

The name index will be a B-tree of order $d = 50$. The key is name and the pointer will be the SSN since records can migrate within the student file. The node size is found to be

$$100 \times 30 + 100 \times 9 + 101 \times 2 = 4102 \text{ bytes}$$

By formula (9.8), the expected number of levels for the tree is 1.76 or 2 for $M = 2000$ and 2.13 or 3 for $M = 10,000$.

The four files for this model of database are summarized in Figure 11.13. These figures include the overhead required for the appropriate load factors.

File Name	File Type	Record Size	Blocking Factor	Block Size	Number of Records	Total Size
Student	Hash w/replacement 90% load factor	93	50	4650	$M/0.9$	103.3M
Course	Hash w/replacement 90% load factor	68	50	3400	$M/(5 * 0.9)$	15.1M
Enrollment	Bit-mapped, relative	29	100	2900	6M	174M
Name index	B-tree	41	$d = 50$	4102	M	54.7M
Total accesses						347.1M

Note: For $M = 2000$, space = 694,200 bytes; for $M = 10,000$, space = 3,471,000 bytes (M, number of students).

Figure 11.13 Summary of file characteristics for network model database.

The files are assumed to be set up before registration begins. All the student and course data have already been entered and the name index has been built. All of the processing needed to provide the five functions will involve adding and deleting enrollments, changing pointers in the student and course files, and reading all the files.

Registration is begun by using the memory resident bit map to find a block of the enrollment file that has enough room for all the enrollments for the student. This block is then read and the enrollments are added to it. The chains between the enrollments for the student are linked, using the student chain. The student record is read, using hashing and the enrollment pointers are updated to point to the first and last enrollments for the student, thus completing the doubly linked circular list.

Linking the enrollments into the course chain is more complicated because each enrollment will be linked to a different course. For each course (average of six per student), the following sequence is executed. First the course record is read and the backward pointer is used to read the last previous enrollment for that course. The forward pointer for that enrollment is updated to point to the new enrollment, and the backward pointer for the course is likewise updated to point to the new enrollment. Both the course record and the former last enrollment record are then written back. When all of the course-enrollment chains have been updated to link the new enrollments, the block containing the new enrollments can be written back, completing the registration for one student.

Changes begin by accessing the student record by SSN. After all the enrollment changes are completed, this record will be written back with the enrollment pointers updated. The enrollment chain is followed to locate all the enrollments for the student, which are all likely to be in the same enrollment file block. For each drop that is made (average of three per student), the course chain must be patched so that it will not be broken. This is done by using the forward and backward course chain pointers to locate the enrollments that precede and follow the deleted enrollment in the course chain. These two enrollments are updated by changing their pointers to point to each other.

The adds (average of two per student) are inserted into the enrollment block. For each add, the course record is accessed and the backward pointer is used to find the last enrollment on the course chain. The pointers in this record and in the course record are then updated to link in the new enrollment. Finally, the student chain is rebuilt by updating the enrollment records with appropriate values for the student chain. The enrollment block is then written back to the file.

Rosters are produced by accessing the course record. From there the course-enrollment chain is followed to access each enrollment for that course. As each enrollment is found, the SSN is used as a key to access the student record to retrieve the name and other data for the student. The grade input function is done exactly as the roster function, except that each enrollment record is updated after the grade has been entered.

The grade reports are produced by traversing the entire name index. As each SSN is found, the corresponding student record is read to get the student information and the pointer to the student's enrollments. The enrollments are probably all in the same block, thus requiring only one physical read for all enrollments. As each enrollment is processed, the corresponding course record is read to retrieve the course title, and so on.

The functions are summarized in Figure 11.14. Notice that the statistics are of order M. This is due partly to the lack of order in the rosters and partly because the maintenance of the name index did not figure in the statistics. Even if these elements had been included, the coefficient of the resulting $M \cdot \log(M)$ term would be negligibly small.

Function	File	Algorithm	Physical Accesses per Record	Number of Records	Mult.	Total
Registration	Enrollment	Read block	1	1	M	M
	Enrollment	Update	1	1	M	M
	Student	6.11	1.026	1	M	$1.026M$
	Student	Update	1	1	M	M
	Course	6.11	1.026	6	M	$6.156M$
	Course	Update ptr	1	6	M	$6M$
	Enrollment	4.2	1	6	M	$6M$
Change	Student	6.11	1.026	1	M	$1.026M$
	Student	Update	1	1	M	M
	Enrollment	4.2	1	1	M	M
	Enrollment	4.2	1	$2 \cdot 3 + 2$	M	$8M$
	Enrollment	Update course changes	1	$2 \cdot 3 + 2$	M	$8M$
	Course	6.11	1.026	2	M	$2.052M$
	Enrollment	Update course changes	1	1	M	M
Rosters	Course	6.11	1.026	1	$2M/5$	$0.410M$
	Enrollment	4.2	1	30	$2M/5$	$12M$
	Student	6.11	1.026	30	$2M/5$	$12.312M$
Grades in	Course	6.11	1.026	1	$M/5$	$0.205M$
	Enrollment	4.2	1	30	$M/5$	$6M$
	Student	6.11	1.026	30	$M/5$	$6.156M$
	Enrollment	Update	1	30	$M/5$	$6M$
Grades out	Name index	8.5	1	$M/75$	1	$0.013M$
	Student	6.11	1.026	M	1	$1.026M$
	Enrollment	4.2	$1/6$	$6M$	1	M
	Course	6.11	1.026	$6M$	1	$6.156M$
						$95.538M$

Note: For $M = 2000$, accesses $= 191,076$; for $M = 10,000$, accesses $= 955,380$ (M, number of students).

Figure 11.14 Function analysis for network model database.

11.4.2 The Student Records Problem Using the Relational Model

Since the normalization process does not take into account the type of model used for the database, the same three entities are used for the relational model that were used for the network model. However, the entity relationships are implicitly established by the indexes that are provided, rather than being explicitly provided by means of pointers. The relational model, with indexes, is shown in Figure 11.15.

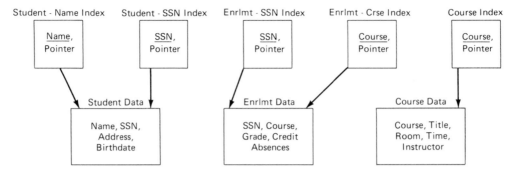

Figure 11.15 Data structure diagram for relational model database.

The files are of just two types: the indexes are B-trees, and the data files are relative files with bit maps used to allocate slots. All pointers, both tree pointers within the B-trees and record pointers from indexes to data files, are assumed to be 2-byte integers.

The student data file contains the following fields:

Field	Length (bytes)
Name	30
SSN	9
Address	40
Birthdate	6
Total record length	85

The blocking factor will again be 50. The file size does not require any extra slots, so the file may be built with M records.

The enrollment data file is organized in the same manner as the student data file. The record contains the following fields:

Field	Length (bytes)
SSN	9
Course	7
Grade	1
Credit	2
Absences	2
Total record length	21

Because the record is so short, the blocking factor can be as large as 200. Again it is assumed that all enrollments for one student can be fit into one block. The number of slots required is the same as the number of enrollments, or 6M.

The course data file organization is the same as that of the other data files. The fields it contains are:

Field	Length (bytes)
Course	7
Title	20
Instructor	20
Time	7
Room	6
Total record length	60

A blocking factor of 50 is appropriate for this size of record. Storage efficiency is the only consideration in selecting the blocking factor. The number of slots required is equal to the number of courses used, or $M/5$.

The indexes are all of the same general structure, differing only in the key used, the file to which they point, and the order of the nodes. The student-name index is of order $d = 50$ and has the following node length

$$100 \times 30 + 100 \times 2 + 101 \times 2 = 3402 \text{ bytes}$$

By applying formula (9.8) we can anticipate the number of levels to be 1.76 or 2 for 2000 students, and 2.13 or 3 for 10,000 students.

The student-SSN index is similar, but the order can be $d = 100$, since the key is smaller. The nodes will be of length

$$200 \times 9 + 200 \times 2 + 201 \times 2 = 2602 \text{ bytes}$$

Formula (9.8) yields expected levels of 1.52 and 1.84 for the two student populations, so that this index will be of two levels for both cases.

The enrollment-SSN index is structured exactly as the student-SSN index. The nodes will be of the same size. However, since there are six enrollments per student, there will be six times as many entries in the index. This will result in the expected number of levels being 1.87 or 2, and 2.19 or 3 for the two student populations.

The enrollment-course index will also be of order $d = 100$ but uses the 7 byte course for a key. The node size is found as

$$200 \times 7 + 200 \times 2 + 201 \times 2 = 2202 \text{ bytes}$$

Because the order and population are the same as for the enrollment-SSN index, formula (9.8) will yield the same numbers of levels, 2 and 3, for the two student populations.

The course index is used to find courses in the course data file. It will be of order $d = 100$ and, because the order and key are the same as the enrollment-course index, it will have the same node size of 2202 bytes. The number of entries is only $M/5$ and, by formula (9.8), the number of levels will be two for both student populations.

File Name	File Type	Record Size	Blocking Factor	Block Size	Number of Records	Total Size
Student name index	B-tree	34	$d = 50$	3402	M	45.4M
Student SSN index	B-tree	13	$d = 100$	2602	M	17.4M
Enrollment SSN index	B-tree	13	$d = 100$	2602	6M	104.1M
Enrollment course index	B-tree	11	$d = 100$	2202	6M	88.1M
Course index	B-tree	11	$d = 100$	2202	0.2M	2.9M
Student data	Bit-mapped, relative	85	50	4250	M	85M
Enrollment data	Bit-mapped, relative	21	100	2100	6M	21M
Course data	Bit-mapped, relative	60	50	3000	0.2M	12M
						375.9M

Note: For $M = 2000$, space $= 751,800$ bytes; for $M = 10,000$, space $= 3,759,000$ bytes (M, number of students).

Figure 11.16 Summary of file characteristics for relational model database.

The five indexes and three data files are summarized in Figure 11.16. Although there are four more files than required by the network model, the space is only about 8% greater.

As with the network model database, we will assume that the course and student data, with their indexes, are already present before registration begins. All of the processing will consist of adding, deleting, and updating enrollments, and reading the other data.

Registration begins by reading a block of the enrollment data file that has enough empty slots to accommodate the student being registered. The enrollments are added to the file and the corresponding entries are added to the two indexes for this file. All of the entries for the enrollment-SSN index will probably be in the same node. Hence there will be $k - 1$ reads to find the node and one to write it back after the entries are added. The entries for the enrollment-course index will be scattered. Therefore, each of the six courses will be added as a separate operation.

Changes are begun by using the enrollment-SSN index to locate the block in which the student's enrollments are stored. This block is read and the enrollments added and deleted as required. The enrollment-course index is updated by deleting an average of three courses, and adding two courses. Finally, the affected node of the enrollment-SSN index is updated and written back.

Rosters are produced by traversing the enrollment-course index for entries for the desired course. As each entry is found, the corresponding enrollment record is read to identify the student. The student's SSN is used to find the corresponding entry in the student-SSN index, and finally, the student's record is read from the student data file to get the name and other data.

Grades are entered by following the same sequence as for the rosters, except that the enrollment record is updated after the grade is entered.

Grade reports are generated by traversing the student-name index. The corresponding student record is read to get the name and other student data. The student's SSN is used to locate his enrollments through the enrollment-SSN index. As each enrollment is found, the corresponding course record is accessed through the course index to get the title and other data.

The functions are summarized in Figure 11.17. The statistics are of order $M \cdot \log(M)$, since k is a logarithmic function of M. The number of accesses is somewhat higher than that for the network model database. This is not unexpected since efficiency is a major advantage of the network model.

11.4.3 Critique

The relational database proved to be slightly less efficient than the network database in both accesses and storage space. This is because indexes will be less efficient than embedded pointers. This does not necessarily mean that the network design is a better choice than the relational one, just that it is more efficient for the given functions. The relational design is more flexible and this advantage may more than compensate for the lower efficiency. Indexes may be added without a major restructuring. With the appropriate keys indexed, nearly any conceivable type of access can be performed with reasonably good efficiency.

Except for ordering the grade reports by name, neither design ordered the outputs. Both rosters and grade inputs can be ordered by name for both designs. The modifications for the relational design are the simpler of the two. The name field must be added to the enrollment data file. The key for the enrollment-course index can then include the name as a secondary key. Thus, when the index is traversed for the enrollments for one course, those enrollments will be found in the order required to produce all the names in alphabetic order. This will give the required order for both the rosters and grade input functions.

Function	File	Algorithm	Physical Accesses per Record	Number of Records	Mult.	Total
Registration	Enrollment	Read block	1	1	M	M
	Enrollment	Update	1	1	M	M
	Enrollment-SSN					
	index	8.2	$k3$	1	M	$k3 \cdot M$
	Enrollment-course					
	index	8.2	$k4$	6	M	$6k4 \cdot M$
Change	Enrollment-SSN					
	index	8.5	$k3 - 1$	1	M	$k3 \cdot M - M$
	Enrollment	4.2	1	1	M	M
	Enrollment	Update	1	1	M	M
	Enrollment-course					
	index	8.3	$k4$	3	M	$3k4 \cdot M$
	Enrollment-course					
	index	8.2	$k4$	2	M	$2k4 \cdot M$
	Enrollment-SSN					
	index	Update	1	1	M	M
Rosters	Enrollment-course					
	index	8.5	$k4 - 1$	1	$2M/5$	$0.4k4 \cdot M - 0.4M$
	Enrollment	4.2	1	30	$2M/5$	$12M$
	Student-SSN					
	index	8.4	$k2 - 1$	30	$2M/5$	$12k2 \cdot M - 12M$
	Student	4.2	1	30	$2M/5$	$12M$
Grades in	Enrollment-course					
	index	8.5	$k4 - 1$	1	$M/5$	$0.2k4 \cdot M - 0.2M$
	Enrollment	4.2	1	30	$M/5$	$6M$
	Student-SSN					
	index	8.4	$k2 - 1$	30	$M/5$	$6k2 \cdot M - 6M$
	Student	4.2	1	30	$M/5$	$6M$
	Enrollment	Update	1	30	$M/5$	$6M$
Grades out	Student-name					
	index	8.5	1	$M/75$	1	$0.013M$
	Student	4.2	1	M	1	M
	Enrollment-SSN					
	index	8.5	$k3 - 1$	M	1	$k3 \cdot M - M$
	Enrollment	4.2	1	$6M$	1	$6M$
	Course index	8.4	$k5 - 1$	$6M$	1	$6k5 \cdot M - 6M$
	Course	4.2	1	$6M$	1	$6M$
Total accesses						$(18k2 + 3k3 + 11.6k4 + 6k5 + 33.4) \cdot M$

Note: For $M = 2000$, $k2 = 2$, $k3 = 2$, $k4 = 2$, $k5 = 2$, accesses = 221,200; for $M = 10,000$, $k2 = 2$, $k3 = 3$, $k4 = 3$, $k5 = 2$, accesses = 1,252,000 (M, number of students; k, number of levels).

Figure 11.17 Function analysis for relational model database.

The network database can also be ordered in a similar, if more complicated, way. Again, the name field must be included in the enrollment file. When an enrollment is added to the course-enrollment chain, it is not appended to the end of the chain as before. Instead, the chain is followed from the beginning, and the name field of each enrollment is compared with the name field of the new enrollment. When the first name is found with a higher value than that of the new enrollment, the new enrollment is linked into the chain just before the record with the higher value. Thus, when the course-enrollment chain is followed, the enrollments will be retrieved in alphabetic order by name.

Both of these modifications have penalties. Each requires the addition of a large field to the enrollment file, increasing the space requirements, and adding redundancy. The network database will also require more accesses since a sequential search must be performed on the enrollment chain each time a new enrollment is added. This will introduce a statistic of order L^2, where L is the length of the average chain. Since L is independent of the number of students, this does not make the statistics of order M^2, but it can be a serious performance problem if L is large.

The database solutions to the student records problem illustrate the advantages of normalization, entity relationships, and the other database concepts. The redundancy and wasted space has been greatly reduced from that found in all single data file solutions. It is not possible to eliminate redundancy totally since the same values may be parts of more than one entity. For example, both the SSN and course in the enrollment file are redundant with fields in the student and course files. However, their values are necessary to identify the student and course to which enrollment is related. In principle they could be replaced with pointers in the network database, but this would not serve any useful purpose since the pointer values would be a function of the data item values.

Further redundancy is added if the ordering is introduced, as described in the preceding subsection. Such compromises of the "pure" normalized model are commonly made when databases are designed. This does not negate the value of the formal normalization process. When such compromises are made, it is done with the full knowledge of the designer, who can weigh the costs and benefits and make an informed decision.

In Figure 11.18 the database designs are compared with the direct access design of Section 6.6.1 and the multi-indexed design of Section 10.4.1. Notice that this plot is done on a linear scale rather than the logarithmic scale used in earlier comparisons. When both space and accesses are compared, the databases are clearly superior to the best of the single-file solutions. It is worth noting that the multi-indexed solution did require fewer accesses than either of the databases, and also performed the roster and grade input functions in alphabetic order. However, it used considerably more space and is not nearly as flexible as the databases.

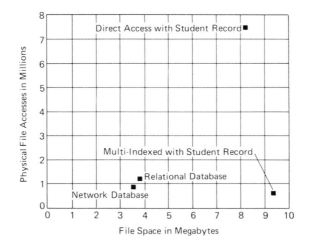

Figure 11.18 Scatter plot of physical accesses vs. storage space for $M = 10,000$.

For these reasons, most problems that involve multiple entities are solved using database concepts, if not database systems. Typically, there will be many data files, even though there are good solutions possible using a single data file. The freedom from redundancy and the flexibility allowed by databases make the multiple file solutions superior even though they are more complicated.

Database systems are available on most computers today. These make the task of using a database relatively simple and straightforward. Consequently, databases are becoming nearly universal in the implementation of file applications.

It must be remembered, however, that database systems must use the same elementary file methods that have been the subject of this book. It is wise to learn how the various features of a database system are implemented. Unless this is well understood, it is very easy to design databases that are inefficient when implemented on a given database system. Compromises in the design are usually necessary to find an efficient solution, and such compromises can be made intelligently only when the methods that underlie the database system are well understood.

11.5 PROBLEMS

11.1. For each of the four files described in Section 3.6, calculate the percent of space that is either occupied by redundant data or is wasted because of extra space allowed for repeating groups.

11.2. Develop a normalized data model for the computer equipment problem described in Section B.2.

11.3. Develop a normalized data model for the parts supply problem described in Section B.3.

11.4. Find three examples of each of the following entity relationships in real or imagined systems
  (a) One-to-one
  (b) One-to-many
  (c) Many-to-many

11.5. For each of your examples of many-to-many relationships from Problem 11.4(c), try to discover the intermediate entity so that all relationships will be one-to-many.

11.6. Calculate the proportion of space required for indexes, pointers, and redundant items that are used to locate records by key, or link entities for
  (a) the network model database of Section 11.4.1.
  (b) the relational model database of Section 11.4.2.

11.7. Determine the amount of additional space that would be required if the databases were modified to do the roster and grade input functions in alphabetic order as described in Section 11.4.3 for
  (a) the network database.
  (b) the relational database.

11.8. Determine the number of additional accesses that would be required by the network database if the alphabetic modification described in Section 11.4.3 were used. Note that the average course-enrollment chain length is 15 during registration and 30 for the other functions.

11.9. Find the proportion of accesses required for each function for both databases. Why is there a difference?

11.10. What structural difference accounts for the multi-indexed solution of Chapter 10 using fewer accesses than the database solutions of Chapter 11?

11.11. Design and analyze a database for the computer equipment problem described in Section B.2.

11.12. Design and analyze a database for the parts supply problem described in Section B.3.

Appendix A

File System Descriptions

This appendix contains descriptions of the file system interface provided by two real operating systems, and one "generic" interface that is used throughout the book to describe algorithms. Other, real operating systems will have different procedures and commands, but they are likely to be similar in function to those found here. The syntactic details will vary, but the principles will be the same. Before attempting to use any file system, the reader should study the manuals that give all the details of that system.

A.1 "GENERIC" FILE SYSTEM

This is an artificial system that is designed to be as simple as possible while providing all the essential primitive operations from which the file processing algorithms can be built. For the most part, details such as the typing of parameters have been left undefined to simplify the algorithms. Operations are initiated by making procedure calls. Hence all operations are defined as procedures.

OPEN(filename)

    Functions: 1. Allows access to the file.

                2. Sets the currency pointer to just before the first record.

    Parameter:

                1. filename—uniquely identifies the file to be opened.

CLOSE(filename)

Function: 1. Terminates access to the file.

Parameter:

      1. filename—uniquely identifies the file to be closed.

READ-NEXT(filename,buffer)

Functions: 1. Advances the currency pointer to the next unflagged (occupied) record.
      2. Copies that record from the file to the user's buffer.
      3. If there is no next record, EOF becomes true and no data is transferred.

Parameters:

      1. filename—uniquely identifies the file being read.
      2. buffer—location in the user's work space to which the record is transferred.

READ-DIRECT(filename,buffer,record-nbr)

Functions: 1. Sets currency pointer to the record whose number equals the value of record-nbr.
      2. Copies that record from the file to the user's buffer.
      3. If the record-nbr is outside the range of the file, or if the slot corresponding to the record number is empty, VALID becomes false and no data is transferred.

Parameters:

      1. filename—uniquely identifies the file being read.
      2. buffer—location in the user's work space to which the record is transferred.
      3. record-nbr—a nonnegative integer whose value equals the record number of the record to be read.

UPDATE(filename,buffer)

Function: 1. Copies a record from the user's buffer to the position indicated by the currency pointer. VALID becomes false if the currency pointer does not point to a valid record.

Parameters:

      1. filename—uniquely identifies the file being read.
      2. buffer—location in the user's work space from which the record is transferred.

APPEND(filename,buffer)

Functions: 1. Sets the currency pointer to the position immediately following the last record in the file.
      2. Adds a new record at the position of the currency pointer.

3. Copies a record from the user's buffer to the position indicated by the currency pointer.

Parameters:

1. filename—uniquely identifies the file to which the record is appended.
2. buffer—location in the user's work space from which the record is transferred.

WRITE-NEXT(filename,buffer)

Functions: 1. Advances the currency pointer to the next record position in the file.
2. Adds a new record at the position of the currency pointer if there is no next record position in the file.
3. Copies a record from the user's buffer to the position indicated by the currency pointer.

Parameters:

1. filename—uniquely identifies the file to which the record is appended.
2. buffer—location in the user's work space from which the record is transferred.

WRITE-DIRECT(filename,buffer,record-nbr)

Functions: 1. Sets the currency pointer to the record whose number equals the value of record-nbr.
2. Copies that record from the user's buffer to the file.
3. If the record-nbr is outside the range of the file, VALID becomes false and no data is transferred.

Parameters:

1. filename—uniquely identifies the file being read.
2. buffer—location in the user's work space from which the record is transferred.
3. record-nbr—a nonnegative integer whose value equals the record number of the record to be written.

logical EOF(filename)

Function: 1. Becomes true if the currency pointer is beyond the last record of the file; otherwise, it is false.

Parameter:

1. filename—uniquely identifies the file being tested.

logical VALID(filename)

Function: 1. Becomes false if any operation fails or if the record has been logically deleted; otherwise, it is true. VALID always tests the most recent operation performed on the named file.

Parameter:

1. filename—uniquely identifies the file being tested.

ALLOCATE(filename,pointer)

Functions:　1. Selects from the file system free-space pool a segment of storage equal to the bucket size for the named file.
2. Assigns this new bucket to the named file.
3. Returns a pointer that points to the new bucket.

Parameters:

1. filename—uniquely identifies the file to which the bucket is added.
2. pointer—a "record number" that allows the read and write primitives to access the new bucket.

DEALLOCATE(filename,pointer)

Functions:　1. Removes the bucket indicated by the pointer from the file.
2. Returns the bucket to the file system free-space pool.

Parameters:

1. filename—uniquely identifies the file to which the bucket is assigned.
2. pointer—a "record number" that identifies the bucket being removed from the file.

A.2 VAX-11 C COMPILER UNIX I/O LIBRARY FUNCTIONS

This is one of several sets of file system interfaces that may be used from C programs. These file functions, in turn, call on facilities of the Record Management Services (RMS). Functions that are used for less common purposes have been omitted from this list. Notice that the function *lseek* must be used to set the currency pointer when using any type of relative file.

int creat(name,mode[,file_attribute,...])

Functions:　1. Creates a new file with the name and attributes given.
2. Opens the new file for read/write access.
3. Returns an integer file descriptor used by subsequent calls.

Parameters:

1. name—a string containing any VAX/VMS file specification and terminated by a NUL.
2. mode—an unsigned value that specifies the file protection mode.

        3. file_attribute—a character string of the form ''keyword = value''. Each file_attribute describes one aspect of the file, such as record length, block size, allocation quantity, etc.

int open(name,mode)

Functions: 1. Opens the file named.

        2. Returns an integer file descriptor used by subsequent calls.

Parameters:

        1. name—a string containing any VAX/VMS file specification and terminated by a NUL.

        2. mode—an integer whose value specifies the type of access: 0 = read only, 1 = write only, 2 = read/write.

int close(file_descriptor)

Functions: 1. Causes all buffers to be written to the file if necessary.

        2. Closes the file.

        3. Returns a value of zero if there were no errors, a -1 is returned if the operation failed.

Parameter:

        1. file_descriptor—integer returned by *creat* or *open*, which identifies the file.

int read(file_descriptor,buffer,nbytes)

Functions: 1. Copies data from the file to the buffer.

        2. Advances the currency pointer.

        3. Returns the number of bytes actually transferred, or:

        0 which indicates end-of-file
        −1 which indicates an error

Parameters:

        1. file_descriptor—integer returned by *creat* or *open*, which identifies the file.

        2. buffer—address of buffer for record.

        3. nbytes—integer that sets upper limit on number of bytes transferred. Buffer must be equal or greater in size than nbytes.

int write(file_descriptor,buffer,nbytes)

Functions: 1. Copies data from the buffer to the file.

        2. Advances the currency pointer.

        3. Returns the number of bytes written.

Parameters:

1. file_descriptor—integer returned by **creat** or **open**, which identifies the file.
2. buffer—address of buffer for record.
3. nbytes—integer giving number of bytes to be written.

int lseek(file_descriptor,offset,base)

Functions: 1. Sets the currency pointer to the beginning of a selected record.
2. Returns the bytes position of the currency pointer relative to the front of the file.

Parameters:

1. file_descriptor—integer returned by **creat** or **open**, which identifies the file.
2. offset—integer value giving the number of bytes by which the currency pointer is to be displaced. The pointer will always be positioned at the beginning of a record for record files.
3. base—gives the location from which the offset is measured:

$$0 = \text{front of the file}$$
$$1 = \text{the current pointer position}$$
$$2 = \text{end of the file}$$

A.3 HP-3000 FILE SYSTEM

The following are seven of the standard MPE procedures or "intrinsics." They are callable directly from most programming languages and are used implicitly by the others. Although there are many other file procedures, these are the ones most commonly used, and constitute a sufficient set for most functions.

INTEGER PROCEDURE FOPEN(formaldesignator,foptions,aoptions.recsize, device,formmsg,userlabels,blockfactor,numbuffers,filesize, numextents, initialloc,filecode)

Functions: 1. Optionally creates the named file as a new file.
2. Opens the file for the mode specified.
3. Returns a file number which is used to identify the file in subsequent calls.
4. Sets the condition code to indicate whether or not there were any errors or exceptional conditions.

Parameters:

1. formaldesignator—byte array containing the MPE file name.
2. foptions—logical word value with bit fields that describe file characteristics and defaults.
3. aoptions—logical word value with bit fields that describe the modes of access to be used with this file.
4. The remaining parameters are used only to describe characteristics of new files.

PROCEDURE FCLOSE(filenum,disp,seccode)

Functions: 1. Writes all buffers to the file, if needed.
2. Closes the file.
3. Optionally, can save a temporary file or purge a permanent file.
4. Optionally, can modify the security provisions of the file.
5. Sets the condition code to indicate whether or not there were any errors or exceptional conditions.

Parameters:

1. filenum—integer value returned by FOPEN to identify the file.
2. disp—integer value of disposition code as follows:

> 0 = no change in file status
> 1 = make file permanent
> 2 = retain as a job temporary file, rewind if tape
> 3 = retain as a job temporary file, do not rewind
> 4 = purge the file

3. seccode—integer value that denotes security provisions:

> 0 = allow access by any user within the normal security
> 1 = allow access only by the creator of the file

INTEGER PROCEDURE FREAD(filenum,buffer,count)

Functions: 1. Advances the currency pointer to the next record.
2. Copies the (now) current record to the user's buffer.
3. Returns the count of the actual number of words or bytes transferred.
4. Sets the condition code to indicate whether or not there were any errors or exceptional conditions.

Parameters:

1. filenum—integer value returned by FOPEN to identify the file.
2. buffer—address of the buffer to which the data is transferred.
3. count—integer value of the maximum number of words or bytes that can be transferred. The buffer must be able to hold this much data.

PROCEDURE FREADDIR(filenum,buffer count,recnum)

Functions: 1. Sets the currency pointer to the record indicated by recnum.

2. Copies the (now) current record to the user's buffer.
3. Sets the condition code to indicate whether or not there were any errors or exceptional conditions.

Parameters:

1. filenum—integer value returned by FOPEN to identify the file.
2. buffer—address of the buffer to which the data is transferred.
3. count—integer value of the maximum number of words or bytes that can be transferred. The buffer must be able to hold this much data.
4. recnum—double integer value giving the number of the record to be read.

PROCEDURE FUPDATE(filenum,buffer,count)

Functions: 1. Copies the data in the buffer to the current record.

2. Sets the condition code to indicate whether or not there were any errors or exceptional conditions.

Parameters:

1. filenum—integer value returned by FOPEN to identify the file.
2. buffer—address of the buffer from which the data is transferred.
3. count—integer value of the number of words or bytes to be transferred.

PROCEDURE FWRITE(filenum,buffer,count,control)

Functions: 1. Advances the currency pointer to the next record.

2. Copies the contents of the user's buffer to the (now) current record.

3. Sets the condition code to indicate whether or not there were any errors or exceptional conditions.

Parameters:

1. filenum—integer value returned by FOPEN to identify the file.
2. buffer—address of the buffer from which the data is transferred.
3. count—integer value of the number of words or bytes to be transferred.
4. control—logical value that indicates carriage control options.

PROCEDURE FWRITEDIR(filenum,buffer,count,recnum)

Functions: 1. Advances the currency pointer to the record indicated by recnum.
2. Copies the contents of the user's buffer to the (now) current record.
3. Sets the condition code to indicate whether or not there were any errors or exceptional conditions.

Parameters:

1. filenum—integer value returned by FOPEN to identify the file.
2. buffer—address of the buffer from which the data is transferred.
3. count—integer value of the number of words or bytes to be transferred.
4. recnum—double integer value giving the number of the record to be written.

Appendix B

Study Problems

B.1 THE STUDENT RECORDS PROBLEM

This is a simplified version of the very real problem common to all colleges and universities of keeping data on student enrollments in courses. While many of the details have been ignored, the basic problem of organizing the data remains. The functions required are sufficiently complex to raise most of the questions of file design and file processing algorithms.

The problem is to organize and maintain records of student registration to allow certain necessary functions to be performed upon them. So that everyone can use and understand common terms, the following definitions will apply to this problem:

> *Student data.* Student data is that which describes a student, including the following:
>> *Name:* 30 bytes, last name first
>> *SSN:* 9 bytes, unique identification number
>> *Home address:* 40 bytes
>> *Birthdate:* 6 bytes
>
> *Course data.* A course is a unique course-section in which one or more students may be enrolled, and which meets at a specific place and time. For example CS 100 01 is a different course from CS 100 02. Course data describes a course and includes the following:
>> *Course number:* 7 bytes, example: MA 203 03
>> *Course Title:* 20 bytes, example: Linear Algebra
>> *Instructor:* 20 bytes consisting of last name and initials

Time: 7 bytes giving time of day

Room: 6 bytes giving building code and room number

Enrollment data. Enrollment data is data required to describe the enrollment of one student in one class. An enrollment must be implicitly or explicitly associated with exactly one student and exactly one course. Other data includes:

Grade: 1 byte, a letter grade for the course

Credit: 2 bytes, an integer representing credit hours

Absences: 2 bytes, an integer representing the number of absences

Population. The population of this system will have a strong influence on the choice of design. However, it is more instructive to generate statistics of usage using a variable population rather than a fixed population. Therefore, the following quantities should be used:

Number of students: N

Number of courses: N/5

Number of courses per student: average of 6, range of 1 to 10

Number of students per course: average of 30, range of 1 to 100

All statistics should be calculated in terms of N. After they are derived in terms of N, a value $N = 2000$ should be substituted to give a representative numerical value.

Functions. Functions are operations performed on the file(s) during a cycle of the system. For this system, a cycle is a full semester. Some are batch processing functions, while others are interactive functions. Reasonable allowances should be made for the mode of the function when selecting algorithms.

1. *Initial registration.* This is done exactly once by each student. It is processed interactively by a clerk and consists of associating each student with 1 to 10 courses. The students appear in random order to be registered and each registration is processed while the student waits. Assume that any needed student or course data is either already in the file or readily available. Do not count the acquisition of student and course data in your statistics.

2. *Change of schedule.* Many students never change their schedules, while others may change them several times. On the average, there is one change per student. A change may be as simple as adding or dropping one course, or as complex as dropping all courses and adding a new group of courses. On the average, a change involves dropping three courses and adding two courses. All registrations are completed before any changes are permitted.

3. *Class rosters.* A class roster is a list of all students enrolled in one course. The students may be listed in any order only if there is no reasonable way to list them in alphabetical order by name. Rosters

are produced separately, interactively, upon demand, for each course. An average of two rosters per course is produced. All registrations are completed before any rosters are produced.

4. *Grade input.* Grades are submitted by instructors with one grade per enrollment. Grades for all enrollments in one course are submitted together. The process is interactive, and the program will prompt the instructor for each grade by printing the name and identification number of each student in the course. The names are to be in alphabetic order unless there is no reasonable way to so order them.

5. *Grade reports.* Grade reports are produced all at one time in batch mode. There is one report for each student, showing the courses in which he is enrolled and the grade received for each. The students are to be in alphabetic order unless there is no reasonable way to so order them. All grades are posted before the grade reports are run.

Solutions. Solutions are to be developed within the constraints of the particular file structures and algorithms assigned. Each solution will consist of three parts as outlined below. Where other functions, such as external sorts or organization of indexes, are required for your solution, statistics for these auxiliary functions may or may not be required by your instructor. However, these functions should always be clearly shown in your function summary table.

1. For each file in your solution, describe the following:
   A. The name of the entity type represented in the file
   B. The type of file structure, including modes of access
   C. The data items in each record
   D. The key(s), if any
   E. The blocking factor
   F. The total number of bytes as a function of N
   G. The storage efficiency

2. For each function in your solution, create a row in a table to summarize the function. Where functions may have subfunctions, use a separate row for each subfunction. The table will show the following for each function. See Figure B.1 for an example.
   A. The name of the function
   B. The algorithm used for the file access
   C. The name of the file used
   D. The number of physical accesses required to find one logical record
   E. The number of logical records required for the function
   F. The total number of logical accesses for the function in terms of N
   G. The total number of physical accesses for all functions in terms of N

H. The total number of physical accesses for all functions for a representative value of N

3. List solutions considered and rejected. All alternative solutions that were, at least briefly, considered should be listed together with the reasons they were not used. It will be very easy to eliminate some candidates as they will be obviously inefficient in their algorithms or use of file space. Others will require more detailed, even complete analysis. In this section you must make the case that your choice of structures and algorithms was the most appropriate one.

Function	File	Algorithm	Physical Accesses per Record	Number of Records	Mult.	Total
Registration	Data	6.11	1.45	6	M	$8.70M$
	Data	Update	1	6	M	$6.00M$
	Name index	9.2	k	6	M	$6Mk$
Change	Data	6.11	1.45	5	M	$7.25M$
	Data	Update	1	5	M	$5.00M$
	Name index	9.3	k	3	M	$3Mk$
	Name index	9.2	k	2	M	$2Mk$
Rosters	Data	6.11	1.45	1	$2M/5$	$0.58M$
Grades in	Data	6.11	1.45	1	$M/5$	$0.29M$
	Data	Update	1	1	$M/5$	$0.20M$
Grades out	Name index	9.5	1	$6M/1.5d$	1	$0.08M$
	Data	6.11	1.45	$M/5$	30	$8.70M$
Total accesses						$11Mk + 36.80M$

Figure B.1 Sample table for summarizing functions.

B.2 THE COMPUTER EQUIPMENT PROBLEM

A computer vendor needs to keep records on the pieces of equipment that its customers have on maintenance contract. The records are kept by each area office on the units supported by that office. The problem is to organize and maintain these records so that the necessary functions can be performed in an efficient and effective manner. The following definitions apply to this problem:

Model data. Model data is data that describes a particular model of equipment, including the following:
Name: 20-byte generic description such as "disk", "printer", etc.
Model number: 8-byte alphanumeric designation unique to each model
Service interval: 2-byte integer giving maximum interval in days between required services

Rate: 4-byte integer giving the monthly basic maintenance cost

Customer data. Customer data is data that describes a customer that has units under a maintenance contract, including the following:

Name: 30 bytes, name of company

Customer number: 4 bytes, unique identification number

Contact: 30 bytes, name of contact person in company

Phone: 18 bytes, includes area code and extension of contact

Contract basis: 1 byte, gives contract coverage as follows:

"B": basic plan, Monday-Friday, 8 AM to 5 PM

"E": extended plan, Monday-Friday, 8 AM to 11 PM

"W": full week plan, Sunday-Saturday, 8 AM to 11 PM

"C": continuous plan, Sunday-Saturday, 24 hours per day

Contract date: 6 bytes, date on which the current contract expires

Unit Data. Unit data is data on each individual unit that each customer has under contract. A unit is associated with exactly one customer and one model. Other data includes:

Serial number: 10 bytes with a unique value for each unit

Installation date: 6 bytes giving date unit was installed

Options: 4-byte bit map indicating which of 32 options are used

Service date: 6 bytes giving date unit was most recently serviced

Costs: 4 bytes giving the total services costs charged to this unit under the current contract

Population. The population of this system will have a strong influence on the choice of design. However, it is more instructive to generate statistics of usage using a variable population rather than a fixed population. Therefore, the following quantities should be used:

Number of customers: N

Number of models: average of 100, varies slightly

Number of units per customer: average of 25, range of 1 to 100

Number of units per model: average of $N/4$, range of 1 to $N/2$

All statistics should be calculated in terms of N. After they are derived in terms of N, a value $N = 500$ should be substituted to give a representative numerical value.

Functions. Functions are operations performed on the file(s) during a cycle of the system. For this system, a cycle is one year. Some are batch processing functions, while others are interactive functions. Reasonable allowances should be made for the mode of the function when selecting algorithms.

1. *Invoices.* Customer invoices are prepared monthly and sent to the customers. Each invoice lists the units that the customer currently has on contract and the monthly service charge. The service charge is calculated by multiplying the basic service charge for that model by a factor dependent on the contract basis. The processing is done in batch mode, once per month.

2. *Maintenance schedule.* Weekly service schedules are prepared for the service people (commonly called customer engineers or CEs). This is done by comparing the date of last service for each unit with the maximum service interval for that model. If the time between the date of last service and the end of the week for which the schedule is being prepared exceeds the service interval, then the unit is scheduled for service. On the average, 6% of all units will be scheduled in any week. The processing is done in batch mode, once per week.

3. *Maintenance reports.* When each unit is serviced, the CE enters the service date for that unit. On the average, 10% of all units are serviced in any week. This is done daily in an interactive mode. mode.

4. *Configuration changes.* When a customer changes configuration, it is necessary to add and delete units associated with that customer. Each customer makes an average of two configuration changes per year, and adds and / or deletes an average of 8 units per change. The changes are made in an interactive mode.

5. *Contract changes.* The average customer makes 1.4 contract changes per year, including renewals and contract basis. These changes are made in the interactive mode.

Solutions: Your solutions to this problem are to be developed as detailed in Section B.1 for the student records problem.

B.3 THE PARTS SUPPLY PROBLEM

A small manufacturer requires a system to track inventory and parts orders. The problem is to organize and maintain records so that parts can be ordered when required and the suppliers of these parts can be paid for parts received. The following definitions apply to this problem:

Parts Data. Parts data is data that describes each part and its inventory status. This includes:
Part number: 4 bytes, unique identification number
Part description: 20-byte alphanumeric field
Monthly requirement: 4 bytes, estimated required quantity
Inventory quantity: 4 bytes, quantity in stock
Quantity on order: 4 bytes, total of quantity now on order, but not yet received
Reorder quantity: 4 bytes, the number of units ordered whenever an order is placed
Unit price: 4 bytes, latest unit price paid

Supplier Data. Supplier data is data describing a vendor of parts including:
  Name: 25 bytes, company name
  Vendor ID: 4 bytes, unique identification number
  Address: 40 bytes
  Current balance: 4 bytes, total owed to vendor for parts received

Part order data: Part order data is data describing one order for one single part type. A part order is associated with exactly one part type and exactly one vendor. Items include:
  Part number: 4 bytes
  Vendor ID: 4 bytes
  Quantity: 4 bytes
  Unit price: 4 bytes, may be unique to this order
  Status: 1 byte, allowed values are:
      "N": needed, not yet ordered from supplier
      "O": ordered from supplier, not yet received
      "R": received, not yet paid

Population. The population of this system will have a strong influence on the choice of design. However, it is more instructive to generate statistics of usage using a variable population rather than a fixed population. Therefore, the following quantities should be used:
  Number of parts: N
  Number of suppliers: $N/10$
  Number of part orders per part per month: average 2, range 0 to 5
  Number of part orders per supplier per month: average 20, range 0 to 100

All statistics should be calculated in terms of N. After they are derived in terms of N, a value $N = 2500$ should be substituted to give a representative numerical value.

Functions. Functions are performed on a monthly cycle. Some are in batch mode, while others are interactive as noted. Make allowances for the mode of the function when choosing algorithms.

1. *Adjust inventory.* This function is performed daily in an interactive mode by a stock clerk. Whenever some quantity of a part is removed from stock, the inventory quantity is reduced by that amount. A check is made to see if the remaining inventory amount plus the quantity on order is less than the monthly requirement. If it is, a part order is placed in the system for the reorder quantity indicated with a status of "N". The supplier and unit price for the order are selected by a clerk based on the best current price. The quantity on order is increased by the amount of the order quantity. This function is performed on each part an average of eight times per month, but a part order is generated on an average of two times per month.

2. *Generate supplier orders.* This function is performed weekly in batch mode. All part orders with a status of "N" for each vendor are grouped together and a consolidated order is sent to each supplier. The order status is changed to "O". In an average week, half of the suppliers are sent orders.

3. *Receive part order.* This function is performed daily, in an interactive mode by a receiving clerk. When a part order is received, the order status is changed to "R", and the inventory quantity is increased by the quantity of the order. The quantity on order is reduced by the same amount.

4. *Accounts payable report.* This report is run once per month in batch mode to determine the amount to be paid to suppliers. It is preferred that it be ordered by supplier name. For each supplier from whom parts were received during the month, a report is produced showing the part number, name, quantity, unit price, and total cost. A grand total is calculated and printed at the bottom of the report. Each part order is removed from the system after it has been reported.

5. *Inventory report.* This report is also run monthly, in batch mode. It lists each part in inventory, the quantity on hand, the unit price, and the total value (inventory quantity times unit price). It is preferred that the report be ordered by part number.

Solutions. Your solutions to this problem are to be developed as detailed in Section B.1 for the student records problem.

Appendix C

Calculating Logarithms

When designing files or making many other calculations in computer science, there is frequently a need to calculate logarithms to bases not usually found on calculators, in library procedures, or in tables. There is a very simple method for computing these values. Probably because such logarithms are seldom needed outside of computer science, this method is not often taught in mathematics courses.

In the following examples, the bases will be shown explicitly for all log functions to avoid confusion. The general method of calculating a logarithm in base b is as follows:

$$\log_b(N) = \log_x(N) \div \log_x(b)$$

where x can be any convenient base, such as 10 or e.

The following are examples worked out using both base 10 and base e logarithms:

$$\log_2(1000) = \log_{10}(1000) \div \log_{10}(2) = 3.00000 \div 0.30103 = 9.96578$$
$$\log_2(1000) = \log_e(1000) \div \log_e(2) = 6.90776 \div 0.69315 = 9.96578$$
$$\log_{50}(123{,}456) = \log_{10}(123{,}456) \div \log_{10}(50) = 5.09151 \div 1.69897 = 2.99682$$
$$\log_{50}(123{,}456) = \log_e(123{,}456) \div \log_e(50) = 11.72364 \div 3.91202 = 2.99682$$

Since a number such as $\log_e(50)$ is a constant, it may be calculated once and used as a constant thereafter. This can be done conveniently in programs, or in calculators with memory.

Appendix D

Conventions Used
for Pseudocode Algorithms

1. Reserved words of the language are shown in uppercase, boldface type. Examples: **IF, THEN, ELSE, WHILE, DO, UNTIL, BEGIN, END**.

2. Function names are shown in regular upper-case type. Examples: READ, EOF, KEY, FWD.

3. Operators and declarations of the language are shown in lowercase, boldface type. Examples: **and, not, or, mod, integer, function, procedure**.

4. Variables and named constants are shown in regular lowercase type. Examples: j, k, oldfile, buffer, true, null.

5. Comments are enclosed with parentheses and asterisks. Example: (* this is a comment *).

6. Occasionally, functions will be stated in plain English where the intent is clear and the actual code would not contribute to an understanding of the algorithm. Examples: process contents of buffer, INSERT middle-entry INTO father-node.

Index